# Hybridity in Contemporary Commercial Organizations

# Hybridity in Contemporary Commercial Organizations:

## *Implications for Employee Trust*

By

Ijeoma Jacklyn Okpanum

**Cambridge Scholars** Publishing

Hybridity in Contemporary Commercial Organizations:
Implications for Employee Trust

By Ijeoma Jacklyn Okpanum

This book first published 2021

Cambridge Scholars Publishing

Lady Stephenson Library, Newcastle upon Tyne, NE6 2PA, UK

British Library Cataloguing in Publication Data
A catalogue record for this book is available from the British Library



ISBN (10): 1-5275-7025-8
ISBN (13): 978-1-5275-7025-2

# TABLE OF CONTENTS


List of Tables ........................................................................ xiii

List of Figures ........................................................................ xv

Abbreviations ........................................................................ xvii

**CHAPTER 1 – BACKGROUND OF STUDY ........................................ 1**

1.1 Introduction ........................................................................ 1

*1.1.1 Organizational hybridity ........................................ 2*

*1.1.2 The institutional logics perspective ........................ 3*

*1.1.3 Organizational trust ........................................ 3*

*1.1.4 The context of the study: Nigeria ........................ 4*

1.2 Statement of the Problem ........................................ 5

1.3 Research Questions ........................................ 6

1.4 Research Aim, Objectives and Propositions ........................ 7

1.5 Research Strategy and Design ........................................ 8

1.6 Research Process ........................................ 9

1.7 Scope of the Study ........................................ 10

1.8 Rationale and Contributions of the Research ........................ 11

1.9 Summary of Empirical Findings ........................................ 12

**CHAPTER 2 – CONCEPTUALISING ORGANIZATIONAL HYBRIDITY .......... 13**

2.1 Introduction ........................................ 13

2.2 Organizational Hybridity: An Overview ........................ 15

*2.2.1 Organizational hybridity: Theoretical background ................ 15*

*2.2.2 Benefits and challenges of organizational hybridity ............. 18*

2.3 Organizational Hybridity: Controversies and Definitions ............... 20

*2.3.1 Organizational hybridity as a combination of multiple identities ........................................ 21*

*2.3.2 Organizational hybridity as a combination of multiple forms ........................................ 22*

*2.3.3 Organizational hybridity as a combination of multiple institutional logics ........................................ 22*

*2.3.4 Definition* ........ *24*
2.4 The Institutional Logics Perspective: Philosophical Background ...... 25
*2.4.1 The nature of institutional logics* ........ *27*
*2.4.2 Institutional logics and individuals' behaviours* ........ *28*
*2.4.3 Applicability of institutional logics in non-Western society: The case of Nigeria* ........ *29*
2.5 Contemporary Commercial Organizations as Carriers of Multiple Institutional Logics ........ 30
*2.5.1 Market-orientated institutional logics* ........ *31*
*2.5.2 Non-market-orientated institutional logics* ........ *31*
*2.5.3 Types of institutional logics embodied by commercial hybrid organizations* ........ *33*
*2.5.4 The coexistence of multiple institutional logics* ........ *40*
*2.5.5 Typology of hybrid organizations* ........ *41*
*2.5.6 Internal tensions and conflicts* ........ *44*
2.6 Dimensions of Organizational Hybridity ........ 46
*2.6.1 Organizational activities* ........ *46*
*2.6.2 Workforce composition* ........ *47*
*2.6.3 Organizational design* ........ *47*
*2.6.4 Inter-organizational relationships* ........ *49*
*2.6.5 Organizational culture* ........ *50*
2.7 Dimensions of Organizational Hybridity in Commercial Hybrid Organizations ........ 51
*2.7.1 Governance* ........ *53*
*2.7.2 Leadership structure/style* ........ *55*
*2.7.3 Organizational culture* ........ *56*
*2.7.4 Intra-organizational relations* ........ *58*
*2.7.5 Trust relations* ........ *60*
2.8 Gaps in Research ........ 65
2.9 Research Propositions and Theoretical Framework for the Implications of Organizational Hybridity for Employees' Trust in Commercial Hybrid Organizations ........ 66
2.10 Summary and Conclusions ........ 69

**Chapter 3 – Commercial Hybrid Organizations in Nigeria ...... 71**
3.1 Introduction ........ 71
3.2 Geographic and Climatic Context ........ 72
3.3 Political Context ........ 73
3.4 Social Context ........ 74

*3.4.1 Population and demography* ... 74
*3.4.2 Languages and ethnic groups* ... 74
*3.4.3 Beliefs and values* ... 75
3.5 Economic Context ... 75
*3.5.1 Economic characteristics* ... 75
*3.5.2 Economic reforms and development policies* ... 77
3.6 The Institutional Environment ... 80
*3.6.1 Institutional logics at play in the Nigerian institutional environment* ... 80
*3.6.2 The capitalist market* ... 81
*3.6.3 The state/professions* ... 82
*3.6.4 The community/family* ... 83
*3.6.5 Religion* ... 83
3.7 Case Study Organizations ... 84
*3.7.1 ASL* ... 85
*3.7.2 BPL* ... 89
*3.7.3 Summary of case studies* ... 94
3.8 Implications of Organizational Hybridity for Commercial Hybrid Organizations in Nigeria ... 96
*3.8.1 Governance challenges* ... 96
*3.8.2 Challenges of creating a leadership structure* ... 97
*3.8.3 Challenges of creating an organizational culture* ... 98
*3.8.4 Behavioural challenges* ... 99
3.9 Implications of Organizational Hybridity for Employees' Trust in Commercial Hybrid Organizations in Nigeria ... 100
3.10 Gaps and Limitations of Organizational Hybridity in the Nigeria Context ... 101
3.11 Summary and Conclusions ... 101

**Chapter 4 – Research Methodology and Methods ... 103**
4.1 Introduction ... 103
4.2 Research Methodology: An Overview ... 104
*4.2.1 Developing the methodological framework* ... 106
*4.2.2 Epistemology and ontology: Positioning this study* ... 107
*4.2.3 Interpretivism: A symbolic interactionist perspective* ... 109
4.3 Research Design ... 112
*4.3.1 The case-study design* ... 113
*4.3.2 The research setting for the data collection process* ... 114
*4.3.3 Case selection process* ... 115

*4.3.4 Negotiating access* ................................................ *116*
*4.3.5 Sampling technique* ................................................ *116*
*4.3.6 The sample size* ................................................ *118*
4.4 Data Collection Methods ................................................ 121
*4.4.1 The semi-structured interview approach* ................................................ *121*
*4.4.2 Conducting the interviews* ................................................ *123*
*4.4.3 Transcribing the interviews* ................................................ *124*
*4.4.4 Documents as data sources* ................................................ *124*
*4.4.5 Analysing documents in context* ................................................ *125*
4.5 Data Analysis Procedure ................................................ 127
*4.5.1 A thematic analysis* ................................................ *128*
*4.5.2 Coding strategy* ................................................ *129*
4.6 Research Governance and Ethics ................................................ 131
*4.6.1 Key ethical considerations* ................................................ *131*
*4.6.2 Ethical access* ................................................ *132*
*4.6.3 Ethical data collection* ................................................ *133*
4.7 Conclusions ................................................ 134

**Chapter 5 – Organizational Hybridity in Practice: The Case Study of ASL ................................................ 136**
5.1 Introduction ................................................ 136
5.2 Profiles of the Interviewees ................................................ 138
*5.2.1 Gender, age and native language of the interviewees* ................................................ *138*
*5.2.2 Work experience in the organization* ................................................ *138*
5.3 Findings Associated with Exploring the Influence of Organizational Hybridity on Specific Organizational Attributes of ASL ................................................ 138
*5.3.1 Interviewees' experiences and knowledge of the goals and objectives of ASL* ................................................ *139*
*5.3.2 Interviewees' experiences and knowledge of the governance of ASL* ................................................ *140*
*5.3.3 Interviewees' experiences and knowledge of the leadership style/structure of ASL* ................................................ *142*
*5.3.4 Interviewees' experiences and knowledge of the organizational culture of ASL* ................................................ *143*
*5.3.5 Interviewees' experiences and knowledge of tensions at ASL* ................................................ *144*
*5.3.6 Behavioural responses to organizational hybridity* ................................................ *148*
5.4 Findings Associated with Understanding the Implications of Organizational Hybridity for Employees' Trust in ASL ................................................ 151

*5.4.1 Integrity as a dimension of trust ........ 152*
*5.4.2 Competence as a dimension of trust ........ 152*
*5.4.3 Job security as a dimension of trust ........ 153*
*5.4.4 Employees' trust in ASL ........ 153*
*5.4.5 The implications of organizational hybridity for employees' trust in ASL ........ 155*
5.5 Findings Associated with Understanding the Influence of Non-Market-Orientated Logics at ASL ........ 156
*5.5.1 The influence of the capitalist market at ASL ........ 156*
*5.5.2 The influence of religion at ASL ........ 158*
*5.5.3 The importance of identification at ASL ........ 159*
5.6 Findings Relevant to Developing Research-Based Recommendations for Sustaining Employees' Trust in ASL ........ 160
*5.6.1 Improved organizational identification ........ 161*
*5.6.2 Improved organizational effectiveness and performance ........ 161*
5.7 Profiles of Analysed Documents ........ 162
5.8 Findings Associated with Exploring the Influence of Organizational Hybridity on Specific Organizational Attributes of ASL ........ 164
*5.8.1 Organizational hybridity in relation to goals and objectives of ASL ........ 164*
*5.8.2 Organizational hybridity in relation to governance of ASL ........ 165*
*5.8.3 Organizational hybridity in relation to leadership style/structure of ASL ........ 166*
*5.8.4 Organizational hybridity in relation to organizational culture of ASL ........ 166*
*5.8.5 Organizational hybridity in relation to tensions at ASL ........ 167*
*5.8.6 Organizational hybridity in relation to employees' behavioural response at ASL ........ 168*
5.9 Findings Associated with Understanding the Implications of Organizational Hybridity for Employees' Trust in ASL ........ 168
5.10 Findings Associated with Understanding the Influence of Non-Market-Orientated Logics at ASL ........ 168
5.11 Findings Relevant to Developing Research-Based Recommendations for Sustaining Employees' Trust in ASL ........ 169
5.12 Summary and Conclusions ........ 169

**CHAPTER 6 – ORGANIZATIONAL HYBRIDITY IN PRACTICE: THE CASE STUDY OF BPL ........ 172**
6.1 Introduction ........ 172
6.2 Profiles of the Interviewees ........ 173
*6.2.1 Gender, age and native language of the interviewees ........ 173*
*6.2.2 Work experience in the organization ........ 173*
6.3 Findings Associated with Exploring the Influence of Organizational Hybridity on Specific Organizational Attributes of BPL ........ 174
*6.3.1 Interviewees' experiences and knowledge of the goals and objectives of BPL ........ 174*
*6.3.2 Interviewees' experiences and knowledge of the governance of BPL ........ 176*
*6.3.3 Interviewees' experiences and knowledge of the leadership style/structure of BPL ........ 177*
*6.3.4 Interviewees' experiences and knowledge of the organizational culture of BPL ........ 178*
*6.3.5 Interviewees' experiences and knowledge of tensions at BPL ........ 179*
*6.3.6 Behavioural responses to organizational hybridity ........ 182*
6.4 Findings Associated with Understanding the Implications of Organizational Hybridity for Employees' Trust in BPL ........ 185
*6.4.1 Integrity as a dimension of trust ........ 185*
*6.4.2 Competence as a dimension of trust ........ 186*
*6.4.3 Benevolence as a dimension of trust ........ 186*
*6.4.4 Employees' trust in BPL ........ 187*
*6.4.5 The implications of organizational hybridity for employees' trust in BPL ........ 188*
6.5 Findings Associated with Understanding the Influence of Non-Market-Orientated Logics at BPL ........ 189
*6.5.1 The influence of the capitalist market at BPL ........ 190*
*6.5.2 The influence of family at BPL ........ 191*
*6.5.3 The influence of religion at BPL ........ 192*
*6.5.4 The importance of identification at BPL ........ 193*
6.6 Findings Relevant to Developing Research-Based Recommendations for Sustaining Employees' Trust in BPL ........ 194
*6.6.1 Improved organizational identification ........ 194*
*6.6.2 Improved organizational effectiveness and performance ........ 195*
6.7 Profiles of Analysed Documents ........ 196

6.8 Findings Associated with Exploring the Influence of Organizational Hybridity on Specific Organizational Attributes of BPL ...................... 198
*6.8.1 Organizational hybridity in relation to goals and objectives of BPL ..................................................................................... 198*
*6.8.2 Organizational hybridity in relation to governance of BPL .. 199*
*6.8.3 Organizational hybridity in relation to leadership style/structure of BPL .................................................................. 200*
*6.8.4 Organizational hybridity in relation to organizational culture of BPL ..................................................................................... 201*
*6.8.5 Organizational hybridity in relation to tensions at BPL........ 201*
*6.8.6 Organizational hybridity in relation to employees' behavioural responses at BPL ..................................................................... 202*
6.9 Findings Associated with Understanding the Implications of Organizational Hybridity for Employees' Trust in BPL ........................ 202
6.10 Findings Associated with Understanding the Influence of Non-Market-Orientated Logics at BPL ....................................................... 203
6.11 Findings Relevant to Developing Research-Based Recommendations for Sustaining Employees' Trust in BPL............................................... 203
6.12 Summary and Conclusions.......................................................... 203

**CHAPTER 7 – DISCUSSION OF FINDINGS ........................................... 206**
7.1 Introduction.................................................................................. 206
7.2 Overview of the Research ............................................................ 207
7.3 Exploring the Influence of Organizational Hybridity on Specific Organizational Attributes of Commercial Hybrid Organizations......... 209
*7.3.1 The influence of organizational hybridity on the governance of commercial hybrid organizations.......................................... 211*
*7.3.2 The influence of organizational hybridity on the leadership style/structure of commercial hybrid organizations .................... 214*
*7.3.3 The influence of organizational hybridity on the organizational culture of commercial hybrid organizations ................................ 217*
*7.3.4 The influence of organizational hybridity on intra-organizational relations ................................................................ 220*
7.4 Understanding the Influence of Non-Market-Orientated Logics in Commercial Hybrid Organizations .................................................. 226
*7.4.1 The tacit acceptance of religion in the commercial hybrid organizations ........................................................................... 228*
7.5 Understanding the Implications of Organizational Hybridity for Employees' Trust in Commercial Hybrid Organizations .................. 236

*7.5.1 Positive implications of organizational hybridity for employees' trust* ... *239*
*7.5.2 Negative implications of organizational hybridity for employees' trust* ... *240*
*7.5.3 The role of religion in the construction of employees' trust* ... *242*
*7.5.4 The role of identification in the construction of employees' trust* ... *243*
7.6 Towards Developing Research-Based Recommendations for Sustaining Employees' Trust in Commercial Hybrid Organizations ... 244
*7.6.1 Challenges limiting employees' trust in commercial hybrid organizations* ... *246*
7.7 The Future of Commercial Hybrid Organizations ... 247

**Chapter 8 – Recommendations and Conclusions ... 249**
8.1 Introduction ... 249
8.2 Summary of the Empirical Findings ... 249
8.3 Recommendations for Improving the Effectiveness and Performance of Commercial Hybrid Organizations ... 254
*8.3.1 Sustaining employees' trust* ... *255*
*8.3.2 Employees' involvement in decision-making* ... *257*
*8.3.3 Clear communication channels* ... *258*
*8.3.4 Barriers limiting the future of commercial hybrid organizations* ... *260*
8.4 Future Research ... 260
8.5 Approaches to Generalisation of Research Findings ... 262
8.6 The Significance of the Study and its Contribution to Knowledge .. 263
8.7 Reflections on the Knowledge Gained from the Research ... 265

**Appendices ... 268**
Appendix A: Interview Schedule for ASL ... 268
Appendix B: Interview Schedule for BPL ... 269
Appendix C: Data Display Format ... 271

**References ... 272**

# List of Tables

Table 1: Primary and Supporting Research Questions ............................... 6

Table 2: Research Aim and Objectives....................................................... 7

Table 3: Key Research Propositions........................................................... 7

Table 4: An Overview of Benefits and Challenges of Organizational Hybridity ..................................................................................................... 20

Table 5: Summary of Institutional Logics embodied in Commercial Hybrid Organizations ....................................................................... 38

Table 6: Economic Development Policies................................................ 78

Table 7: Summary of Case Studies........................................................... 95

Table 8: Developing the Research Methodology Framework ............... 107

Table 9: A Comparative Representation of Research Paradigms........... 111

Table 10: Interviewees' Profiles............................................................. 119

Table 11: Interviewees' Age (ASL) ....................................................... 120

Table 12: Interviewees' Length of Service (ASL).................................. 120

Table 13: Interviewees' Age (BPL)........................................................ 120

Table 14: Interviewees' Length of Service (BPL).................................. 121

Table 15: Research Objectives and Methods.......................................... 127

Table 16: Data Analysis Procedure Summary........................................ 131

Table 17: Coding System for ASL ........................................................ 137

Table 18: Documents Collected and Used............................................. 163

Table 19: Summary of Emerging Themes.............................................. 171

Table 20: Coding System for BPL ..... 173

Table 21: Documents Collected and Used ..... 197

Table 22: Summary of Emerging Themes ..... 205

Table 23: Summary of Empirical Findings Associated with Exploring the Influence of Organizational Hybridity on Specific Attributes of Commercial Hybrid Organizations ..... 210

Table 24: Summary of Empirical Findings Associated with Understanding the Influence of Non-Market-Orientated Logics on Commercial Hybrid Organizations ..... 227

Table 25: Summary of Empirical Findings Associated with Understanding the Implications of Organizational Hybridity for Employees' Trust in Commercial Hybrid Organizations ..... 238

Table 26: Summary of Empirical Findings Associated with Developing Research-Based Recommendations for Sustaining Employees' Trust in Commercial Hybrid Organizations ..... 245

Table 27: Summary of Overall Empirical Findings ..... 252

Table 28: Summary of Research Contributions ..... 264

# List of Figures

Figure 1: The Research Cycle (Phase 1) ........ 13

Figure 2: Mind Map of Literature Review ........ 14

Figure 3: Various Perspectives in the Definition of Organizational Hybridity ........ 25

Figure 4: The Ideal Types of Hybrid Organizations (Besharov and Smith, 2014) ........ 42

Figure 5: Dimensions of Organizational Hybridity in the Literature ........ 46

Figure 6: Dimensions of Organizational Hybridity in Commercial Hybrid Organizations ........ 52

Figure 7: Proposed Theoretical Framework for the Implications of Organizational Hybridity for Employees' Trust ........ 68

Figure 8: The Research Cycle (Phase 2) ........ 71

Figure 9: The Institutional Framework of the Nigerian Finance Sector ... 86

Figure 10: ASL's Hybrid Type (Besharov and Smith, 2014) ........ 89

Figure 11: The Institutional Framework of the Nigerian Oil and Gas Sector ........ 91

Figure 12: BPL's Hybrid Type (Besharov and Smith, 2014) ........ 94

Figure 13: The Research Cycle (Phase 3) ........ 103

Figure 14: Research Choices ........ 105

Figure 15: Overview of Sampling Approach ........ 118

Figure 16: The Research Cycle (Phase 4) ........ 136

Figure 17: The Research Cycle (Phase 5) ........ 206

Figure 18: Synergic Behavioural Response ........................................... 224

Figure 19: Progressive Behavioural Process .......................................... 240

Figure 20: Retrogressive Behavioural Cycle .......................................... 242

# ABBREVIATIONS

ASL – Alter Securities Limited

BPL – Barak Petroleum Limited

CBN – Central Bank of Nigeria

CHO – Commercial hybrid Organizations

IL – Institutional logics

ILP – Institutional logics perspective

JOA – Joint operating agreement

JV – Joint venture

NNPC – Nigerian National Petroleum Corporation

NSE – Nigerian Stock Exchange

OH – Organizational hybridity

PMS – Premium Motor Spirit

PSC – Production sharing contract

SEC – Securities and Exchange Commission

# CHAPTER 1

# BACKGROUND OF STUDY

## 1.1 Introduction

Times of extensive institutional pressure challenge the existence of contemporary commercial organizations as entities that reproduce a single coherent market-orientated institutional template to achieve effectiveness (Greenwood et al., 2010; DiMaggio, 1988; Karré, 2011; Billis, 2010; Suddaby et al., 2010; Battilana et al., 2012). Indeed, "markets are constantly on the move as tastes change and advanced products and services raise expectations about future products and prices" (Snow, 2015:5). In tune with pressure from the changing markets, contemporary commercial organizations adopt various combinations of skills, templates and processes for new sources of competitive advantage (Day, 1998, 1999; Foreman and Whetten, 2002). This continuous combination of skills and processes for competitive advantage enabled the rise in the "hybridisation movement", as postulated by Battilana et al. (2012:54). Janus-faced or multidimensional commercial organizations, which in some sense incorporate non-commercial principles, are commonly referred to as hybrid organizations (Karré, 2011; Billis, 2010; Greenwood et al., 2010; Battilana et al., 2012).

At a conceptual level, hybridisation embraces the notion that contemporary commercial organizations may embody multiple templates, logics or values to secure legitimacy and achieve effective organizational performance (Pache and Santos, 2013; Thornton, 2004; Suddaby et al., 2010; Alter, 2007; Foreman and Whetten, 2002; Haigh and Hoffman, 2012). A good number of scholars have supported the idea of hybridity, suggesting that it has the potential for generating effective outcomes for organizations. Such outcomes include making the organizations more enduring, sustainable and innovative (Kraatz and Block, 2008; Jay, 2013). However, other scholars have argued that the concept presents tensions, inconsistencies and contradictions for organizations; a state of affairs that could have adverse consequences for employees' behaviour and trust in the organization (Pache and Santos, 2010; Pache and Santos, 2013; Karré, 2011; Mangen and Brivot, 2014; Reay and Hinings, 2009; Brandsen and Karré, 2011).

This book, therefore, explores the implications of organizational hybridity for employees' trust in commercial hybrid organizations, with a view to making a contribution to theory by providing a fresh perspective for understanding individual-level responses to organizational hybridity. In particular, this is in terms of identifying, among other things, the major tensions faced by employees of these organizations. This study aims to address the gap in the literature between institutional logics and trust, by highlighting the role of religion in influencing employees' behaviour and trust in commercial hybrid organizations. Furthermore, this work addresses the gaps in knowledge relevant to organizational hybridity by extending on the frameworks of Battilana and Lee (2014), and Besharov and Smith (2014). This study extends Battilana and Lee's (2014) framework by highlighting governance, organizational culture, leadership, intra-organizational relationships and trust relations as core attributes of commercial hybrid organizations. In addition, it addresses a gap in Besharov and Smith's (2014) hybrid typology framework, showing how tensions are experienced within hybrid organizations. Finally, this study also makes practical recommendations on how to improve the overall effectiveness and performance of commercial hybrid organizations.

### 1.1.1 Organizational hybridity

In the literature that forms the background of this study, organizational hybridity has been characterised as: A concept developed from research and practice-based evidence for achieving effective organizational performance through the embodiment of multiple institutional logics in a unified strategy (Pache and Santos, 2013; Besharov and Smith, 2014; Battilana and Lee, 2014; Greenwood et al., 2010). The concept of organizational hybridity has attracted much scholarly attention across different disciplines in recent years (Besharov and Smith, 2014; Jäger and Schröer, 2014; Battilana and Lee, 2014; Battilana et al., 2012; Ebrahim et al., 2014; Karré, 2011; Battilana and Dorado, 2010; Mars and Lounsbury, 2008; Lee and Lounsbury, 2015). This growing attention in organizational studies cuts across a variety of fields including healthcare (Dunn and Jones, 2010), micro-finance (Battilana and Dorado, 2010), eco-entrepreneurship (Mars and Lounsbury, 2008), public administration (Skelcher, 2012), toxic waste (Lee and Lounsbury, 2015) and social enterprise (Battilana and Lee, 2014; Battilana et al., 2012; Ebrahim et al., 2014; Doherty et al., 2014). However, the study of hybridity in organizational studies appears to focus mainly on social enterprises (Battilana et al., 2012; Smith et al., 2013b; Doherty et al., 2014). Thus, this study attempts to advance the understanding of organizational hybridity in the sense proposed by Boyd et al. (2009:243): “Hybrid organizations are for-profit organizations which create social value, but are mainly driven by profits and capitalist incentives.” Despite the documented challenges posed by organizational hybridity, research suggests that wider adoption of the growing concept may hold promise for effectively addressing modern-day economic, environmental and social challenges, which traditional organizational practices have increasingly failed to meet (Billis, 2010; Karré, 2011; Boyd et al., 2009).

### 1.1.2 The institutional logics perspective

Institutional logics appears to be one of the most promising perspectives for understanding organizational hybridity and, more specifically, for an understanding of the phenomenon that pays due attention to actors' responses to hybridity (Binder, 2007). Institutional logics has been argued to connect meaning with action by linking internal mental cognitions to external institutions, rituals and practices, and in doing so, provide prescriptions that help actors to make sense of their social reality (Friedland and Alford, 1991; Thornton et al., 2012; Greenwood et al., 2010; Thornton, 2004; Gawer and Phillips, 2013). Thus, this research adopts institutional logics as a meta-theory to explore the implications of organizational hybridity for employees' trust in commercial hybrid organizations. An institutional logics perspective is defined in this study as the intellectual current in sociology and organization theory that places at centre stage: “The socially constructed, historical patterns of material practices, assumptions, values, beliefs, and rules by which organizations and individuals produce and reproduce their material subsistence, organize time and space and provide meaning to their social reality” (Thornton and Ocasio, 1999:804). The general direction of this research lies in showing how employees, who are exposed to multiple institutional logics within commercial hybrid organizations, make sense of, interpret and respond to these logics embodied within the organizations.

### 1.1.3 Organizational trust

Trust has many definitions. In an organizational context I have drawn on the definition of trust provided by Mayer et al. (1995:712): “The willingness of a party to be vulnerable to the actions of another party based on the expectation that the other will perform a particular action important to the trustor, irrespective of the ability to monitor or control that other party.” Trust in an organization has been argued to have a positive influence on employees' workplace attitudes, behaviour, effectiveness and performance (Jones and George, 1998; Rousseau et al., 1998; Mayer et al., 1995; Dirks and Ferrin, 2002). This is because when employees trust the organization, they are more willing to suspend doubts about it and carry out the tasks and objectives set by the leaders towards a common goal (Burke et al., 2007). Thus, trust appears to be a social imperative for the sustainability and effectiveness of contemporary (commercial hybrid) organizations (Fukuyama, 1995). However, so far, research linking organizational hybridity and institutional logics to trust appears to be scarce (Karré, 2011). Nevertheless, literature posits that institutional logics can influence individuals' behaviour (Thornton et al., 2012; Pache and Santos, 2013; Pache, 2010; Battilana, 2006; Farrell and Knight, 2003), as well as foster the development of trust (Bachmann and Inkpen, 2011; Fuglsang and Jagd, 2015). Further empirical research is required to understand how trust might be influenced by multiple logics that prescribe different values for individuals' behaviour. Moreover, very little attention has been paid to the consequences of non-market-orientated institutional logics on employees' trust in commercial hybrid organizations. Hence, this study attempts to address these gaps.

### 1.1.4 The context of the study: Nigeria

Nigeria was chosen as the context for this study for two main reasons. Firstly, judging from my past experiences as a Nigerian who has worked in the country, the Nigerian institutional environment provides a rich context for learning about trust. Moreover, it is an environment that has suffered from a severe trust deficit in previous years (Omeje, 2006). Secondly, Nigeria is a complex, pluralistic and highly institutionalised environment in which competing logics are almost palpable. Its history reflects ongoing regional, community and religious tensions, which reveal the dominance of non-market institutional logics within the society. Thus, Nigeria exemplifies the contextual institutional elements implicit within the research purpose. Nigeria, the largest single geographical unit in West Africa, originated from the merger of the Southern Nigeria Protectorate and the Northern Nigeria Protectorate in 1914 (Central Intelligence Agency, 2013). The country consists of 36 states carved out from seven regions - the North Central, the North East, the North West, the South East, the South-South and the South West, plus the Federal Capital Territory (FCT) (Omeje, 2006). Like Western society as depicted by Friedland and Alford (1991), Nigeria is infused with various institutional logics derived from dominant institutions, such as the capitalist market, religion, family and community, that provide values and meaning to actors' social realities (Omeje, 2006; Ibrahim, 1991).

However, some of these institutions have been argued to fuel recurring conflicts in Nigerian society and the strong influence of factors such as religious affiliation on actors' behaviours make the Nigerian context an interesting subject of consideration in a study, like this one, informed by the institutional logics perspective. Despite the ethnic and political conflicts, even civil war, in the later decades of the 20th century, Nigeria has experienced strong economic growth in recent years, thanks to the dynamism of the private sector (Effoduh, 2014; Kolawole and Omobitan, 2014). The private sector comprises large commercial organizations alongside small- and medium-scale enterprises and self-employment of all kinds (Osemeke, 2011; Kolawole and Omobitan, 2014; Okonjo-Iweala and Osafo-Kwaako, 2007). The case studies for this research are both private sector commercial hybrid organizations, namely ASL and BPL, both of which are located in the FCT Abuja, Nigeria.

## 1.2 Statement of the Problem

In this thesis, I argue that organizational hybridity can offer a promising flexible vehicle for understanding the creation of socially and economically sustainable organizations in both developing and developed countries (Battilana et al., 2012; Boyd et al., 2009). However, despite this potential as a device for scholarly analysis, the literature shows that commercial hybrid organizations could face various tensions as a result of the embodiment of multiple logics, which may prescribe contradictory values for actions. These tensions may take the form of conflicting and mixed messages to employees (Pache and Santos, 2013). Such messages could have implications for employees' behaviour and trust in an organization, as well as affecting its overall performance in the long run.

Interestingly, social enterprise organizations emerged as the most favourable contexts for the study of organizational hybridity in recent years (Battilana et al., 2012; Ebrahim et al., 2014; Smith et al., 2013b; Doherty et al., 2014). This tendency has generated questions regarding the theoretical assumptions surrounding the conceptualisation of organizational hybridity. Researchers such as Besharov and Smith (2014) have argued that the focus on social enterprise is inadequate for advancing the understanding of organizational hybridity. The focus neglects the potential research interest of a broader spectrum of hybrid organizations and their distinguishing dimensions, such as commercial hybrid organizations which are more market focused (Battilana and Lee, 2014; Smith et al., 2013b). By analysing the dynamics of organizational hybridity across a broader spectrum of hybrid organizations, we may get a better understanding of the concept, the tensions posed by hybridity, and how employees working within these organizations make sense of, interpret and respond to the multiple logics prescribed to them. Thus, the overall aim of this study is to understand the implications of organizational hybridity for employees' trust in commercial hybrid organizations, with a view to making both theoretical and practical recommendations.

## 1.3 Research Questions

Yin (2003) suggests that robust research questions guide the research process and methodology, helping the researcher decide upon the type of data required, how best to collect it and the particular focus that the analysis will take. However, while it is important to know what one is looking for (see Table 2), this initial focus should not divert attention from other unanticipated questions that are perhaps more attractive, relevant or manageable than the initial one(s) (Bryman, 2012). The process of developing the research questions (see Table 1) and the research propositions (see Table 3) was based on an extensive review of the literature on organizational hybridity, institutional logics and organizational trust. The research questions were formulated to address the overall research aim, identify objectives of the research and guide the empirical research. The questions were improved by discussions with specialists in the field during conferences and workshops. The questions were revised throughout all phases of the research to ensure that the aim and objectives were achieved.

**Table 1: Primary and Supporting Research Questions**

| **Primary research question:**<br>What are the implications of organizational hybridity for employees' trust in commercial hybrid organizations? |
|---|
| **Supporting research questions:** |
| 1. To what extent does organizational hybridity influence specific attributes of commercial hybrid organizations? |
| 2. What role does religion play in influencing employees' behaviour and shaping other organizational attributes of commercial hybrid organizations? |
| 3. How does organizational hybridity affect the level of employees' trust in commercial hybrid organizations? |
| 4. How can employees' trust in commercial hybrid organizations be sustained for improved effective organizational performance? |

## 1.4 Research Aim, Objectives and Propositions

The overall aim of this research and the research objectives are summarised in Table 2, while the key research propositions are depicted in Table 3.

**Table 2: Research Aim and Objectives**

| **Overall research aim:**<br>The aim of this research is to understand the implications of organizational hybridity for employees' trust in the commercial hybrid organization. |
|---|
| **Research objectives:** |
| 1. To explore the influence of organizational hybridity on specific organizational attributes including governance, leadership, organizational culture, organizational structure and intra-organizational relationships of commercial hybrid organizations. |
| 2. To understand the influence of non-market-orientated institutional logics on commercial hybrid organizations. |
| 3. To shape an understanding of the implications of organizational hybridity for employees' trust in commercial hybrid organizations, with particular attention to those implications having a plausible relationship to organizational effectiveness. |
| 4. To develop research-based recommendations for sustaining employees' trust in commercial hybrid organizations. |

**Table 3: Key Research Propositions**

| **Propositions:** |
|---|
| 1. The more extensive the tensions associated with organizational hybridity, the greater the likelihood of negative behavioural responses by employees. |
| 2. The greater the tensions produced by multiple logics, the less likely it becomes that employees of commercial hybrid organizations will trust their organizations. |
| 3. The greater the employees' trust in commercial hybrid organizations, the more effective the organizational performance. |
| 4. The stronger the employees' affiliations to religious logics, the greater the influence of such logics on employees' behaviour and trust in commercial hybrid organizations. |

## 1.5 Research Strategy and Design

Research can be designed and conducted using various methods and approaches. According to Yin (2003), the appropriateness of a particular research strategy is dependent on the type of investigation. The early stages of this study established that the most important issue to consider was that of determining the best context in which to conduct the study. The key findings from the early literature review revealed that it was essential to carry out the study in a context that best suits the research aim and objectives. The Nigerian institutional environment was selected for this research for the reasons detailed in Section 1.1.4 and Chapter 4.

To answer the research questions shown in Table 1, I conducted an exploratory investigation using qualitative research methods. Owing to the lack of previous studies, it was clear that a qualitative case-study research design was the most appropriate strategy for this study (see Section 4.3.1 The case-study design). A multiple case-study design was chosen for this research, as it would allow the opportunity for a holistic and comparative analysis of the research context. This approach has been used in many fields of social science research and by several researchers (Grix, 2010; Bryman, 2012; Bryman and Bell, 2011). A qualitative case-study research design was appropriate since it provides an excellent opportunity to explore and understand the subjective experiences of the participants. The two case organizations selected for this study – ASL and BPL – were chosen using Besharov and Smith's (2014) framework. This framework was utilised in this study to analyse and assess the nature of hybridity in both organizations.

The initial intention was to select four hybrid organizations operating in Nigeria's private sector that were consistent with Besharov and Smith's hybrid typology. However, due to limited resources and time restrictions, only two hybrid criteria were met: the contested hybrid type and the dominant hybrid type. The detailed justifications for the case-study selection are discussed in Section 3.7 and further detailed in Section 4.3.3. Data collection was undertaken using semi-structured interviews. This research method was chosen based on my interest in the interviewees' subjective interpretations of reality, views and experiences within a naturalistic organizational setting. A total of 20 interviewees were recruited heterogeneously across different levels of the employment hierarchy, including top management executives, middle managers and employees from each of the organizations (ASL and BPL). This was achieved through purposive and snowball sampling. A total of 40 interviews were conducted from both organizations. The estimated duration of each interview was one hour, and data was analysed and interpreted using a thematic approach (Miles and Huberman, 1994; Grix, 2010; Bryman, 2012; Bryman and Bell, 2011; Blaikie, 2009; Symon and Cassell, 2012). Also, online documents from the websites of both companies were analysed for additional information.

## 1.6 Research Process

Research, as defined by Patton (2002:32), is "a systemic process of enquiry whose goal is communicable knowledge". As Yin (2003:21) affirms: "Unless research activity has been carefully planned, data analysis made through established protocols and an effort to disseminate knowledge [made]…it cannot be classed as research."

Reflecting on the above definition, the research process was planned and structured into six continuous, interlinked, reflective and progressive phases, as follows:

1. The initial phase involved an extensive review of literature, analysing current knowledge on the topic and identifying any gaps therein. This phase is presented in Chapter 2.
2. The second phase focused on the formulation of the research problem, questions, propositions and identification of the research context (the Nigerian institutional environment). The conclusion of the first and second phases established the philosophical, theoretical and methodological framework for the study. The second phase is presented in Chapter 3.
3. The third phase is linked to the outcome of the second phase and entailed the development of the empirical research strategy, projecting the conduct of fieldwork, data collection and selecting appropriate techniques for analysis. This phase is presented in Chapter 4.
4. The fourth phase included the fieldwork, using qualitative methods for data collection strategies, namely semi-structured interviews and a review of company documents. This phase is also detailed in Chapter 4.
5. The fifth phase included the analysis and interpretation of the data from both organizations, which included categorising the data into themes and coding. This stage is presented in Chapter 5 and Chapter 6.

6. The final phase summarised the research findings, including making a synthesis of theoretical perspectives and empirical findings, drawing conclusions, and formulating recommendations.

## 1.7 Scope of the Study

To answer the focal research question of “What are the implications of organizational hybridity for employees’ trust in commercial hybrid organizations?” a multiple case-study approach was employed. However, owing to geographical, technical, time, and human and financial resource limitations, the study was focused on only two case studies: ASL and BPL.

The study was constrained by a number of factors, the most important of which were as follows. Firstly, there is a lack of empirical evidence on the activities and performance of commercial hybrid organizations. More so, most of the research on organizational hybridity is based on social enterprises, and the dimensions of organizational hybridity are not well established empirically. Secondly, most of the research investigating organizational hybridity builds on the organizational level of analysis. Thus, there is limited research on individual-level responses to organizational hybridity based on the institutional logics perspective. Furthermore, there is limited literature on organizational hybridity and institutional logics in the Nigerian context. Thirdly, there were delays and difficulties in obtaining approval from case organizations and the timing of the interviews coincided with the suppression of the insurgency (Boko Haram) in the FCT of Nigeria. The restrictions involved in this emergency made movement within the city difficult. Finally, conducting the interviews within the workplace was very stressful for some of the employees, because of the nature of their jobs.

To address these theoretical limitations, a literature review was conducted drawing on a vast body from independent fields such as institutional theory, corporate governance and strategic management. Furthermore, caution was taken during fieldwork, which included scheduling multiple interviews per day and pre-informing the interviewees about the interviews to avoid unnecessary movements around the city. Also, breaks were given to the interviewees when required, to minimise stress. Details of how these limitations were addressed are further discussed in Chapter 4 and Chapter 8.

## 1.8 Rationale and Contributions of the Research

The limited understanding of the concept of organizational hybridity from an institutional logics perspective, especially with particular reference to its implications for understanding employees' trust in the organizations operating in developing countries, provides a compelling rationale for this research. The significance of this study is essentially theoretical as it provides a fresh perspective for understanding individual-level responses to organizational hybridity. In addition, it highlights, among other things, how employees of commercial hybrid organizations experience tensions. Specifically, this study attempts to revive religion as an important institution that strongly influences behaviour at the individual level of analysis; therefore, this is an element that should not be ignored in organizational trust literature. Furthermore, this study contributes to existing knowledge, embodied in the literature relevant to organizational hybridity and the tensions it presents for contemporary organizations, by extending Battilana and Lee's (2014) and Besharov and Smith's (2014) frameworks, which should be of interest to researchers in hybrid organizations. The study provides a different perspective to understand organizational hybridity by highlighting governance, leadership, organizational culture, intra-organizational relations and trust relations as core attributes of commercial hybrid organizations where tensions are likely to occur. However, it also has a practical intent and the recommendations may be of interest to practising managers.

Further reasons why the study is justified and significant are summarised below.

1. This study advances knowledge on organizational hybridity by focusing on another spectrum of it: commercial hybrid organizations. This knowledge could help yield research-based knowledge aimed at developing strategies for the effectiveness and sustainability of these organizations.
2. This study contributes to understanding the relationship between organizational hybridity and trust. Most importantly, it explores the links between institutional logics and trust. Furthermore, it contributes to the very limited knowledge on the role of non-market-orientated institutional logics, such as religious logics, in influencing employees' behaviours and trust in commercial hybrid organizations. Thus, it could help these organizations to understand how to sustain employees' trust.

3. The research contributes to existing knowledge on organizational hybridity by exploring the individual level of analysis – more specifically, individual responses to organizational hybridity. It focuses on the continent of Africa – more specifically Nigeria, which is an environment that is often ignored in management and organizational research.
4. The findings and recommendations from this study, as well as the research methodology, can be used as a reference and point of departure for studies in a similar contextual background. The data and information gathered through this research may suggest and inform future studies.

## 1.9 Summary of Empirical Findings

This study makes a significant contribution to knowledge, with the key empirical findings as follows.

Firstly, organizational hybridity may lead commercial hybrid organizations to use flexibility in adopting distinctive attributes in relation to governance, leadership and organizational culture, which may trigger various degrees of tension. These tensions may result in both positive and negative behavioural responses by the employees. Regarding the positive responses, the data showed that organizational hybridity may have triggered a high level of trust in the organizations and the subsequent progressive behavioural responses from the employees (see Figure 19). However, the data also unveiled a paradoxical effect. Specifically, organizational hybridity may have also triggered distrust in the organizations and the subsequent retrogressive behavioural responses from the employees (see Figure 20). These negative behavioural responses emerged in the form of employee disengagement, opportunism, insubordination and resignation, which may have affected the overall performance of the commercial hybrid organizations.

Secondly, the data also showed that non-market-orientated institutional logics, such as religious logics, played a role in influencing positive employee behaviours in terms of commitment, honesty and trust; and, conversely, it may also promote unethical behaviours such as bribery and corruption (see Section 7.4.1d The influence of religion on employees' behaviours). Finally, the overall findings pointed to the need to sustain employees' trust, which may be achieved through involving the employee in decision-making and clearly communicating organizational values and goals to them to avoid misinterpretation of multiple logics.

# CHAPTER 2

# CONCEPTUALISING ORGANIZATIONAL HYBRIDITY

## 2.1 Introduction

Figure 1: The Research Cycle (Phase 1)

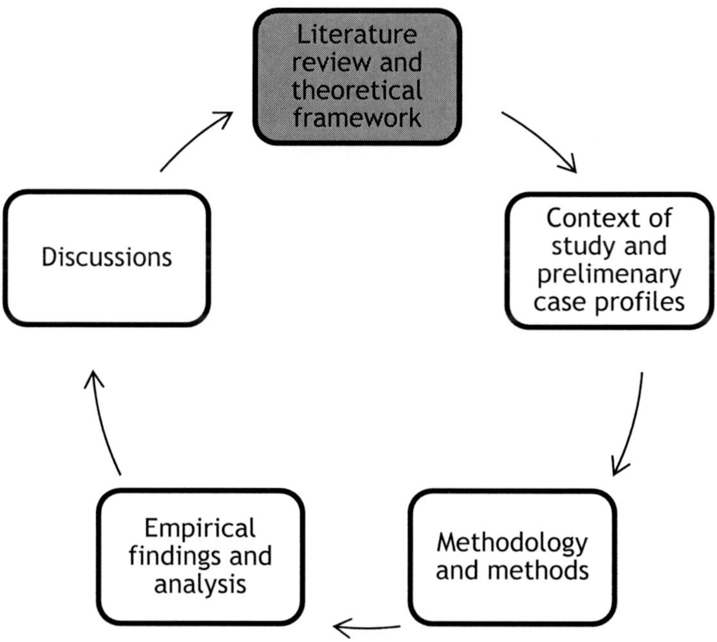


This chapter develops the philosophical and theoretical framework for the study, as illustrated in Figure 1. It introduces an outline of the literature review and discussion of the concept of organizational hybridity, mentioning the benefits and challenges that arise under conditions of hybridity. It proceeds to review how hybridity in organizations has been conceptualised and defined. Particular attention is paid to the institutional logics perspective, which appears to be the most powerful way of conceptualising organizational hybridity. The chapter then goes on to specifically discuss commercial hybrid organizations and raises the particular problem of fostering the trust of employees in such organizations. An overview of this chapter is illustrated in Figure 2: Mind Map of Literature Review. The chapter ends with the main propositions, and an outline of a theoretical framework in which conditions of employees' trust in a commercial hybrid organization are spelt out for development and exploration in later chapters.

Figure 2: Mind Map of Literature Review

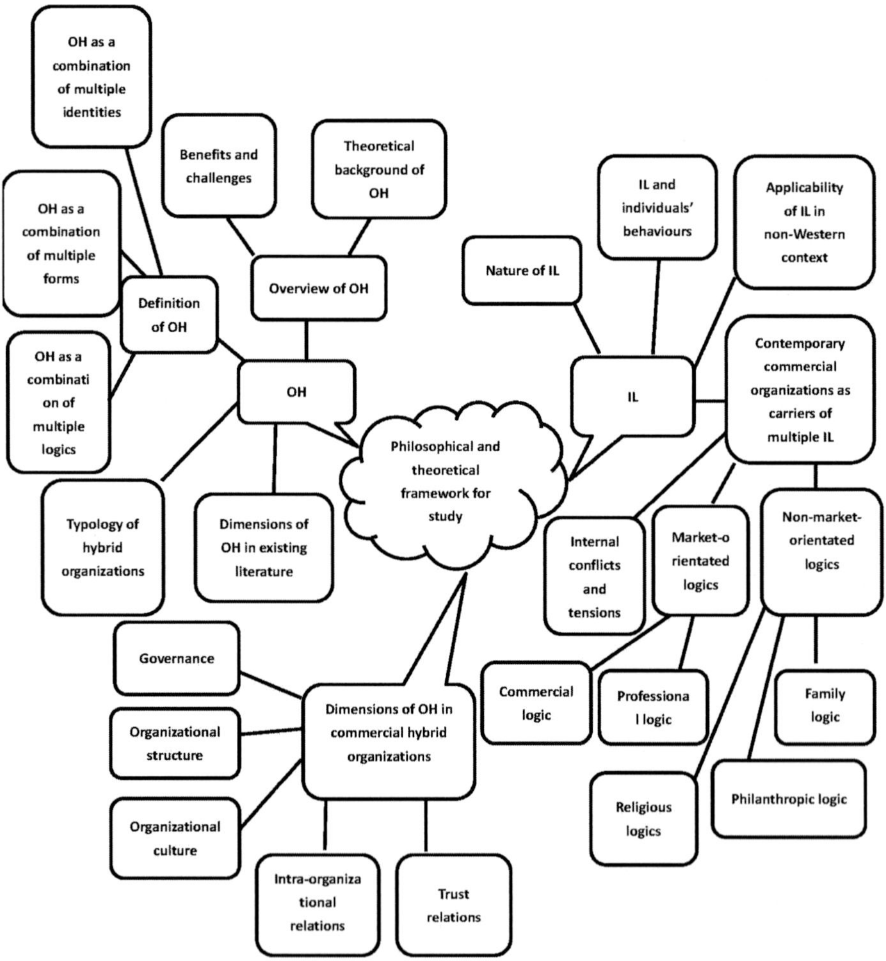

## 2.2 Organizational Hybridity: An Overview

The ways that contemporary organizations operate have evolved significantly in recent times due to constant social, economic, environmental and technological pressure from the institutional environment (Greenwood et al., 2010; Dunn and Jones, 2010; Romanelli, 1991; Shane, 1996). This evolution has led to a rise in the "hybridisation movement" (Battilana et al., 2012:54). A quarter of a century ago DiMaggio (1988) posited that external pressure towards effectiveness and efficiency is pushing more organizations towards hybridity. Such Janus-faced or multidimensional organizations are commonly referred to as hybrid organizations (Karré, 2011; Billis, 2010; Greenwood et al., 2010; Battilana et al., 2012; Martin et al., 2016). In fact, "Hybrid entrepreneurs are opening the ways for a reformation of the current economic order, combining principles, practices and logics of modern capitalism with inclusive humanitarian ideals" (Battilana et al., 2012:55). However, some researchers claim that even though organizational hybridity appears to have burgeoned in recent years, it has long been in existence, as many organizations in the past have innovatively combined various organizational elements to reap economic, governance and performance benefits (Borys and Jemison, 1989; Karré, 2011; Billis, 2010; Alter, 2007; Battilana et al., 2012; Jäger and Schröer, 2014). Nevertheless, this relatively new concept could be essential for understanding the reconfiguration of multiple organizational objectives from completely separate fields to a common space. Such an improved understanding may even be expected to facilitate the real-world development of suitably flexible organizational vehicles for social and economic change in both developing and developed countries (Battilana et al., 2012; Boyd et al., 2009).

### 2.2.1 Organizational hybridity: Theoretical background

Hybridity as a concept is used across various academic disciplines. In all these contexts, though used distinctively, hybridity always implies the combination of multiple elements, which may be contradictory (Brandsen and Karré, 2011). Organizational hybridity has attracted a great deal of scholarly attention in recent years (Besharov and Smith, 2014; Jäger and Schröer, 2014; Battilana and Lee, 2014; Battilana et al., 2012; Ebrahim et al., 2014; Karré, 2011, Battilana and Dorado, 2010; Mars and Lounsbury, 2008; Reay and Hinings, 2009; Tracey, 2012; Pache and Santos, 2013; Lee and Lounsbury, 2015). This growing attention cuts across a variety of fields, including healthcare (Dunn and Jones, 2010; Reay and Hinings, 2009), micro-finance (Battilana and Dorado, 2010), Islamic banking (Tracey,

2012), eco-entrepreneurship (Mars and Lounsbury, 2008), public administration (Skelcher, 2012; Karré, 2011), toxic waste (Lee and Lounsbury, 2015), education (Townley, 1999), music (MacLean and Webber, 2015) and social enterprise (Battilana and Lee, 2014; Battilana et al., 2012; Ebrahim et al., 2014; Tracey et al., 2011). However, the limited literature on organizational hybridity and the distinctive duality of hybrid organizations make them particularly difficult to analyse. For this reason, a large body of the literature used in this review is drawn from the wider fields of corporate governance, institutional theory and strategic management.

An extensive review of the literature shows that social enterprise has emerged as one of the most favourable organizational contexts for the study of organizational hybridity in recent years (Battilana and Lee, 2014; Battilana et al., 2012). Indeed, social enterprises have been argued to exemplify the perfectly aligned hybrid organizations that provide a functional solution towards fulfilling the traditional non-profit social mission in a financially sustainable way (Battilana and Lee, 2014; Battilana et al., 2012). For example, a study by Battilana et al. (2012:51) explored the case of The Hot Bread Kitchen, a social enterprise, which combined social welfare to guide its mission and revenue generation to guide its financial activities. In their study, they highlighted various tensions and conflicts faced by hybrid organizations, classifying these challenges along four organizational dimensions: the legal structure, financing, customer and beneficiary interests, and organizational culture. They concluded that hybrid organizations might require innovation, a distinctive leadership style and persistence to survive.

Similarly, Battilana and Lee's (2014:412) study proposed five key dimensions of hybrid organizing for managing conflicts and tensions posed by organizational hybridity. These dimensions are core organizational activities, workforce composition, organizational design, inter-organizational relationships and culture. According to the authors, hybrid organizing is "the activities, structures, processes and meanings by which organizations make sense of and combine aspects of multiple organizational forms" (Battilana and Lee, 2014:398). Furthermore, like Battilana et al. (2012) and Battilana and Lee (2014), a study by Ebrahim et al. (2014) focused on the key challenges facing the governance of hybrid organizations. They suggested effective means for managing tensions in the governance of hybrid organizations and called for further research for a better understanding of the challenges of organizational hybridity. However, these previous researchers explored organizational hybridity from an organizational level perspective.

On this basis, there appears to be a need to explore organizational hybridity from the micro level of analysis, to understand its implications for employees' behaviour and trust in the organization. Moreover, the attention on social enterprise has, among other things, led people to question the conceptualisation of some of the theoretical assumptions made regarding organizational hybridity. As suggested by Besharov and Smith (2014), a focus on social enterprise will be inadequate for advancing the understanding of organizational hybridity if it fails to capture a broader spectrum of hybrid organizations.

At this point, it is necessary to ask questions such as: Would the experience of these tensions and conflicts be different within the organizations in the event that the degree of misalignment among the multiple objectives embodied by the organizations was greater? In particular, would this be so if the organizations were more market focused? Such ambiguity presents a gap in research on organizational hybridity, which this study attempts to address. Particularly, this research attempts to advance understanding of the various challenges facing hybrid organizations in the sense proposed by Boyd et al. (2009:243): "Hybrid organizations are for-profit organizations which create social value, but are mainly driven by profits and capitalist incentives." Therefore, to restrict ambiguity and unnecessary generalisation, this study is focused primarily on commercial hybrid organizations.

## Commercial organizations as hybrid organizations

While little has been written on organizational hybridity in areas such as commercial organizations, a larger body of literature used in this review is drawn from independent fields such as corporate governance and strategic management. From a strategic management perspective, it is clear that commercial organizations are strongly influenced by market forces (Day, 1998). According to Day, contemporary commercial organizations are proficient in predicting and acting on market shifts and emerging opportunities ahead of competitors. Indeed, "markets are constantly on the move as tastes change and advanced products and services raise expectations about future products and prices" (Snow, 2015:5). In tune with the changing markets, these organizations adopt various combinations of skills and processes for new sources of competitive advantage (Day, 1998, 1999; Foreman and Whetten, 2002).

However, Boyd et al. (2009:202) argued that these organizations may also take a hybrid form by embodying "market-orientated goals and common-good mission goals" to achieve organizational effectiveness and to secure legitimacy. This is because the ultimate form of organizational effectiveness, deeply entrenched in neoliberal thinking in recent years, is to use business and market forces as tools to solve the world's challenges (Boyd et al., 2009). In so doing, they create social value, even though they are mainly driven by market forces and are accountable to shareholders (Boyd et al., 2009:243). Moreover, it is also necessary to note that these hybrid organizations could fall into any part of the hybrid typology suggested by Besharov and Smith (2014) (see Section 2.5.5 Typology of hybrid organizations). Thus, drawing on the study by Boyd et al. (2009), commercial hybrid organizations have the following characteristics:

- They are legally registered
- They provide products and services in the marketplace at competitive prices
- They may be privately held by connected individual investors, such as families
- They employ innovative products in niche markets to increase organizational effectiveness and performance
- They integrate business practices that enable the organization to meet multiple objectives, which may include both commercial and social goals.

### 2.2.2 Benefits and challenges of organizational hybridity

At a conceptual level, hybrid organizations contest the notion of organizations as entities that reproduce a single coherent institutional template to gain legitimacy and secure support from external institutional referents (Pache and Santos, 2013; Thornton, 2004; Suddaby et al., 2010; Battilana et al., 2012; Alter, 2007; Foreman and Whetten, 2002; Haigh and Hoffman, 2012). At a more practical level, many commercial hybrid organizations challenge the notion that the primary objectives of businesses are financial benefits and welcome the idea of balancing economic objectives with social objectives (Battilana and Lee, 2014). In so doing, they offer an infusion of humanitarian principles into modern-day capitalism, which can be seen as promising both economic and social benefits (Battilana et al., 2012). Furthermore, they embody alternative ways of expanding an organization's capabilities, which makes them unusual; however, they present different management challenges than those found in conventional commercial organizations (Borys and Jemison, 1989). These challenges and benefits, which are categorised as economic and social objectives, are discussed next.

### *Economic aspect*

Like conventional commercial organizations, commercial hybrid organizations may be expected to seek to benefit economically by getting access to new markets to increase their financial turnover (Battilana et al., 2012). Such adaptive strategies might appear to be a corollary of an inherent flexibility that allows them to blend into different markets. However, Battilana et al. (2012) warn that the ability to blend into different markets might be perceived as a threat by incumbent organizations that enact institutionalised forms within the same field, provoking reactive responses, which could affect the effectiveness and sustainability of the hybrid entity. Furthermore, regarding the acquisition of financial capital, the rigidity of a single organizational form may be problematic for the hybrid organizations, as well as encouraging mission drift (Battilana et al., 2012; Battilana and Dorado, 2010; Ebrahim et al., 2014). According to Ebrahim et al. (2014), mission drift involves neglecting certain tasks and allowing one task to gain dominance over time. Unfortunately, this could threaten the sustainability of commercial hybrid organizations in the sense that organizations experiencing mission drift could compromise their hybrid nature (Battilana et al., 2012; Battilana and Dorado, 2010; Ebrahim et al., 2014).

### *Social aspect*

While commercial hybrid organizations seek to enjoy financial autonomy, they also strive to be connected to the non-financial social systems in which they operate (Haigh and Hoffman, 2012; Karré, 2011; Battilana et al., 2012; Battilana and Dorado, 2010; Ebrahim et al., 2014). According to Haigh and Hoffman (2012), the flexible nature of hybrid organizations allows them to create positive relationships with stakeholders, based on trust. Indeed, hybrid organizations may create credible trusting relationships and a sense of family for employees through the values they embody. In this way, employees can identify with different values embodied by the organization. This value identification leads to a mutually beneficial relationship (Haigh and Hoffman, 2012:128). However, tensions and conflicts may arise, especially when the objectives set by the organizations espouse contradictory value systems for guiding action (Pache and Santos, 2013; Reay and Hinings, 2009). This could have adverse consequences for employees' trust in the organization (Karré, 2011; Brandsen and Karré, 2011).

Such a problem calls for further investigation, as commercial hybrid organizations are likely to continue to pursue multiple objectives, including those which prescribe contradictory values due to pressure from their environment (Greenwood et al., 2010; Romanelli, 1991). Nevertheless, the main practical issue raised by organizational hybridity is not whether it provides more benefits than challenges, or vice versa, but how to make the "best of both sides of the coin" and increase the sustainability, effectiveness and performance of hybrid organizations (Karré, 2011:16).

Table 4 summarises the benefits and challenges of organizational hybridity.

**Table 4: An Overview of Benefits and Challenges of Organizational Hybridity**

| ***Criteria*** | ***Benefits*** | ***Challenges*** |
|---|---|---|
| ***Economic aspect*** | Increases access to new markets (Battilana and Lee, 2014; Battilana et al., 2012) and financial turnover (Karré, 2011). Increases sustainability, innovativeness (Jay, 2013; Kraatz and Block, 2008) and organizational effectiveness (Karré, 2011). | Unpredictability (Battilana and Lee, 2014; Karré, 2011). May threaten hybrid nature (Battilana and Dorado, 2010) by resulting in mission drift (Ebrahim et al., 2014; Battilana et al., 2012; Battilana and Dorado, 2010). |
| ***Social aspect*** | Enables trust and mutually beneficial intra-organizational relationships (Haigh and Hoffman, 2012; Karré, 2011). | May result in internal conflicts and tensions, and negative implications for employees' trust in the organization (Pache and Santos, 2013; Karré, 2011). |

## 2.3 Organizational Hybridity: Controversies and Definitions

As this study seeks to understand the implications of organizational hybridity for employees' trust in contemporary organizations, an important initial task is to define organizational hybridity. In organizational studies, organizational hybridity has been commonly discussed from three main perspectives: organizational identity, organizational forms and institutional logics (Battilana and Lee, 2014). These perspectives are discussed in turn.

### 2.3.1 Organizational hybridity as a combination of multiple identities

According to Kodeih and Greenwood (2014:10), identity is that which indicates what organizations stand for and allows them to ask themselves "who they are before following a course of action." It is often referred to as the enduring characteristics of organizations that differentiate them from others (Gioia et al., 2000). Organizational hybridity from this perspective requires that organizations combine multiple identities to achieve certain goals (Pratt and Foreman, 2000; Albert and Whetten, 1985; Glynn, 2000; Foreman and Whetten, 2002). Foreman and Whetten (2002) emphasise this point in their terminology of "hybrid-identity organizations". Such organizations are those "whose identity is composed of two or more types that would not normally be expected to go together…it is not simply an organization with multiple components, but it considers itself, alternatively or even simultaneously, to be two different types of organizations" (Albert and Whetten, 1985:270). This dual identity gives the organization the capacity to meet a wider range of expectations than similar organizations with one identity, especially when faced with complex institutional challenges (Pratt and Foreman, 2000). For example, Foreman and Whetten's (2002) study revealed how a rural cooperative combined both normative (supportive of traditional folkways) and utilitarian (supportive of realistic approaches) identities. This unusual combination enabled the organization to gain acceptance from stakeholders.

However, the embodied identities were incompatible because they prescribed different values. While the normative identity emphasised tradition and symbols associated with the community, church and family, the utilitarian identity emphasised economic rationality and profit maximisation. The literature supports the view that this incompatibility could condition identity conflict, since the values prescribed by the embodied identities may not normally go together (Foreman and Whetten, 2002; Pratt and Foreman, 2000). This is not to say that such conflict can never be controlled or turned to account. Pratt and Foreman (2002) suggested compartmentalisation, aggregation, deletion and integration as schemes for managing multiple identities in hybrid-identity organizations. However, caution is necessary here because the literature on organizational identity is vast, and the debate is ongoing regarding the distinction in meaning between organizational identity and organizational image. It would be a pity if such uncertainty were to undermine the theoretical usefulness of the hybrid-identity concept in the context of this research (Whetten, 2006; Gioia et al., 2000).

## 2.3.2 Organizational hybridity as a combination of multiple forms

According to Romanelli (1991:82), "Organizational form refers to those characteristics of an organization that identify it as a distinct entity". From this perspective, organizational hybridity is recognised as a unique combination of multiple strategies, designs and structures (Romanelli, 1991), which becomes institutionalised and taken for granted over time within organizations (Schein, 1984). Such a combination might be planned and deliberate – for example, a strategy to access new markets for new opportunities – or it might be an unintentional innovative combination that occurred by accident (Battilana and Lee, 2014; Jay, 2013; Kraatz and Block, 2008). For example, Battilana and Dorado's (2010) study of the micro-finance industry illustrated how the need to achieve a balance between commercial goals and developmental mission favoured the combination of different strategies in hiring employees. However, as organizational forms vary between similar organizations, so do the organizations' responses to pressure from the organizational field, which makes it difficult to understand the nature of organizational hybridity from this perspective (Romanelli, 1991). Furthermore, the possibility that organizational forms are manifestations of institutional logics, as suggested by Greenwood et al. (2010), implies that to understand organizational forms, there may be the need to understand the underlying institutional logics. This makes the institutional logics perspective a more attractive construct for understanding organizational hybridity in this research.

## 2.3.3 Organizational hybridity as a combination of multiple institutional logics

From the above discussion, the institutional logics perspective appears to be the most promising one for the understanding of organizational hybridity and in particular its implications for employees' trust in commercial hybrid organizations. Organizational hybridity from this perspective entails rejecting the view that organizations are dominated by a single logic (Suddaby et al., 2010). It perceives organizations as entities that combine multiple logics, which concurrently influence the organizational objectives, goals and activities (Pache and Santos, 2010; Besharov and Smith, 2012; Battilana and Lee, 2014; Greenwood et al., 2010; Reay and Hinings, 2009; Seo and Creed, 2002; Thornton and Ocasio, 1999; Thornton et al., 2012; Greenwood et al., 2011). For example, Reay and Hinings' (2009) study examined how healthcare organizations in a market-dominant economy, like that of the Anglo-Saxon countries, combined multiple institutional logics of market and professionalism in novel ways to achieve effective organizational objectives.

Among other studies that have investigated organizational hybridity from this perspective, research by Tracey et al. (2014) showed how two social entrepreneurs created a company named "Aspire" by innovatively combining charity and commercial logics. Other authors have explored the interaction of institutional logics in greater or less generality, including banking logic and social value logic (Battilana and Dorado, 2010), banking logic and religion (Tracey, 2012), philanthropic logic and commercial logic (Alter, 2007), market logic and social activist logic (Mars and Lounsbury, 2008), market logic and environmental sustainability logic (Haigh and Hoffman, 2012), managerial logic and professional logic (Townley, 1997; McCourt and Moores, 2007), orchestral logic and philanthropic logic (MacLean and Webber, 2015), commercial logic and professional logic (Willmott, 1995), and social welfare logic and commercial logic (Battilana et al., 2012). However, studies by Reay and Hinings (2009) and Pache and Santos (2013) challenge the argument that organizational hybridity may be the ideal practice for achieving organizational effectiveness, as suggested by Battilana et al. (2012). These critics point to the fact that the flexibility claimed to inhere in combinations of multiple institutional logics may not yield beneficial results in practice. However, suggesting that the multiplicity of logics would yield benefits ignores the fact that institutional logics may not always be compatible (Friedland and Alford, 1991).

Similarly, Besharov and Smith (2014) have cautioned that even though the benefits of organizational hybridity may have been tried and tested in practice, situations evidencing such favourable outcomes in the case of one organization might produce an entirely different outcome in another, depending on the compatibility and centrality of the multiple institutional logics embodied by the organization (see Section 2.5.4 The coexistence of multiple institutional logics). The point is that there is potential for institutional logics to contradict each other, causing internal tensions especially when the logics prescribe incompatible values for actions and behaviour (Greenwood et al., 2011; Pache and Santos, 2010; 2013; Reay and Hinings, 2009; Townley, 2002; Mangen and Brivot, 2014). For example, combining market logic (which emphasises commercialisation of resources for economic returns) with social welfare logic (which underlines a humanistic approach to achieving public welfare goals) could all too readily result in what it is natural to describe as contradictions (situations where the organization fails to act coherently and where it is not even clear what goal its actions are meant to address). However, what this suggests is that there may be the need for hybrid organizational leaders to ensure that these challenges posed by organizational hybridity are managed effectively to avoid future conflicts (Karré, 2011; Ebrahim et al., 2014; Battilana and Lee, 2014; Battilana et al., 2012). One way of overcoming these challenges, as suggested by Mangen and Brivot (2014), is by understanding the logic identification process of organizational actors, which this research attempts to contribute to.

### 2.3.4 Definition

The above discussion reveals an evidence-based argument regarding the economic and social benefits of organizational hybridity, as well as the potential challenges it presents (Battilana et al., 2012; Karré, 2011; Besharov and Smith, 2014; Battilana and Lee, 2014; Ebrahim et al., 2014). These challenges include the possibility that organizational hybridity could trigger internal tensions and conflicts, which some researchers argue could have implications for employees and their trust in the organization (Karré, 2011; Pache and Santos, 2013). For now, there is limited empirical evidence supporting these assumptions; hence, this research will attempt to contribute to this limited body of knowledge. Despite such possible dangers, there seems to be a consensus that organizational hybridity holds promises for addressing modern-day economic, environmental and social challenges, which conventional organizational practices have failed to address (Billis, 2010; Karré, 2011; Alter, 2007; Battilana et al., 2012).

For the purpose of this research, I propose the following definition of organizational hybridity from an institutional logics perspective: *A concept developed from research- and practice-based evidence for achieving effective organizational performance through the embodiment of multiple institutional logics in a unified strategy.* Embodiment in this context can be defined as the inclusion or adoption of multiple logics in the organizational functioning (Besharov and Smith, 2014). However, to make this position clearer, there is the need for a better understanding of the institutional logics perspective. Figure 3 summarises the various perspectives taken in the definition of organizational hybridity.

Figure 3: Various Perspectives in the Definition of Organizational Hybridity

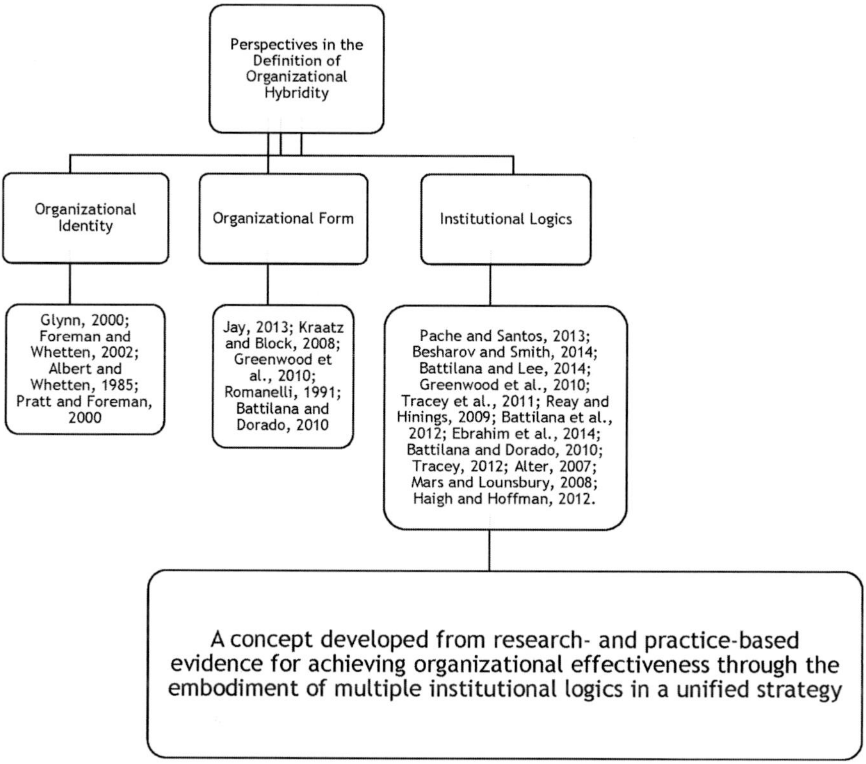


## 2.4 The Institutional Logics Perspective: Philosophical Background

Institutional logics are defined as "the socially constructed, historical patterns of material practices, assumptions, values, beliefs, and rules by which individuals produce and reproduce their material subsistence, organize time and space and provide meaning to their social reality" (Thornton and Ocasio, 1999:804). This definition develops the view that institutional logics connect meaning with action by linking internal mental cognitions to external rituals and practices (Friedland and Alford, 1991; Thornton et al., 2012; Thornton, 2004; Gawer and Phillips, 2013). In doing so, it provides prescriptions that help actors to make sense of their social reality (Friedland and Alford, 1991; Thornton et al., 2012; Greenwood et al., 2010). Sense-making can be understood as "the ongoing retrospective development of plausible images that rationalise what people are doing" (Weick et al., 2005:409). On this basis, the institutional logics approach appears to offer a well-articulated systematic method for understanding how employees experience, interpret, make sense of and sustain trust in hybrid organizations. The institutional logics perspective, since developed within the wider field of institutional theory, was first introduced in Roger Friedland and Robert Alford's work "Powers of Theory" in 1985. It was extended in their 1991 seminal work titled "Bringing Society Back In: Symbols, Practices, and Institutional Contradictions" in *The New Institutionalism in Organizational Analysis* edited by Powell and DiMaggio (Friedland and Alford, 1991). In this article, they highlighted five institutional orders of contemporary Western society that influence actors' behaviour by helping them to make sense of their social reality: the capitalist market, the bureaucratic state, the nuclear family, democracy and the Christian religion.

According to Friedland and Alford (1991), each institutional order is constituted of material and symbolic elements which make up a set of unique organizing principles, values, rules and practices that influence individual and organizational behaviour. For example, the capitalist market prescribes logics, like market and commercial logics that emphasise values that are concerned with the commodification of human and organizational activities (Friedland and Alford, 1991). The central logic of family emphasises values such as unreserved loyalty to those considered as family members. Religion, on the other hand, prescribes logics that are concerned with transcendent values such as honesty and truth (Friedland and Alford, 1991).

The *material* elements of an institutional order refer to the prescribed structures and observable practices, while the *symbolic* elements refer to the values and unobservable meanings anchored within the institution (Friedland and Alford, 1991). For example, the modern-day Christian religion tends to interpret all issues as expressions of moral values and principles of truth, while God is materialised through prayers and other ritualistic behaviours such as communion (Friedland and Alford, 1991). However, this influential work by Friedland and Alford (1991) was criticised by Thornton (2004) who drew attention to, among other things, the fact that their conceptualisation limited religion to Christianity alone leaving out other religions that may exist in other parts of the world. Building on Friedland and Alford's (1991) work, Thornton (2004) and Thornton et al. (2012) revised their conception of institutional order, taking into account a broader definition of the value sphere of religion. They proposed a seven-fold institutional order comprising the market, the corporation, the professions, the state, family, community and religion. On lines similar to Friedland and Alford's (1991) work, they argued that each of the institutional orders has a central logic that prescribes values. These values influence the behaviours of actors and also form part of the actors' identities (Friedland and Alford, 1991; Thornton, 2004; Thornton et al., 2012). For example, the state emphasises the regulation of organizational and human activities through the enforcement of law, financial support, investment policies and legal structures as a means of controlling these actors' behaviours (Cloutier and Langley, 2013; Friedland and Alford, 1991; Lee and Lounsbury, 2015).

The institutional logics can be seen to provide meaning to actors' social reality by constraining not only the ends to which their behaviour is directed but also the means by which those ends are achieved (Friedland and Alford, 1991; Lee and Lounsbury, 2015). Friedland and Alford's (1991) work has contributed heavily to the redirection of scholarly attention toward other institutional logics that could be in play in the context of capitalist society (Hirsch and Lounsbury, 2015). For example, the growth of Islamic banking provides an interesting case of how religion could influence capitalist processes. Similarly, studies have also shown the influence of family logic on an organization's economic performance (Tomes, 1985; Greenwood et al., 2010). Other studies have shown how religion can encourage employees' trustworthy behaviour within organizations (Wagner-Marsh and Conley, 1999). However, how various institutional logics shape individuals' and organizational behaviour calls for further empirical investigation (Tracey, 2012). This, therefore, presents a gap that I propose to address with this empirical research.

### 2.4.1 The nature of institutional logics

Although Friedland and Alford's (1991) original conceptualisation was focused on societal-level phenomena, the concept has evolved across different levels of analysis such as organizational fields, organizations, markets, industries, communities and inter-organizational networks, which allows room for a wider variety of theoretical development (Thornton and Ocasio, 2008). For Friedland and Alford (1991:243), "The society is composed of multiple institutional logics, which are available to individuals and organizations as basis for action", and therefore, rather than privileging one logic over the other, they see these logics as manifest in multiple forms and at multiple levels of analysis (Friedland and Alford, 1991). For example, the organizational fields have their logics, which are derived from societal-level logics. Organizations and individuals situated within these fields draw from those societal- and field-level institutional logics available to them to interpret their social reality (Friedland and Alford, 1991; Thornton et al., 2012; Thornton, 2004; Besharov and Smith, 2014). However, as a result of constant interaction, an institutional logic at one level could be completely taken over by another institutional logic at another level (Thornton et al., 2012; Thornton and Ocasio, 1999; Lounsbury, 2007). For example, Thornton and Ocasio's (1999) case study of higher education textbooks revealed the move from professional editorial logic to corporate profitability logic. On the other hand, logics could alternatively be combined as hybrids by actors harnessing meaning for their identities, actions and behaviours (Besharov and Smith, 2014, Battilana and Lee, 2014; Battilana et al., 2012; Battilana and Dorado, 2010; Pache and Santos, 2013). The process of combining logics takes us back to the concept of organizational hybridity, which is favourable to the view that organizations combine multiple institutional logics to achieve goals, as discussed in Section 2.3.3. However, for unknown reasons, most of the institutional logics literature appears to be focused on the societal, field and organizational levels of analysis with very little attention paid to the individual level. Thus, this research focuses on the individual level of analysis.

### 2.4.2 Institutional logics and individuals' behaviours

The institutional logics perspective emphasises how "societal level institutional orders provide distinct sources of meaning and practices" (Lee and Lounsbury, 2015:1), which are instantiated through behaviours and actions of actors who act as carriers of these institutional logics. Indeed, since "logics are not purely top-down, real people [actors], in real contexts with consequential past experiences of their own, play with them, question them, combine them with institutional logics from other domains, take what they can use from them and make them fit their needs" (Binder, 2007:568). These actors include organizations and individuals (Friedland and Alford, 1991). A number of studies lend support to the view that institutional logics could influence individuals' behaviour (Thornton et al., 2012; Friedland and Alford, 1991; Pache and Santos, 2013; Pache, 2010; Battilana, 2006; Farrell and Knight, 2003; Bachmann and Inkpen, 2011). For example, a religious logic has been shown to influence honest behaviour (Weaver and Agle, 2002; Wagner-Marsh and Conley, 1999), a community logic has been shown to influence philanthropic behaviour (Galaskiewicz, 1997), a family logic has been shown to influence commitment behaviour (Greenwood et al., 2010) and a professional logic has been shown to influence stewardship behaviour (Davis et al., 1997). Furthermore, there have been studies that have argued institutional logics could foster the development of trust and trustworthiness (Bachmann and Inkpen, 2011; Farrell and Knight, 2003; Wagner-Marsh and Conley, 1999). For example, Wagner-Marsh and Conley (1999) theorised that the presence of religious logics within organizations could support the development of mutual trust and honesty among employees.

However, it remains unclear how being exposed to multiple institutional logics can generate stable patterns of employees' behaviour within hybrid organizations. Empirical research may be required to understand its influence on employees' trust dispositions, especially in more market-focused hybrid organizations like the commercial hybrid organizations as they continue to embody multiple logics that may prescribe contradictory values for action. I attempt to address this gap in this research. In summary, the above discussion highlights two assumptions that are critical to this research:

a) Institutional logics are based on institutions (Scott, 1995), which are available to actors in multiple forms and at multiple levels with each bearing its own unique material practices and symbolic construction, providing various values and belief systems that both enable and constrain actors' behaviour (Friedland and Alford, 1991; Thornton and Ocasio, 2008).
b) Since most organizations are situated in environments where multiple institutional logics exist, these organizations may embody multiple institutional logics that prescribe contradictory values for actions, which could have substantial implications for employees' behaviour and trust relations (Farrell and Knight, 2003; Bachmann and Inkpen, 2011; Greenwood et al., 2011; Haigh and Hoffman, 2012).

### 2.4.3 Applicability of institutional logics in non-Western society: The case of Nigeria

Like the Western society as depicted by Friedland and Alford (1991), non-Western societies are permeated by various institutional logics derived from dominant institutions that infuse actors' social realities with values and meaning. Nigeria, for example, is a country dominated by institutional logics prescribed by the family and the capitalist market. However, existing literature shows that other non-market-orientated institutions such as religion are also deeply embedded in the Nigerian society, and as such provide prescriptions for individuals and organizations that operate within these institutional environments (Omeje, 2006). For example, a study by conducted by PEW Research Center in 2013 revealed that over 80% of Nigerians believe that religion plays an important role in their daily lives (Gao, 2015). This is consistent with observations by Tomes (1985) and Hoge et al. (1982) that religion is part of culture acquired during childhood in some societies as a result of its embeddedness. Indeed, the self-perception of many religious individuals includes a belief that their daily and business decisions are guided by their religious prescriptions and convictions (Nash, 1994).

This dominance of religion in the Nigerian institutional environment has led most organizations to be "religion accommodating organizations" (Mazumdar and Mazumdar, 2005); that is, non-religious organizations that show tolerance and consideration for religion. Such consideration includes allowing prayers to be said at the start of work every morning, or having prayer rooms within the organization's premises (Tracey, 2012). Indeed, the institutional order of religion in Nigeria is deeply embedded and very pervasive. This being the case, it is hard to recognise, especially from within the culture. Research-based approaches can only help to make headway in understanding the dynamics of hybrid organizations in Nigeria if they come up with solid results, which people can evaluate. In the absence of such results, the challenges associated with organizational hybridity may never be adequately understood, especially in the Nigerian context. So far, there is only very limited research addressing these issues. This comes as no surprise as Africa, as a research context, is often ignored in management research (Zoogah et al., 2015). Thus, I highlight this as yet another gap that I propose to address with this research.

## 2.5 Contemporary Commercial Organizations as Carriers of Multiple Institutional Logics

Since institutional logics provide distinct sources of meaning, which are instantiated through behaviours and actions of actors, it makes sense to argue that "Organizational forms and managerial practices are manifestations of, and legitimated by institutional logics" (Greenwood et al., 2010:1). This suggests that to understand how multiple institutional logics manifest within commercial hybrid organizations, it is necessary to trace the institutional logics that are embedded within the institutional environment, which organizations may embody (Greenwood et al., 2010). For the purpose of this research, these institutional logics, based on Friedland and Alford's (1991) conceptualisation, can be broadly classified as market-orientated institutional logics and non-market-orientated institutional logics.

### 2.5.1 Market-orientated institutional logics

Market-orientated logics, broadly reflecting the influence of the capitalist market, can be classified as institutional logics that emphasise marketisation and commercialisation of human and organizational resources and activities (Friedland and Alford, 1991). According to Lee and Lounsbury (2015:8), market-orientated logics "have helped fuel processes of financialisation, commensuration, and marketisation" for a very long time. For example, from a corporate governance theory perspective, the traditional purpose of commercial organizations was to maximise profit and shareholders' wealth (Aguilera and Jackson, 2010; Davis et al., 1997; Zajac and Westphal, 2004). This emphasis on financial performance has become a driving force for most businesses, thanks to the widening of markets and removal of anti-competitive barriers associated with the dominance of Western capitalism (Aguilera and Jackson, 2010). Organizations driven by market-orientated logics approach their employees guided by the notion that human resources should be managed for revenue and profit maximisation in the same way as other resources (Aguilera and Jackson, 2010). For example, downsizing is often linked to a thoughtful response to market forces (Zajac and Westphal, 2004). In other words, employees are arguably perceived as part of the environment that can be exploited for the sole purpose of maximising shareholders' returns (Davis et al., 1997; Friedland and Alford, 1991; Day, 1998, 1999).

### 2.5.2 Non-market-orientated institutional logics

As distinct from market-orientated logics, the non-market-orientated logics prescribe values that are not focused on commodification and commercialisation of resources. Such logics are rather based on a normative perspective that is open to considering moral commitments, good citizenship, value creation, stakeholder involvement and ethical responsibility, trust, fairness, and corporate social responsibility (Friedland and Alford, 1991). From a corporate governance theory perspective, Freeman (1984) argued against the idea that business organizations show a predominantly capitalist orientation, pointing out that organizational activities are also rooted in a network of social relationships, and their existence is dependent on the stakeholders' consent, not just that of the shareholders. Indeed, Freeman (1994) argued that non-market values are a substantial part of doing business. This is close to the view that "each stakeholder group merits consideration for its own sake and not merely because of its ability to further the interests of some other group, such as shareholders" (Donaldson and Preston, 1995:67). On this basis, from this perspective employees are unlikely to be perceived as merely part of an environment to be exploited solely for economic objectives (Freeman, 1984). However, evidence of the role of non-market-orientated logics in influencing economic behaviour at the individual level appears to be scarce (Mars and Lounsbury, 2008). So far, research illustrates these influences at the organizational level. For example, interesting studies by Tomes (1985) from an economics perspective illustrated how non-market institutional logics influenced economic organizational performance. In their studies, family and religious logics respectively influenced the overall performance of the organizations in terms of production, distribution, and consumption of goods and services in an environment where these logics are dominant, even though they are not typically considered as part of the economic compass.

There is no denying that commercial organizations are joining the "hybridisation movement", as speculated by Battilana et al. (2012), because of institutional pressures triggered by market developments. Based on the discussion so far, it appears that contemporary commercial organizations are likely to embody both market- and non-market-orientated logics as they respond to changing markets and fulfil organizational goals (Lee and Lounsbury, 2015; Battilana et al., 2012; Greenwood et al., 2011). However, dealing with multiple institutional logics could be most challenging for commercial hybrid organizations, as internal tensions and conflicts are likely to be provoked, thanks to contradictory values prescribed by embodied logics as discussed in Section 2.5.3 (Battilana and Dorado, 2010). These tensions are discussed next, along with the implications of these tensions for employees' behaviours. It is also implied that institutional logics may have fundamental incompatibilities, which may become noticeable when they are combined (Pache and Santos, 2013). This assertion is consistent with Friedland and Alford's (1991) initial conceptualisation, which argues that institutional logics highlight the heterogeneity that materialises when diverse social orders interact with one another across varied contexts. As such, this provides insights into the contradictions that emerge in values and practices (Thornton and Ocasio, 2008; Besharov and Smith, 2014; Hirsch and Lounsbury, 2015). However, to thoroughly understand how these contradictions occur, it is important to explore specifically the types of logics that could be embodied by commercial hybrid organizations.

### 2.5.3 Types of institutional logics embodied by commercial hybrid organizations

Some of the frequently discussed logics in the literature are commercial logic, professional logic, family logic, philanthropic logic and religious logic. Each of these logics could be categorised as either market orientated or non-market orientated, as specified above. These logics are now discussed in turn.

#### 2.5.3a Commercial logic

Commercial logic is underpinned by the values of capitalism, which prescribe marketisation and commercialisation of resources (Friedland and Alford, 1991; Lee and Lounsbury, 2015). More so, capitalism emphasises revenue generation (Mangen and Brivot, 2014). The influence of commercial logic is nowhere more evident than in the *Fortune 500* organizations, where marketisation and commercialisation of resources are perceived as central to organizational functioning, reinforced by the expectations of shareholders and customers (Besharov and Smith, 2014; Battilana and Dorado, 2010). Furthermore, research reveals that commercial logic may be reinforced and supported by other institutional logics derived from institutional orders that prescribe consistent values, like a professional logic (Besharov and Smith, 2014). A professional logic is in line with market principles as it emphasises historically warranted norms of payment, e.g. the equitable treatment of all executives (Crombie, 2013). Employees in commercial hybrid organizations are often motivated by economic and financial rewards prescribed by professional norms to keep their goals aligned with the organization's goals of profit maximisation (Aguilera and Jackson, 2010). Referring to such "professional" perquisites as stock options, Lee and Lounsbury (2015:1) argued: "market [commercial] logics can press actors to focus attention on shareholder value maximisation through stock price appreciation and dividend increases". However, the influence of commercial logic has generated much critical discussion regarding its effects on both organizational and individual levels. Research argues that it encourages adverse consequences, such as self-interest at the individual level and opportunistic behaviour at that of the organization (Lee and Lounsbury, 2015; Farrell and Knight, 2003; Davis et al., 1997; Eisenhardt, 1989). Further research is needed to understand more fully its implications for employees' behaviour when combined with other logics that prescribe contradictory values for actions.

### 2.5.3b Professional logic

Professional logic is argued to draw legitimacy from the institutional order of the professions (Thornton et al., 2012; Mangen and Brivot, 2014). The latter essentially means an insistence that control and management of work should be based on expertise (Freidson, 2001). According to Mangen and Brivot (2014), professional logic shapes the identity and values of actors according to their profession's norms. It emphasises "unique strategic knowledge that is required for efficient allocation [and management] of corporate resources" (Zajac and Westphal, 2004:436). Professional logic exercises its influence over members' behaviour and actions through prescribed codes of conduct, norms and rules (Besharov and Smith, 2014). Interestingly, researchers have argued that the values prescribed by professional logic are consistent with the stewardship theory of corporate governance (Davis et al., 1997). This is because, like the stewardship theory, professional logic emphasises the need for maximisation of shareholder/stakeholder value through efficient and effective management of the organization's resources (Davis et al., 1997; Zajac and Westphal, 2004). This line of argument suggests that professional logics are likely to reinforce commercial logic rather than contest it due to the compatibility of the values prescribed (Besharov and Smith, 2014).

On the other hand, there are recent arguments that a professional logic may not always reinforce a commercial logic. For example, while professional logic may have been classified as a market-orientated logic in the financial sector due to the ability to reinforce market or commercial logics, professional logic could conflict with market-orientated logics in other sectors, like the medical field. In Reay and Hinings' (2009) study, medical professionals rejected the idea that patient care should be provided on a basis of cost-effectiveness. They also found objectionable the idea of their behaviours being guided by market-orientated principles and the commercialisation of their professional services, which led them to reject the "business-like healthcare" system proposed by the government. Moreover, when multiple professional groups are active within the same sphere, they may compete for power and legitimacy since each group emphasises its own logic as unique and superior to that of the other group. This may be because well-established links to the values prescribed strengthen a logic's influence over members' behaviour, whereas weaker ties limit its influence (Greenwood et al., 2010). Again, Reay and Hinings

(2009) showed how resilient links to multiple professional groups resulted in the centrality of both logics – of medical professionalism and "business-like healthcare" – within hospitals and health services organizations in Canada.

### 2.5.3c Family logic

The importance of family as an institutional order implies that family logic is likely to have a strong influence on organizational and employees' behaviour, as suggested by Friedland and Alford (1991). Family-influenced organizations have unique attributes derived from patterns of ownership and governance that may influence the value and belief systems of the organizations, as contrasted with non-family-influenced organizations (Payne et al., 2011). However, the role of family logic and how far it represents a distinct approach in business "has largely escaped serious comparative historical analysis" (James, 2006:2). Family logic could influence employees to the extent that organizational values are considered as part of the family identity (Chung and Luo, 2008). This could be a result of the paternalistic approach often adopted by family businesses, which minimises grievances by developing a strong internal sense of solidarity and goodwill (James, 2006:145). Dyer and Whetten's (2006:797) study supports this by arguing that family firms are more likely to be socially responsible actors than non-family-owned firms. An identity thus generated could promote employees' commitment to the organization.

Similarly, the study by Payne et al. (2011) supports this line of argument by suggesting that family firms are more likely to reflect empathy, warmth and zeal than non-family firms. The study by Greenwood et al. (2010) articulates this line of argument differently, maintaining that the influence of family logic promotes a "mild version" of employees' commitment to the organization. However, according to research, this "relationship-based capitalism" may not easily survive in a market-focused family organization because of the inherent tension between the underlying contradictory values of family and business logics (Foreman and Whetten, 2002). On the other hand, arguing from an identity perspective, Foreman and Whetten's (2002) study showed that, where an organization combined business and family identities, such identity congruence had a significant positive effect on employees' commitment. This suggests that an employee's identification with family values prescribed by a family-orientated organization is likely to increase the employee's commitment. However, further empirical investigation is required to legitimise this conjecture.

### 2.5.3d Philanthropic logic

The community as an institutional order may also exert a strong influence on organizational activities to the extent that it could shape corporate executives' decisions, especially in the area of corporate social responsibility and philanthropy (Galaskiewicz, 1997:467). Indeed, Galaskiewicz's (1997) study argued that an organization's affiliations to the community may trigger social engagement and philanthropic activities towards a group of people. The community as an institutional order emphasises "social fitness", drawing upon mental models and value systems shared by a group of individuals, and by raising the salience of these shared values to exert control on the behaviour of actors (Marquis et al., 2011; Marquis and Lounsbury, 2007; Bachmann and Inkpen, 2007). For example, Marquis and Lounsbury's (2007) study revealed how the strong influence of community enabled local banking professionals to resist market logics prescribed by the national banks, resulting in the creation of new community banks to preserve the community logic of banking.

This suggests that the influence of community could enable interpretations that become adopted at the organizational level and in so doing could reinforce commitment to a particular group of people (Lee and Lounsbury, 2015). Recent research has focused on how shared values and traditions could increase commitment to a particular group of people. This could manifest in the form of generous philanthropic activities, stakeholder involvement, corporate social responsibility and fairness (Lee and Lounsbury, 2015; Greenwood et al., 2010; Marquis and Lounsbury, 2007; Thornton et al., 2012). However, like professional logic, philanthropic logic is likely to fall into synch with, or be activated by, logics that have compatible underlying values, such as family logic, that in itself triggers a sense of communal identity and oneness (James, 2006; Greenwood et al., 2010; Lee and Lounsbury, 2015). Future research will need to investigate further how logics with similar values may enable each other within hybrid organizations.

### 2.5.3e Religious logics

Finally, religion continues to play an important role in contemporary urban societies, and in some societies, religion plays a preponderant role in shaping the way people construct their social realities and take actions (Mazumdar and Mazumdar, 2005). Based on this assumption, research in psychology and sociology has investigated various behavioural influences and the implications of religious logics for individuals and organizations

(Weaver and Agle, 2002; Tracey, 2012). For example, Weaver and Agle (2002) found that religion could influence actors' behaviour as a result of their strong affiliations to it. The self-perception of many religious executives includes a belief that their business decisions are guided by their religious values and commitments (Nash, 1994). Furthermore, religious logics are likely to be activated by family logic within organizations, especially in societies where religion forms part of the family or cultural values acquired during childhood (Tomes, 1985; Hoge et al., 1982). For example, in Weaver and Agle's (2002:77) study, Aaron Feuerstein, CEO of Malden Mills, cited his Jewish religious convictions among the reasons for continuing to pay his production workers even after his manufacturing facilities burned down.

However, even though religion is assumed to influence socially constructed positive behaviours such as humility, honesty and trustworthiness (Wagner-Marsh and Conley, 1999), empirical research has revealed inconclusive findings regarding its relationship with unethical behaviour. Nevertheless, given the profound dominance of religion in some societies (Friedland, 2011), its influence on commercial hybrid organizations and their employees is still under-studied and calls for further empirical research. Thus, this research attempts to address this gap by assessing the accuracy of assumptions concerning the influence of religious logic on both individual and organizational behaviours.

Table 5 summarises the above logics embodied by commercial hybrid organizations and their implications for actors' behaviour.

**Table 5: Summary of Institutional Logics embodied in Commercial Hybrid Organizations**

| **Criteria** | **Market-orientated institutional logics** (Instrumental perspective that involves marketisation and commodification of human and organizational resources (Aguilera and Jackson, 2010; Davis et al., 1997; Zajac and Westphal, 2004) | | **Non-market-orientated institutional logics** (Normative perspective that considers moral commitments, good citizenship, value creation, stakeholder involvement and ethical responsibility, trust, fairness, and corporate social responsibility (Friedland and Alford, 1991; Freeman, 1984) ⟷ | | |
|---|---|---|---|---|---|
| **Institutional logics in commercial hybrid organizations** | Commercial logic | Professional logic | Family logic | Philanthropic logic | Religious logics |
| **Links to institutional order** | The capitalist market | The profession | The family | The community | Religion |

| | | | | | |
|---|---|---|---|---|---|
| **Assumptions about prescribed values** | The control and management of work are based on marketisation and commercialisation of resources, which are perceived as central to organizational functioning, reinforced by the expectations of shareholders and customers (Besharov and Smith, 2014; Battilana and Dorado, 2010) | The control and management of work are based on expertise and unique strategic knowledge that are required for efficient allocation of corporate resources (Zajac and Westphal, 2004; Mangen and Brivot, 2014) | The control and management of work are based on family identity, and the paternalistic approach often adopted makes for a strong internal sense of solidarity, commitment and goodwill (James, 2006; Payne et al., 2011) | The control and management of work are based on value systems sharing a commitment to a particular community (Marquis and Lounsbury, 2007; Lee and Lounsbury, 2015) | The control and management of work are based on religious values and commitments (Nash, 1994; Tomes, 1985) |
| **Assumptions about implications for actors' behaviour** | Opportunistic and self-interested behaviour (Lee and Lounsbury, 2015; Farrell and Knight, 2003; Davis et al., 1997; Eisenhardt, 1989) | Stewardship behaviour (Davis et al., 1997; Zajac and Westphal, 2004; Davis et al., 1997) | Solidarity and loyal behaviour (Chung and Luo, 2008; James, 2006; Payne et al., 2011) | Philanthropic and charitable behaviour (Lee and Lounsbury, 2015; Greenwood et al., 2010; Marquis and Lounsbury, 2007; Thornton et al., 2012) | Humble, empathetic and concerned behaviour (Weaver and Agle, 2002; Wagner-Marsh and Conley, 1999) |

### 2.5.4 The coexistence of multiple institutional logics

How hybrid organizations embody multiple logics – such as commercial, professional, religious, philanthropic and family logics – in a unified strategy has been variously addressed in recent studies (Pache and Santos, 2013; Battilana and Dorado, 2010; Tracey et al., 2011). The embodiment of multiple logics simply means the inclusion or adoption of these logics in the organizational functioning (Besharov and Smith, 2014). However, Besharov and Smith (2014), in particular, have argued that the extent to which multiple logics coexist within hybrid organizations is likely to differ based on the degree of compatibility and the degree of centrality of the logics. Therefore, commercial hybrid organizations have to be prepared to contend with the potential tensions and contradictions that may arise, especially when the embodied logics are incompatible (Battilana and Lee, 2014).

***The degree of compatibility of multiple institutional logics***

The degree of compatibility refers to the extent to which multiple logics provide consistent prescriptions for actors' behaviour and actions (Besharov and Smith, 2014). For example, a study by Greenwood et al. (2010) illustrated how both family and community logics embodied in Spanish companies prescribed compatible guidelines for action by providing consistent values, which enabled them to reinforce each other rather than contradict each other. They argued that market logics and professional logics may be considered to be relatively more compatible than market logics and state logics; thus, the conflicts and tensions that may arise under conditions in which such pairings of logics are in play are likely to be less severe in the former case and more severe in the latter case. In other words, logics that prescribe relatively similar values are more likely to be compatible than logics that prescribe dissimilar values (Besharov and Smith, 2014).

Logics are incompatible, however, when they provide inconsistent and contradictory prescriptions for actions. According to Ford and Ford (1994:763), "phenomena are seen as contradictory when opposing processes and principles coexist and each taken separately would have an opposite effect". For example, Pache and Santos's (2013) study of integrated enterprises in France revealed the incompatibility between commercial logic and social welfare logic, which resulted in contradictions when both logics governed the same situation since each one prescribed values for actions that were inconsistent with the other. Thus, compatibility is high when the logics prescribe similar values and it is low when they prescribe dissimilar values for actions and behaviour (Besharov and Smith, 2014).

***The degree of centrality of multiple institutional logics***

According to Besharov and Smith (2014:369), the degree of centrality is the "extent to which multiple logics are each treated as valid and relevant to organizational functioning". For example, social enterprise organizations embody social logics and commercial logics through their core work values, mission, strategy and routines, which are equally central to organizational functioning (Pache and Santos, 2013; Battilana and Lee, 2014). Thus, centrality is high when organizations embody within their core organizational features multiple logics that are equally central to organizational functioning and it is low when the logics are not equally central to core organizational functioning (Besharov and Smith, 2014). When centrality is low, other logics embodied by the organization are embedded through peripheral activities that may or may not be linked to core organizational functioning (Besharov and Smith, 2014). To further understand how multiple institutional logics coexist within hybrid organizations, Besharov and Smith (2014) developed a typology of hybrid organizations.

### 2.5.5 Typology of hybrid organizations

Besharov and Smith (2014:367) suggested four ideal types of hybrid organizations – *dominant*, *estranged*, *contested* and *aligned* – to illustrate how multiple logics coexist within hybrid organizations (see Figure 4). However, the authors warned that the lines between these types are blurry, such that organizations can be located at any point along each dimension over time, as changes in the organization and institutional environment occur. This typology is useful for analysing and identifying the extent of hybridity in the commercial hybrid organizations selected as the case studies for this research in the subsequent chapter.

Figure 4: The Ideal Types of Hybrid Organizations (Besharov and Smith, 2014)

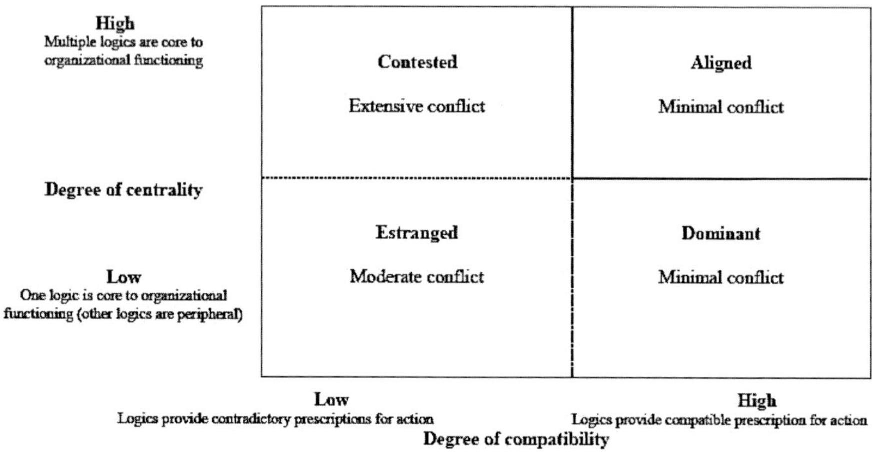


## 2.5.5a Dominant

Organizations in this category represent high compatibility and low centrality of multiple logics (Besharov and Smith, 2014). High compatibility means that the embodied logics prescribe consistent and similar values for actions, rendering the logics compatible as stated earlier. An example would be using professional logic to achieve financial goals (Zajac and Westphal, 2004; Aguilera and Jackson, 2010). Low centrality, on the other hand, suggests that the embodied logics are not equally central to organizational functioning. Because centrality is low, the most prominent logic appears to be dominant in the organization's structure, culture, mission, work practices and identity, while being reinforced by peripheral logic(s) (Besharov and Smith, 2014). For this reason, dominant hybrid organizations are likely to experience a low level of internal conflicts, since one logic appears to be dominant with the other embodied logics providing values for actions consistent with those of the dominant logic (Besharov and Smith, 2014).

## 2.5.5b Estranged

Organizations in this category represent low centrality and low compatibility of multiple logics (Besharov and Smith, 2014). While low centrality implies that the embodied logics are not equally central to organizational functioning, low compatibility, on the other hand, suggests that the embodied logics prescribe inconsistent values for organizational actions.

The low compatibility between embodied logics suggests that actors are likely to be put in a position of using means, or promoting ends, that are incompatible with other values prescribed within the organization. However, Besharov and Smith (2014) argued that the level of conflict is moderate rather than extensive. This is because, as in the case of dominant hybrids, low centrality ensures that the most prominent logic dominates the organization's structure, mission, processes, culture and identity. As a result, when internal conflict arises, this is likely to be resolved in favour of the dominant logic. This was illustrated in Townley's (2002) study on a Canadian cultural organization. This study revealed how pressure from the institutional environment led an organization – Cultural Facilities and Historical Resources (CFHR) – to embody a professional logic of culture preservation and education and market logic as equally central to the organizational functioning. However, employees' strong adherence to the old values of cultural preservation and education meant that both logics were not equally central, i.e. it was a situation of low centrality of logics. As a result, market logic did not equally influence organizational functioning with the other logics.

### 2.5.5c Contested

Organizations in this category represent low compatibility and high centrality of multiple logics (Besharov and Smith, 2014). High centrality means that the embodied logics are equally central to the organizational functioning, while low compatibility suggests that the embodied logics prescribe incompatible values for actions. In other words, although the embodied logics are equally central to organizational functioning, they prescribe inconsistent values for actions due to their incompatibility. As a result, the core of the organization is continually disputed, leading to extensive conflicts; internal conflict in contested hybrid organizations is widespread and intractable (Besharov and Smith, 2014). As these organizations have high centrality, multiple logics are equally incorporated in their mission, culture, structure, identity and core work practices. This is likely to result in employees' lacking clarity as to which goals to prioritise, which could threaten the hybrid nature of the organization (Besharov and Smith, 2014; Battilana and Dorado, 2010). Battilana and Dorado's (2010) study showed just such a course of events. Their case-study organization, BancoSol, embodied banking logic for profit maximisation and development logic in pursuit of alleviating poverty by serving members of the community in need of support; its corporate mission thus prescribed contradictory values for actions, yet both prescriptions were central to organizational functioning. The organization reasonably enough hired employees who had experience in either social welfare or banking. However, this approach resulted in extensive internal conflicts promoted by both groups as each one advocated practices consistent with the values prescribed by its professional affiliations – a situation that led in the long run to the resignation of the CEO (Battilana and Dorado, 2010).

#### 2.5.5d Aligned

Finally, organizations in this category represent high compatibility and high centrality of multiple logics (Besharov and Smith, 2014). High compatibility implies that multiple logics prescribe consistent values for action. Like the contested hybrid organizations, high centrality means that multiple logics equally exert a strong influence over organizational functioning. As a result, the core of the organization is integrated even as it reflects goals, culture, identities and practices associated with multiple logics, resulting in minimal conflicts (Ebrahim et al., 2014; Besharov and Smith, 2014). Extensive research has been conducted in the area of social enterprises, as tokens of what has been argued to be the perfectly integrated hybrid type (Battilana and Lee, 2014; Battilana et al., 2012; Ebrahim et al., 2014). Such an assumption is reasonable given that social enterprises fulfil social objectives through commercial revenue generation using an integrated strategy (Battilana et al., 2012). The study by Battilana et al. (2012) on The Hot Bread Kitchen, which embodied social welfare logic to guide its development mission and commercial logic to guide its revenue generation activities, is exemplary here. However, to fully understand how tensions are experienced within hybrid organizations, future research will need to be extended to other types of hybrid organizations, especially the contested, estranged and dominant hybrid types.

### 2.5.6 Internal tensions and conflicts

According to Schumpeter (2009), the biggest problem with hybrid organizations is that they are inherently conflicted organizations stricken by all sorts of contradictory pressures. This means that their internal operations can be hard to understand and their behaviour difficult to predict. However, as Besharov and Smith (2014) point out, internal tensions experienced within hybrid organizations are likely to vary between organizations. These tensions are likely to be pervasive, given the fact that institutional logics are operative in both symbolic and material systems (Friedland and Alford, 1991; Scott, 2001; Pache and Santos, 2013; Besharov, 2014). The literature attests to the effects upon employees: Pache and Santos (2013) specifically noted tensions that could occur upon employees’ reception of mixed or inconsistent messages, where incompatible logics become manifest in the form of contradictions. Contradictions contribute to the destruction of meaning by constraining and limiting the construction of certain meanings (Karré, 2011). For example, adopting structures of decentralised and centralised decision-making within the same organization could generate value conflicts for employees as these structures evaluate actions in contradictory ways. Similarly, in a "business-like healthcare" system, a doctor may be torn between offering his/her patients every possible treatment and the need to cut costs when both logics are embodied within the same organization (Karré, 2011).

According to Farrell and Knight (2003), employees' responses to these tensions could manifest in forms of opportunistic behaviour and disregard for rules, which may include challenging, for their own advantage, the values on the basis of which their identities are formed within the organization. Additionally, distrust in the organization is likely to develop as employees' goals no longer appear to be aligned with the organizational goals, which is a situation that could compromise the effectiveness of the organization (Friedland and Alford, 1991; Pache and Santos, 2013; Karré, 2011; Reay and Hinings, 2009; Karré, 2011; Seo and Creed, 2002; Greenwood and Hinings, 1996; Marquis and Lounsbury, 2007; Battilana et al., 2012). Furthermore, it is clear that technology, innovation and management alone do not guarantee the effectiveness of the commercial hybrid organizations; trust is equally important because it facilitates effective performance by employees (Dirks and Ferrin, 2002; Sharkie, 2009). Moreover, several studies have found that trust in the organization can have highly beneficial consequences for the organization; for example, where it motivates employees' commitment (Bhattacharya et al., 1998; Holton, 1994; Mayer et al., 1995; Shockley-Zalabak et al., 2010). Since this is the case, it is likely that maintaining employees' trust in the organizations could help manage these internal tensions and conflicts, and improve the overall performance of commercial hybrid organizations (Battilana and Lee, 2014; Ebrahim et al., 2014; Ménard, 2011; Kam, 2009; Hosmer, 1995). For now, this is only an inconclusive conjecture and the implications of these tensions for employees' trust in organizations remain unclear (Pache and Santos, 2013; Bjerregaard and Jonasson, 2013). This creates another gap to be addressed empirically. However, it is possible to conclude from the literature that organizational hybridity requires constant vigilance due to the high risks of enabling internal tensions and conflicts. I turn now to discuss the dimensions of organizational hybridity, based on the literature.

## 2.6 Dimensions of Organizational Hybridity

As stated earlier, recent research on organizational hybridity has focused on various underlying interplays resulting in the varying levels of internal conflicts and tensions experienced within hybrid organizations (Thornton and Ocasio, 2008; Ebrahim et al., 2014; Haigh and Hoffman, 2012; Battilana et al., 2012; Lounsbury, 2007; Thornton, 2004; Greenwood et al., 2011; Thornton and Ocasio, 1999; Reay and Hinings, 2009; Dunn and Jones, 2010; Thornton and Ocasio, 2008; Pache and Santos, 2013; Besharov and Smith, 2014; Battilana and Lee, 2014). Based on the literature in organizational hybridity, and primarily using Battilana and Lee's (2014) framework, these tensions are prominent in five organizational attributes: organizational activities, workforce composition, organizational design, inter-organizational relationships and organizational culture, as illustrated in Figure 5.

Figure 5: Dimensions of Organizational Hybridity in the Literature

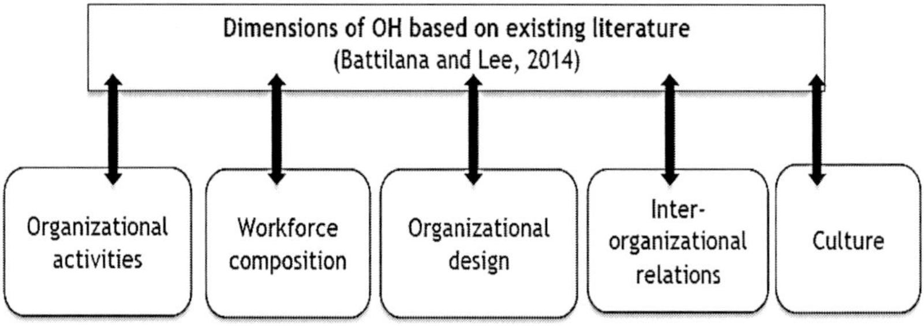


### 2.6.1 Organizational activities

According to Battilana and Lee (2014), hybrid organizations are likely to face constant tensions and conflicts arising from the type of activities they engage in. As shown in Section 2.5, conflicts are more likely to be prominent when the embodied logics prescribe incompatible values for actions, as may happen with social welfare and commercial logics (Besharov and Smith, 2014). Since hybrid organizations are typically designed to achieve multiple objectives, Battilana and Lee (2014) suggested that increasing the centrality of core organizational activities could help hybrid organizations to avoid mission drift, which is a likely result of incompatibility of embodied logics. However, one major concern about their work that I highlight is the vagueness of the term "organizational activities." It raises questions about what this term comprises; does it include organizational goals, objectives, missions or processes? Future work in the area may need to provide some clarity by deconstructing the meaning of the term "organizational activities" for a better understanding of how tensions are experienced in this context.

### 2.6.2 Workforce composition

Workforce composition also appeared to be a relevant dimension in Battilana and Lee's (2014) study. According to them, since hybrid organizations aim to achieve multiple objectives by combining multiple logics, there is sense in the argument that they are likely to hire employees from different fields to achieve maximum effectiveness. However, problems may arise where individuals' values are strongly linked to field-level institutions, which could result in rivalrous or obstructive behaviour between actors who espouse incompatible logics. Problems of this sort can be expected because employees are likely to reject prescriptions within the organization that are not consistent with the institutional logics they espouse (Pache and Santos, 2010; Reay and Hinings, 2009; Battilana and Dorado, 2010); for example, Battilana and Dorado's (2010) study on BancoSol. A major problem in workforce composition may occur with attempts to disconnect the individual's ties with field-level logics, which could generate further contradictions. Thus, it would become problematic for employees who have strong ties to field-level logics to trust their employer organization when it embeds logics that are inconsistent with whatever logics the employee espouses. In this context, Battilana and Lee (2014) suggested developing mechanisms for aligning employees' identities with the organizational identity as an effective way of improving employees' commitment to the organization (Pratt and Foreman, 2000; Foreman and Whetten, 2002). However, further research is needed to discover whether hybrid organizations in general experience such trust issues as a result of the multiple logics they exemplify.

### 2.6.3 Organizational design

Organizational design is how leaders translate organizational strategy into action, which comprises organizational structure, incentives and control systems, and governance (Battilana and Lee, 2014).

### 2.6.3a Organizational structure

In hybrid organizations, tensions and conflicts are likely to be experienced in the organizational structure. This is because it is within the organizational structure that decisions about the embodied institutional logics and multiple activities are made (Battilana and Lee, 2014; Ebrahim et al., 2014). For example, deciding if multiple organizational activities can be addressed by the same unit or compartmentalised into different sub-units within the organization is a structural question. This decision is likely to rely heavily on the level of integration or separation of those organizational activities that are likely to generate contradictions if they prescribe dissimilar values (Kraatz and Block, 2008; Ménard, 2011). However, one limitation of Battilana and Lee's (2014) study is that it paid insufficient attention to organizational structure as a core attribute of hybrid organizations, considering its importance in organizational research. In their study, organizational structure was vaguely addressed as a sub-dimension of organizational design, which I argue is insufficient in understanding organizational hybridity. Future research may need to investigate empirically how tensions are experienced in various specific elements of the organizational structure in hybrid organizations, such as leadership and the power structure.

### 2.6.3b Incentives and control systems

Incentives and control systems dictate types of acceptable and unacceptable behaviours within organizations, and how these behaviours are measured and rewarded (Jensen and Meckling, 1992). Tensions are likely to occur here considering that institutional logics have different prescriptions for behaviour and actions (Friedland and Alford, 1991). Thus, hybrid organizations are likely to be faced with the challenge of measuring employees' performance based on their affiliations to the embodied multiple logics (Battilana and Lee, 2014). According to Battilana and Lee (2014), an integrated system that measures and rewards both economic and social performance effectively may offer a solution to this foreseeable issue. However, the achievement of an integrated system may pose more problems, since hybrid organizations may not all be perfectly integrated (Besharov and Smith, 2014). Thus, further research is needed to proffer solutions to these challenges.

### 2.6.3c Governance

Governance plays a unique role in ensuring, by enacting specific mechanisms, that hybrid organizations do not deviate from their main activities and experience mission drift (Ebrahim et al., 2014; Battilana et al., 2012; Billis, 2010; Karré, 2011; Anheier, 2011; Battilana and Lee, 2014). According to Ebrahim et al. (2014), governance mechanisms are means through which boards and managers seek to balance organizational objectives. This implies that governance of hybrid organizations may face tensions in mitigating risks associated with balancing multiple objectives. Given this, and considering the relevance of governance in organizational studies (Aguilera and Jackson, 2010; Westphal and Zajac, 2013; Davis et al., 1997), Battilana and Lee's (2014) framework paid insufficient attention to governance as a core attribute of hybrid organizations. Extensive research shows that the governance challenges of hybrid organizations are largely unaddressed. This is evident in Battilana and Lee's (2014) study where governance was addressed as a sub-dimension of organizational design, which I argue is insufficient for understanding the governance challenges posed by organizational hybridity. Several questions arise, such as: How, in the hybrid organization, do board members make strategic decisions? What influences strategic decisions and how can they be better managed? All of these questions need to be thoroughly addressed empirically, considering that institutional logics may influence management decisions, especially when the management team members are strongly affiliated to the given logic.

## 2.6.4 Inter-organizational relationships

As observed earlier, since hybrid organizations embody multiple logics, they may appeal to different sectors, which may give them access to new markets resulting in economic benefits (Karré, 2011). Snow (2015:8) named this practice "link and leverage", which is an allusion to the idea that linkages to other organizations may offer access to external resources. Thus, hybrid organizations may also engage in inter-organizational relationships to fulfil objectives (Battilana and Lee, 2014). However, such colonisation of new resource fields may stimulate competition from incumbent organizations in that field, which may pose an existential threat to the colonising organization, or at least threaten its hybrid nature, as its legitimacy may be questioned in the new territory. This line of thought raises questions such as: Can conventional commercial organizations partner with commercial hybrid organizations? Do commercial hybrid organizations risk their hybrid nature by going into relationships with nonhybrid organizations? What roles do employees play in these relationships? Surprisingly, Battilana and Lee's (2014) study, as well as Battilana et al. (2012) and Ebrahim et al. (2014), failed to recognise the importance of intra-organizational relations as a potential locus of tensions when engaging in inter-organizational relations. This is unfortunate, especially considering that the whole idea of institutional logics rests on the premise that sets of values, behaviours and practices are realised by people. 'People' in this research context are the employees and representatives of the hybrid organization who somehow have to come to terms with the contrasting values and practices of organizations. So far, research provides limited answers to these questions, which call for further empirical investigation.

### 2.6.5 Organizational culture

Finally, like governance, organizational culture plays a major role in ensuring that employees' values are in line with organizational values (Schein, 1984). However, the adoption of a unique culture in hybrid organizations is likely to be problematic since they embody multiple logics (Foreman and Whetten, 2002; Pratt and Foreman, 2000). A key concern in this dimension is whether a unified organizational culture integrating multiple logics is possible at all. If it is possible, how then can an employee – especially one espousing strong links to a logic – identify with the multiple logics embodied within the organization when it espouses values that contradict his/her values? (Battilana and Lee, 2014) Can employees trust the hybrid organization even when they know their respective values are not aligned? Even though Battilana and Lee (2014) indicated that leadership might play a role in reinforcing organizational culture within hybrid organizations, the role of leadership in constructing systems of meaning for employees of hybrid organizations remains problematic. It is important to note that the context in which hybrid organizational culture has been discussed is that derived from the study of social enterprise, which is held to exemplify a perfectly aligned hybrid type and, therefore, the associated tensions and conflicts are likely to be minimal, as suggested by Besharov and Smith (2014). This implies that the organizational attributes in other hybrid organizational types where tensions and conflicts are prominent, such as commercial hybrid organizations, may have different characteristics from those highlighted in the literature. For now, this is just a conjecture; further research is required to support or dismiss it.

Building on the above existing dimensions, I propose five specific organizational attributes that are relevant to when tensions are likely to be experienced in commercial hybrid organizations. These are discussed in the next section.

## 2.7 Dimensions of Organizational Hybridity in Commercial Hybrid Organizations

This section draws attention to five organizational attributes that are relevant to when tensions are prominent in commercial hybrid organizations: governance, leadership structure/style, organizational culture, intra-organizational relations and trust relations (see Figure 6). It is important to note that the tensions experienced in each of these attributes would need to be effectively managed by commercial hybrid organizations to achieve the desired positive outcomes. These attributes are discussed in turn.

Figure 6: Dimensions of Organizational Hybridity in Commercial Hybrid Organizations

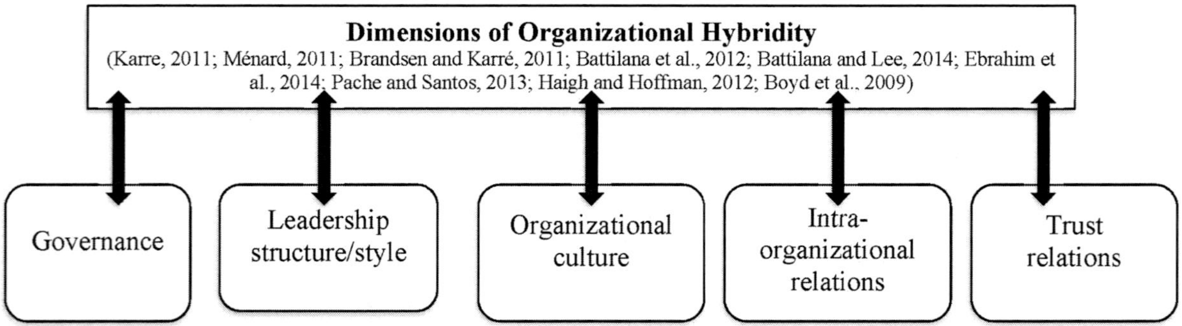

### 2.7.1 Governance

Governance plays a major role in ensuring that commercial hybrid organizations avoid the risk of mission drift and internal conflicts, and good governance is likely to form the basis of their performance success, since they are likely to conform to demands from external pressures and market changes (Karré, 2011; Battilana and Lee, 2014; Battilana et al., 2012; Ebrahim et al., 2014; Martin et al., 2016). According to Ebrahim et al. (2014), governance is the internal means through which organizational resources are deployed, conflicts are resolved, and organizational leaders seek to balance organizational objectives and goals. The fundamental task of governance is to determine what kind of policies, culture, control, power structure and strategy is appropriate for the organizational context (Ebrahim et al., 2014; Martin et al., 2016; Aguilera et al., 2006). These policies reflect values and norms espoused within the organization, and this plays an important role in shaping its identity and employees' perception of it (Sharkie, 2009).

However, while extensive research has been conducted into the governance of conventional organizations in organizational studies, very little research is available on the governance of commercial hybrid organizations (Battilana and Lee, 2014; Ebrahim et al., 2014). Although Battilana and Lee (2014) and Ebrahim et al. (2014) addressed this dimension in the context of the social enterprise, many unanswered questions concerning the governance of commercial hybrid organizations remain, such as: Can governance influence the sustainability of commercial hybrid organizations over time? How can multiple contradictory logics be embodied effectively in governance to minimise conflicts? Does the balance of power in governance affect employees' interpretation of the embodied logics? (Battilana et al., 2012; Battilana and Lee, 2014; Ebrahim et al., 2014); all these questions call for further empirical research. Future research may also need to investigate the extent to which non-market-orientated logics influence the decisions of directors of commercial hybrid organizations, which is an area this research will attempt to investigate empirically.

***Balance of objectives and goals***

When it comes to governance, the board of directors, in particular, plays a key role in piloting the objectives of a commercial hybrid organization to avoid challenges that might prevent it from thriving (Ebrahim et al., 2014; Aguilera et al., 2006; Adekoya and Ekpenyong, 2009). Moreover, the board of directors has the responsibility for ensuring that the organization and its employees do not digress from core market-focused goals under its leadership (Ebrahim et al., 2014). Having stated the above, one of the major challenges of commercial hybrid organizations is how to strategically measure and balance both financial and non-financial objectives by the board of directors to achieve positive outcomes (Battilana et al., 2012; Besharov and Smith, 2014; Battilana and Lee, 2014). For example, commercial hybrid organizations could face challenges when balancing financial objectives derived from sales, profits and high returns on investments with social objectives derived through philanthropic activities in the knowledge that there is no standardised benchmark for measuring social performance, and that the organization's success may be predominantly dependent on financial returns. However, some objectives could pose certain types of risks for the organization, especially when the value that they embody contradicts the overall mission of the organization (Ebrahim et al., 2014). Unfortunately, the board could fail to recognise these risks, which could lead at the very least to further conflicts at both the organizational and individual levels.

***Balance of power and control structures***

A literature review reveals that the primary source of structural conflict in commercial hybrid organizations is likely to be based upon the distribution of power in governance (Gray, 1985; Clarke, 2007). For example, commercial hybrid organizations may experience tensions regarding which power and control structure to adopt, such as the centralised structure where decisions are passed down the chain of command and those at the higher levels of authority are immune to significant questions by those at the lower levels, or a more decentralised structure where lower-level employees contribute to the decision-making process, or a combination of both approaches (Eisenhardt, 1989; Fox, 1974). It is also important to note that each of these approaches presents different challenges. Tensions experienced in this dimension are likely to occur against a background in which actors' power statuses contribute to the way institutional logics are interpreted within the organizations (Besharov and Smith, 2014). In that context, employees are more likely to be receptive to logics when the organizational member espousing that logic has a high level of power within the organization. However, too much power could enable opportunism (Jensen and Meckling, 1992). For example, assuming that various organizational leaders have different preferences over the set of possible managerial tasks within the organization, each leader is likely to encourage employees to perform best in the task that he/she views as the most important, which is a recipe for endemic conflict; it is not to be excluded that a leader may under such circumstances pursue his/her own interests (Friedland and Alford, 1991; Greenwood and Hinings, 1996). Thus, arguably it is paramount to balance power in a way that it reduces inherent tensions. So far, there is limited evidence supporting this argument, which highlights the need for further empirical research.

### 2.7.2 Leadership structure/style

Leadership structure is the hierarchical arrangement of authority within an organization (Jensen and Meckling, 1992). To maintain legitimacy, commercial hybrid organizations have to set up effective leadership structures and ways of disseminating information across the adopted structure (Jensen and Meckling, 1992). However, since leadership might play a role in reinforcing organizational culture within hybrid organizations, one of the structural challenges for commercial hybrid organizations is how employees may interpret and respond to multiple objectives (Battilana and Lee, 2014). This is because differences in employees' adherence to the institutional logics in play could trigger some level of conflicts and tensions (Pache and Santos, 2013). For example, when members adhere strongly to a particular logic, they are more likely to be receptive to, and supportive of, that logic inside the organization and incorporate it into core operations (Besharov and Smith, 2014). On the other hand, when members identify weakly with a logic, they are less receptive to it and are less likely to enact the associated practices inside the organization (Pache and Santos, 2013). Thus, conflicts are likely to occur in the leadership structure of commercial hybrid organizations.

Leadership style, however, can be defined as the behaviour of organizational actors that gives organizational activities meaning and purpose (Kraatz, 2009). It plays a major role in constructing meanings, building trust and shaping how employees interpret the logics embodied within organizations (Creed and Miles, 1996; Battilana and Lee, 2014; Haigh and Hoffman, 2012). Leadership style could ensure that the logics embodied by commercial hybrid organizations are communicated effectively, making sure that the values prescribed are well understood by all the employees, which could play a role in influencing trust in organizations (McAllister, 1995; Creed and Miles, 1996). For example, research by Gillespie and Mann (2004) shows that strong leadership practices, clear communication of the organization's goals and shared values accounted for the high level of trust that employees had in their supervisor. However, according to Misangyi et al. (2008), some leaders may authorise unethical behaviours by imposing structures that promote corrupt practices, or ignoring such practices when they occur, which could result in opportunist wrongdoing. These corrupt practices may become embedded within organizational processes and become problematic to eliminate in the long run.

This raises questions such as: What type of leadership style should be adopted to maximise the effectiveness of commercial hybrid organizations? Should commercial hybrid organizations adopt transactional or transformational leadership, or a hybrid leadership as suggested by Martin et al. (2015)? With regard to this, it should be noted that a majority of hybrid leaders adopt a transformational leadership style, which reflects participative management and a focus on driving the organization to exceptional levels of achievement, as argued by Haigh and Hoffman (2012). So far, findings regarding the effect of leadership structure/style upon hybrid organizations have been inconclusive, and the relationship between transactional leadership and trust is still under-studied (Dirks and Ferrin, 2002). More so, since commercial hybrid organizations are exposed to multiple institutional logics, they could face a greater challenge – that of adopting a leadership structure/style appropriate to maintaining their hybrid nature (Battilana and Lee, 2014). Thus, further research is required to explore empirically how commercial hybrid organizations may deal with these glaring issues and to develop strategies for managing them.

### 2.7.3 Organizational culture

Organizational culture can be defined as "the pattern of basic assumptions that a given group has invented, discovered, or developed in learning to cope with its problems of external adaptation and internal integration, and that have worked well enough to be considered valid, therefore, to be taught to new members as the correct way to perceive, think, and feel in relation to those problems" (Schein, 1984:3). It "is a critical means by which values and beliefs are communicated and maintained within organizations" (Battilana et al., 2012:54). Organizational culture shapes how employees interpret, identify and manifest within the organization the multiple logics available to them, and its development is embedded in the daily activities of the organization (Battilana and Lee, 2014). For this reason, organizational culture becomes a critical means by which multiple logics, beliefs and values are communicated and maintained in commercial hybrid organizations (Battilana et al., 2012). However, some of the cultural assumptions within commercial hybrid organizations may be influenced by the various professional backgrounds of the employees and their links to the values they prescribe, which is likely to generate conflicts especially when the employees are unable to identify with the values embodied within the organization (Schein, 1984). This is because identity strongly influences and motivates individuals' behaviour (Weaver and Agle, 2002). For example, individuals who are economically orientated will be likely to consciously adopt courses of action in their own self-interest, which is part of their identity (Friedland and Alford, 1991; Misangyi et al., 2008). One of the biggest challenges for a commercial hybrid organization may come down to making employees understand and identify with its culture of hybridity. At this point, building employees' trust could increase their acceptance of the organization's culture by fostering their identification with the embodied logics (Fukuyama, 1995; Dietz and Gillespie, 2012).

### *Identification with embodied logics*

One important mechanism by which institutional logics exert their influence on individuals is that of identification (Thornton and Ocasio, 2008; Ashforth et al., 2008; Weaver and Agle, 2002; Whetten, 2006). Identification can be defined as "the degrees to which members define [themselves] by the same attributes that [they] believe define the organization" (Dutton et al., 1994). It relates to the sense of oneness between an employee and the organization, based on the latter's core values, goals and beliefs and how well the employee identifies with them (Shockley-Zalabak et al., 2010; Puusa and Tolvanen, 2006; Albert and Whetten, 1985; Whetten, 2006). For example, research revealed that employees' identification with an organization's values increased their commitment to the organization (Foreman and Whetten, 2002), caused them to be keener to take risks for it (Thorgren and Wincent, 2011; Lewicki et al., 1998; Puusa and Tolvanen, 2006) and enhanced their loyalty to it (MacLean and Webber, 2015). Research reveals that individuals are likely to cooperate with, trust and protect the interests of the members of the social group they identify with against contending parties (Tyler, 1999; Brickson, 2000).

Identification with shared values could create trust within organizations (Puusa and Tolvanen, 2006) as well as enable positive behaviours by employees that could help organizations accomplish their objectives (Besharov, 2014). This is supported by Jones and George's (1998) study that argued that shared values are vehicles that enable people to experience unconditional trust. However, Gillespie and Mann's (2004) study raised serious questions about the role of identification in trust building. When applied to commercial businesses, issues such as the following are raised: What triggers employees' identification in commercial hybrid organizations? How do employees select which values to identify with, even though they may embody logics that emphasise contradictory values for actions? What happens when employees are unable to identify with some or all of these values? These questions call for further empirical research.

From the above, it is evident that commercial hybrid organizations are likely to experience tensions while attempting to build a culture that employees can identify with (Battilana et al., 2012; Besharov, 2014). Problematic areas are likely to include employees' adoption of the appropriate value system that will reinforce the organizational goals and alignment of employees' values with the organizational values (Jäger and Schröer, 2014). So far, there is limited research on these areas and thus there is the need for further empirical investigations. Most importantly, future research will need to investigate the employees' identification process with prescribed logics in commercial hybrid organizations and how hybridity affects this process (MacLean and Webber, 2015).

### 2.7.4 Intra-organizational relations

The assemblage of social and individual factors also contributes to the functioning and performance of commercial hybrid organizations. According to Baluch et al. (2013), organizational performance is enhanced through employees' contributions; thus, this dimension highlights the behavioural responses at the individual level within commercial hybrid organizations (Farrell and Knight, 2003; Battilana, 2006; Besharov and Smith, 2014). This attribute is highlighted as important in this study because "individuals' willingness and ability to act vary from one individual to another" (Battilana, 2006:659) and therefore this could contribute to the tensions within the organization. In other words, since intra-organizational relations are expected to validate the material-symbolic nature of institutional logics (Binder, 2007), this attribute encompasses the individual-level social interactions and relations within commercial hybrid organizations.

By being exposed to multiple institutional logics, employees are more aware of alternative courses of action to follow or not – to obey, alter, ignore or reject – in order to satisfy both their identity and the needs of organizational legitimacy (Oliver, 1991; Friedland and Alford, 1991). Moreover, Battilana (2006) argued that employees' willingness to act depends on what interests them, while their ability to act depends on the resources at their disposal. This implies that tensions are likely to be experienced in intra-organizational relations in commercial hybrid organizations as employees may espouse various values or respond differently to multiple logics embodied by the organization. These responses could be negative or positive (Thornton et al., 2012; Oliver, 1991; Pache and Santos, 2013).

Negative responses could be manifested in the form of disregard for set rules, defiance or opportunism (Eisenhardt, 1989; Jensen and Meckling, 1992; Pache and Santos, 2013; Reay and Hinings, 2009), while positive responses could be manifested in the form of honest or rule-following behaviour within the organization (Gray, 1985; Cook et al., 2009; Hardin, 2002; Farrell and Knight, 2003). However, even with the growing research on organizational hybridity, the implications of it at the individual level of analysis, more specifically in influencing intra-organizational dynamics of practice and employees' behaviours (both positive and negative), remains under-investigated (Kraatz and Block, 2008). For now, some of the behavioural responses described in the literature are broadly discussed below under two types of behaviours.

### 2.7.4a Defiant behaviours

According to research, employees' responses to hybridity in commercial hybrid organizations may manifest in the form of defiance (Oliver, 1991; Pache and Santos, 2013). Defiance is referred to as an individual's explicit rejection of the values, norms and practices prescribed by a given logic within the hybrid organization (Pache and Santos, 2013). This could be as a result of incompatible prescriptions for actions generated by contradictory logics, in particular for those who profess allegiances to one logic and not the other; for example, in healthcare (Reay and Hinings, 2009; Glynn, 2000; Van Gestel and Hillebrand, 2011). Defiance responses may vary in their degree of resistance, ranging from total refusal at one extreme to subtle connivance with more active attempts at contradicting the obnoxious logics so that they can fade away (Pache and Santos, 2013). For example, Townley (1997) illustrated how academics in some UK universities totally resisted the introduction of a new managerial logic emphasising the practices of performance appraisal and time management, whose values were a contradiction to the existing dominant academic logic that emphasised professional autonomy. Exposure to multiple logics enabled these academics to exercise a greater level of strategic choices (Battilana, 2006). Nevertheless, further empirical research is needed to understand fully how employees display their loyalty to institutional logics that they are committed to and how they respond to logics that they do not identify with.

Furthermore, research argues that hybridity could also encourage certain types of opportunism, which may be extremely damaging to trust development within organizations (Cook et al., 2009). Even though this may be the case, commercial hybrid organizations could mitigate certain types of opportunism by embodying logics that provide alternative courses of action and thus allowing trust to develop (Cook et al., 2009; Hardin, 2002). However, these alternative courses of action could encourage further opportunism (Werder, 2010). In this context, Pratt and Foreman (2000) suggested that the alignment of employees' identity and organizational identity is likely to reduce opportunism, enable positive behaviours and improve employees' trust in the organization. This is because identity plays a major role in how employees interpret and respond to institutional logics (Thornton et al., 2012). So far, there is limited evidence supporting this argument and thus there is the need to further explore this conjecture empirically.

#### 2.7.4b Rule-following behaviours

As well as displaying negative responses, it is possible that employees may respond positively to hybridity by identifying with the multiple institutional logics embodied by the organization. According to Farrell and Knight (2003), this may happen in scenarios where employees are aware of the values prescribed by the institutional logics embodied within the organization. For example, if Mr A is mindful of the fact that he will be punished for engaging in a certain type of dishonest behaviour, his optimal strategy might be to remain honest. In this case, Mr A's recognition of the values prescribed by these institutional logics embodied by the organization encouraged his honest behaviour (Farrell and Knight, 2003). By knowing the content of the institutional logics, Mr A was able to use that information to develop expectations about what is expected from him. This suggests that employees are likely to remain committed to an organization by developing compatible ways of manifesting an institutional logic incompatible with their own when they can identify with it, or at least understand its requirements, even though the logics may remain incompatible at the field level (Besharov and Smith, 2014). However, it is still unlikely that the embodiment of multiple logics by commercial organizations will entirely remove the risk of other types of opportunism and promote honesty or trust (Mishra, 1996). However, for now, the discussion above is at the level of inconclusive conjecture, which requires further empirical evidence. Hence, this research attempts to contribute to this body of research by empirically investigating these conjectures.

### 2.7.5 Trust relations

One crucial organizational attribute that seems to have been largely ignored by research on organizational hybridity is that of trust relationships. The extensive literature review shows that trust in the organization is likely to be a social imperative for the sustainability and effectiveness of contemporary (commercial hybrid) organizations (Fukuyama, 1995); thus, this is the reason why I highlight it as an important dimension in this study. However, for an in-depth understanding of this dimension, this research pays close attention to employees' trust in the organization. Employees' trust in organizations has been argued to have a positive influence on their workplace attitudes, behaviour and performance (Jones and George, 1998; Rousseau et al., 1998; Mayer et al., 1995; Dirks and Ferrin, 2002). This is because when employees trust the organization, they are more willing to suspend doubts about it and carry out the tasks and objectives set by the leaders towards a common goal (Burke et al., 2007). For example, Mayer and Gavin's (2005) study posited that trust in management allowed employees to focus on their responsibilities to add value to their organization. However, a lack of trust in management undermined attempts to direct employees' attention toward specified roles. Furthermore, trust in the organization is an excellent facilitator of open communication, increases the acceptance of its culture by employees (Shockley-Zalabak et al., 2010) and increases employees' satisfaction (Dirks and Ferrin, 2001, 2002), while it also promotes effective leadership, high performance, bottom-line results and organizational learning (Dirks and Ferrin, 2002; Shockley-Zalabak et al., 2010). Therefore, it must be encouraged within the commercial hybrid organizations.

Mayer et al. (1995:712) defined trust as "the willingness of a party to be vulnerable to the actions of another party based on the expectation that the other will perform a particular action important to the trustor, irrespective of the ability to monitor or control that other party". This definition implies that the trustor (the employee) accepts certain risks and uncertainties associated with the relationship, believing that the trustee (the organization) will not harm the trustor at such time as the trustor is vulnerable (Hodgetts, 1996; Möllering, 2001; Fulmer and Gelfand, 2012; Mayer et al., 1995; Dirks and Ferrin, 2002). Some of the risks that employees face in commercial hybrid organizations include job loss, exploitation and diminished identity (Holtz, 2013).

While there seems to be a consensus in the literature concerning the importance of trust in organizations, a few dissenting voices have been heard. One example is Rosaci et al. (2012) who argued that trust can morph into blind faith, which maintains the trustor in a state of satisfied ignorance even as the trustee fails to perform as expected. Moreover, one should not forget that any unjustifiable act between the parties could turn an existing trust relationship into distrust (Jones and George, 1998; Mishra, 1996). All these reservations highlight the tensions that are likely to be experienced in an employee–organization trust relationship. However, even though the relevance of employees' trust in hybrid organizations has been acknowledged by a few researchers like Karré (2011) and Pache and Santos (2013), the relationship between organizational hybridity and trust gets little attention in the literature. Among the few who have explored this territory are Haigh and Hoffman (2012). In their study, they argued that hybrid organizations instil a sense of family, real empathy and concern by creating trust relationships through participative management and support for community service (2012:128). Against this evidence of a positive effect of hybridity on trust, a few studies have argued that organizational hybridity could disrupt positive working relations (Pache and Santos, 2013). Future research may need to investigate these assertions further empirically.

### 2.7.5a Dimensions of trust

Trust has been popularly argued to be a multidimensional concept, meaning that various characteristics are taken into consideration in trust relationships (Shockley-Zalabak et al., 2010; Mayer et al., 1995). For example, the popular study titled "An Integrative Model of Organizational Trust" by Mayer et al. (1995) highlighted three important dimensions of trust: ability, benevolence and integrity. In the employee–organization relationship, ability refers to the trustor's (employee's) overall perception of the trustee's (organization's) competence, capacity to perform duties and effectiveness in achieving goals. For example, employees may consider the timely payment of salaries as an action demonstrating competence. The interesting thing about this dimension is that commercial organizations are often characterised by their competence in pursuing their objectives (Mishra, 1996). This implies that commercial hybrid organizations could be trusted by employees based on the competence of the former. Benevolence, on the other hand, is the perception by the trustor of empathy, tolerance, safety and care from the trustee. Such trust is an essential element in constructive social relationships that give employees a feeling of security (Mayer et al., 1995). Trust in terms of this dimension suggests that opportunistic interest is balanced by the interest in the welfare of others (Freeman, 1984). Finally, integrity involves the elements of sincerity, openness and honesty, and is demonstrated by actions that adhere to morals, ethics and codes of conduct. Integrity does not only involve "the amount and accuracy of information shared but also how sincerely and appropriately it is communicated" (Shockley-Zalabak et al., 2010:9).

The interesting aspect about the framework of Mayer et al. (1995) is that it suggests that levels of trust within the same relationship may vary based on these different dimensions, and each dimension may vary independently of the others; in other words, the dimensions are separable. For example, employees could place their trust in an organization because they believe that it is concerned about their welfare, on the basis of its adoption of policies that reflect benevolence. On the other hand, policies and managerial practices that reflect incompetence are likely to stifle and undermine stronger bonds of trust (Rousseau et al., 1998; Schoorman et al., 2007). However, either way, employees constantly have to depend on the ability, benevolence and integrity of their organization for their daily operations (Mayer et al., 1995). Moreover, these dimensions are widely used in most comparative studies in the literature (Serva et al., 2005). Thus, the framework of Mayer et al. (1995) is useful in analysing varying levels of employees' trust in commercial hybrid organizations.

### 2.7.5b Implications of organizational hybridity for employees' trust

Trusting commercial hybrid organizations, in particular, could expose the vulnerability of employees to the risks associated with hybridity, which could generate various consequences for employees' trust in the organizations, namely high trust or distrust. Issues may arise specifically because employees of these organizations are required to carry out corporate functions by translating multiple logics to make sense of what is expected from them (Thornton et al., 2012).

#### *High trust*

A positive interpretation of reality may enable individuals to suspend their disbelief and make a "mental leap of faith" (Möllering, 2001:412) and thus create opportunities for interactions that might not be possible normally (Bachmann and Inkpen, 2011). According to research, positive expectations are likely to be generated based on shared values, identity and clear communication (Nooteboom, 2002; Li et al., 2012a, 2012b). Indeed, value congruence between the trustor and the trustee has been found to positively encourage trust in organizations (Fulmer and Gelfand, 2012). Shared values between employee and organization have been accorded extraordinary power to secure competitive advantage by management textbook writers (Jones and George, 1998). Similarly, Farrell and Knight (2003) argued that high-trust relations might rely on aligning employees' identity with organizational identity through institutional logics. According to them, by knowing the content of institutional logics embedded within an organization, employees can establish stable expectations about modes of action within it. This suggests that employees' identification with organizational values, alongside other characteristics of the organization such as ability, integrity and benevolence, may play a role in enabling employees' trust in commercial hybrid organizations (Puusa and Tolvanen, 2006).

However, when employees cannot identify with the values prescribed by the institutional logics, they are likely to base their trust on their perception of the leadership of the organization, which is an essential element for creating a trust-based organization (McAllister, 1995; Creed and Miles, 1996; Gillespie and Mann, 2004). Surprisingly, considering that trust is partly based on vulnerability, only a small body of research has investigated its relationship with power; for example, Bachmann (2001), and Bachmann and Inkpen (2011). Nevertheless, research suggests that both concepts could be interrelated and one may likely serve as an alternative to the other (Bachmann, 2001; Fulmer and Gelfand, 2012). For now, this is only a conjecture with limited studies supporting the argument. However, this conjecture could provide a fresh approach to understanding employee trust relations within hybrid organizations. Moreover, since research has argued that institutional logics gain symbolic power through identification, it is of paramount importance to explore this conjecture empirically, so as to understand the role of identification in encouraging employees' trust in hybrid organizations that embed multiple logics possibly prescribing contradictory values.

***Distrust***

Unfortunately, institutional pressures and especially market forces lead commercial hybrid organizations to adopt institutional logics that may prescribe values that could disrupt employees' trust in the organization (Sharkie, 2009; Pache and Santos, 2013; Reay and Hinings, 2009; Sharkie, 2009; Sitkin and Roth, 1993; Karré, 2011). This could impair the effectiveness of these organizations, as already suggested (Pache and Santos, 2013; Karré, 2012; Reay and Hinings, 2009; Seo and Creed, 2002; Greenwood and Hinings, 1996; Marquis and Lounsbury, 2007; Battilana et al., 2012). For example, organizations that embody certain types of institutional logics that prescribe certain values could lose the grounds for employees' trust and to this extent employees may not be willing to take risks for the organization (Child and Rodrigues, 2004). Moreover, as trust decreases, the probability of terminating the relationship increases and the sense of solidarity ceases to function (Lewis and Wegert, 1985). Moreover, any unjustifiable act between the parties could turn an existing trust relationship into one of distrust (Jones and George, 1998; Mishra, 1996). All of this highlights the negative implications for employees' trust in hybrid organizations. However, studies by some researchers, such as Saunders et al. (2014) and Lewicki et al. (1998), argue that trust and distrust are likely to coexist in the same relationship. Further empirical research is needed to explore if this assertion is applicable in the context of commercial hybrid organizations.

## 2.8 Gaps in Research

The general direction of this research lies in showing how employees, working within commercial hybrid organizations, make sense of their reality against the background of incompatible institutional logics embedded in the organizations. Prior research has shown that multiple institutional logics are embodied by commercial hybrid organizations, which may pose challenges for organizations and their employees by enabling internal conflicts and tensions, especially when the embodied logics contradict each other (Pache and Santos, 2013). Other studies have shown that conflicts and tensions could result in mission drift or in organizations' inability to access new markets (Battilana and Lee, 2014; Battilana et al., 2012; Ebrahim et al., 2014; Jäger and Schröer, 2014; Thornton et al., 2012). A few studies have shown how employees respond to these tensions (Pache and Santos, 2013; Reay and Hinings, 2009; Karré, 2011; Farrell and Knight, 2003). However, most researchers on organizational hybridity have limited their research to social enterprises, which are argued to have perfectly aligned corporate objectives. This, I believe, calls for concern.

Future research should seek to explore the implications of conflictual institutional logics more widely across the hybrid spectrum. Moreover, the relationship between organizational hybridity, institutional logics and organizational trust remains under-explored. Therefore, in addition to the highlighted gaps in this review, possible avenues for future research are as follows. Future research could empirically examine the implications of organizational hybridity for the diffusion of employees' trust during mergers and acquisitions; for example, investigating the extent to which employees of conventional commercial organizations can trust a commercial hybrid organization in the context of an impending merger or acquisition. Future research could examine the extent to which multiple institutional logics are deeply embedded in the beliefs, vocabularies and practices of board members during decision-making in hybrid organizations. Understanding this wider range of opinion and practice will shed light on the concept of organizational hybridity at the individual level of analysis.

## 2.9 Research Propositions and Theoretical Framework for the Implications of Organizational Hybridity for Employees' Trust in Commercial Hybrid Organizations

The literature suggests that the concept of organizational hybridity is complicated because hybrid organizations are shaped by multiple objectives that are instantiated in many varieties. Thus, informed by the literature, this study advances the following key propositions:

**Proposition 1:** *The more extensive the tensions associated with organizational hybridity, the greater the likelihood of negative behavioural responses by employees.*

**Proposition 2:** *The greater the tensions produced by multiple logics, the less likely it becomes that employees of commercial hybrid organizations will trust their employers.*

**Proposition 3:** *The greater the employees' trust in commercial hybrid organizations, the more effective the organizational performance.*

**Proposition 4:** *The stronger employees' affiliations to religious logics, the greater the influence of such logics on employees' behaviour and trust in commercial hybrid organizations.*

These propositions provide the basis for the empirical research, data analysis and discussion in the following chapters. The theoretical framework illustrates how employees working in commercial hybrid organizations make sense of, interpret and respond to hybridity. As suggested by Besharov and Smith (2014), the embodiment of multiple logics – such as market-orientated and non-market-orientated institutional logics in this case – is likely to trigger various tensions across core organizational attributes of commercial hybrid organizations, which may manifest as extensive, moderate or minimal tensions. These tensions have been argued to be likely to have implications for employees' behaviour and trust (Pache and Santos, 2010, 2013; Karré, 2012; Mangen and Brivot, 2014; Reay and Hinings, 2009; Townley, 1997; Brandsen and Karré, 2011).

In Figure 7 below, various employees' responses to hybridity are organized as being either negative and positive. The negative behavioural responses include the display of deviant behaviours. When exposed to multiple institutional logics, employees are likely to become distressed due to the extensive tensions this presents and begin to reject the logics that prescribe values that are contradictory to those prescribed by the logics they are strongly affiliated to (Pache and Santos, 2013; Besharov and Smith, 2014). This may eventually lead to distrust of the organization. However, the possibility of sense-making and interpretation of the multiple logics prescribed by commercial hybrid organizations to employees reminds us that there is not a fixed response to hybridity. Hence, I advance the following propositions: *1) The more extensive the tensions associated with organizational hybridity, the greater the likelihood of negative behavioural responses by employees*; and *2) The greater the tensions produced by multiple logics, the less likely it becomes that employees of commercial hybrid organizations will trust their employers.*

Various constellations of meanings could manifest as employees individually or collectively make sense of what is expected from them, which may lead to positive behavioural responses such as commitment, trust in the organizations, and subsequently improvement of the effectiveness and performance of commercial hybrid organizations. Employees' trust in organizations has been argued to increase the overall organizational effectiveness and performance (Dirks and Ferrin, 2001; Burke et al., 2007); therefore, trust should not be ignored in hybrid-organization-focused research as they constantly struggle to balance multiple objectives and pressure from the institutional environment where they operate to secure legitimacy (Borys and Jemison, 1989; Karré, 2012; Billis, 2010; Alter, 2007; Battilana et al., 2012; Jäger and Schröer, 2014). Hence, I propose: *The greater the employees' trust in commercial hybrid organizations, the more effective the organizational performance*. Furthermore, through the sense-making process, employees may identify with familiar logics embodied within the organization that prescribe values that are consistent with those prescribed by logics that they are firmly affiliated to – such as religious logics – which they then use as a source of guidance for actions and behaviours. This identification process could lead to a feeling of mutual purpose, which encourages honesty, trust and commitment (Wagner-Marsh and Conley, 1999).

Figure 7: Proposed Theoretical Framework for the Implications of Organizational Hybridity for Employees' Trust

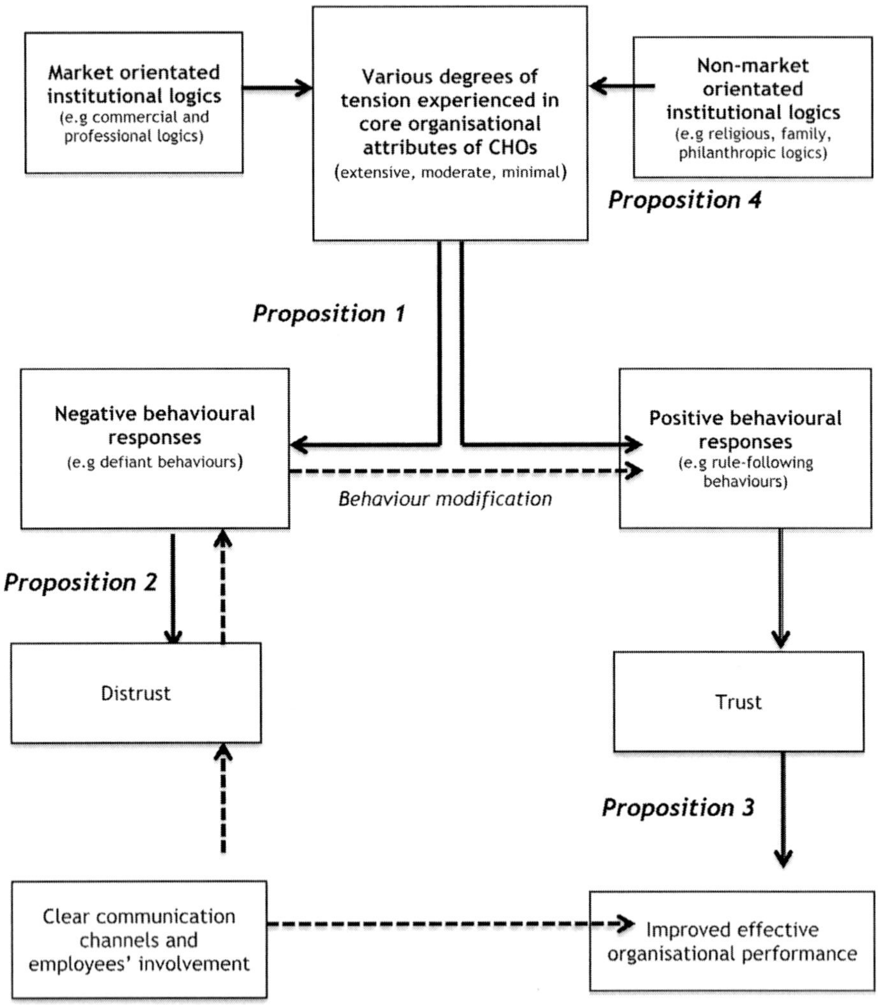

Moreover, clearly communicating the prescriptions of the embodied logics to employees, as well as involving the employees in the decision-making process, could foster the identification process and the feeling of mutual purpose within the organization. It is reasonable to expect that this could modify the negative behavioural responses towards positive responses, as employees – who are more familiar with the embodied logics – are less prone to the misinterpretation of values that these logics prescribe, and this would serve to increase employees' trust in the commercial hybrid organization as well as improving its overall performance in the long run (Foreman and Whetten, 2002; Thorgren and Wincent, 2011; Lewicki et al., 1998; Puusa and Tolvanen, 2006; MacLean and Webber, 2015). Besharov and Smith (2014) argued that employees are likely to remain committed to a hybrid organization by developing compatible ways of understanding the requirements of unfamiliar logics, even though they may remain incompatible at the field level. However, earlier research attempts at linking religion to trust have only served to highlight relevant gaps, making clear the need for exploring the role of religion in the construction of employees' trust in hybrid organizations. The study by Wagner-Marsh and Conley (1999) is an illustration of an early attempt to link religion and trust. Thus, I propose: *The stronger employees' affiliations to religious logics, the greater the influence on employees' behaviour and trust in commercial hybrid organizations.*

## 2.10 Summary and Conclusions

In summary, the review of literature reveals that the concept of organizational hybridity still poses many unanswered questions. This review laboured under limitations in existing theoretical and empirical research on organizational hybridity. One main concern is that the dimensions of organizational hybridity are not well established empirically. For example, insufficient attention has been paid to key organizational attributes in hybrid organizations, such as governance, organizational culture, leadership structure/style, intra-organizational relations and trust relations. Regarding actors' responses to hybridity, prior research has mostly focused on field- and organizational-level consequences of the tensions posed by organizational hybridity, and it has failed to empirically establish the implications of these tensions for organizational actors at the individual level of analysis. Nevertheless, drawing on the wider literature on institutional logics, it is possible to say that many academics have made efforts to ensure that the concept is well understood (Besharov and Smith, 2014; Battilana and Lee,

2014; Pache and Santos, 2013; Battilana et al., 2012; Friedland and Alford, 1991; Jäger and Schröer, 2014; Ebrahim et al., 2014; Thornton et al., 2012).

On the theoretical side, the literature suggests that organizational hybridity provides unique opportunities for contemporary organizations to be more innovative, sustainable, effective and efficient. However, academics have argued that combining multiple logics may result in internal conflicts, tensions and contradictions. These tensions and internal conflicts, if unmanaged, might compromise the effectiveness of a commercial organization by negatively affecting employees' trust in it.

On the empirical side, the literature exploring the implications of these tensions posed by organizational hybridity at the individual level appears to be sparse, with even less attention being paid to links between organizational hybridity and trust. This underscores the need to empirically explore organizational hybridity further to understand its implications for employees' behaviour and trust in hybrid organizations – an area that this research argues to be imperative for the effectiveness and sustainability of commercial hybrid organizations.

Despite the limitations of research, there seems to be a broad consensus that commercial hybrid organizations are an important feature of economic life, and they will continue to evolve as they pursue new opportunities and overcome emerging challenges. However, it remains under-studied how organizational hybridity may provide an environment conducive to fostering employees' trust in the organizations, as they continue to embody multiple logics that prescribe various values. Based on this literature review, it is clear that the definition of organizational hybridity needs to be constantly and continuously assessed, to reflect new knowledge gained through research-based evidence and with due attention to the high risk of tensions inherent in the clash of incompatible institutional logics. Moreover, it is essential for commercial hybrid organizations to take action towards maintaining employees' trust through clear communication and involvement. Based on these findings, the context of the study is discussed next.

# CHAPTER 3

# COMMERCIAL HYBRID ORGANIZATIONS IN NIGERIA

## 3.1 Introduction

Figure 8: The Research Cycle (Phase 2)

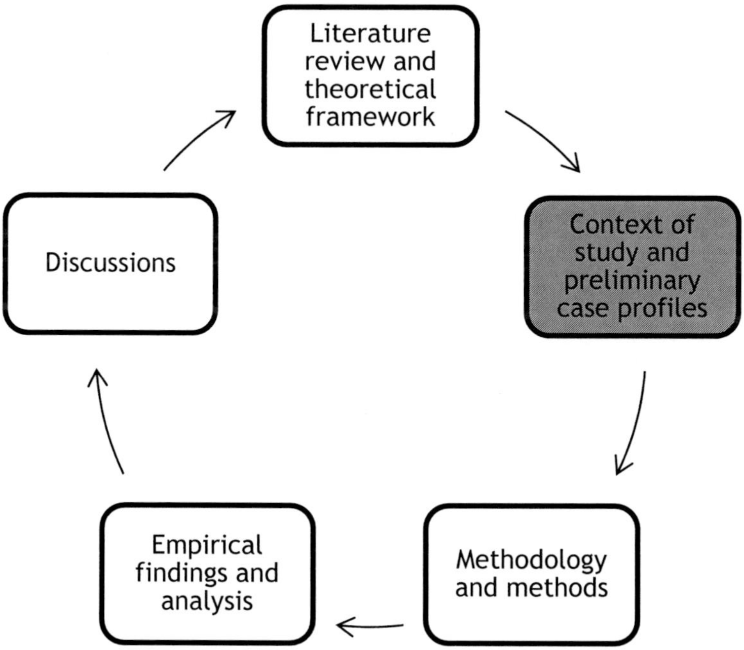


This chapter presents the geographical context of study (see Figure 8), Abuja, which is situated within the FCT in Nigeria, where the two organizations studied – ASL and BPL – are located. The chapter has three main sections. Section A sets out the research context. Section B explores the institutional environment, the commercial hybrid organizations in Nigeria, and the dominant institutional logics influencing individual and organizational behaviours within this environment. Section C discusses the emerging issues and implications of organizational hybridity for employees' trust in commercial hybrid organizations in Nigeria.

## Section A: The Research Context

The study of organizational hybridity in Nigeria requires consideration of its geographical, political, social-cultural and economic background, which are all discussed below.

## 3.2 Geographic and Climatic Context

Nigeria is the single largest geographical unit in West Africa, originating from the merger of the Southern Nigeria Protectorate and the Northern Nigeria Protectorate in 1914 (Central Intelligence Agency, 2013). It is located along the Atlantic coast of West Africa, and bordered by neighbouring countries such as the Benin Republic to the west, Cameroon to the east, and Niger and Chad to the north. Apart from crude oil, the country is rich in numerous natural resources, such as gas, tin, iron ore, coal, limestone, lead, zinc and arable land (OPEC, 2020). Nigeria occupies a land area of about 923,768 square kilometres, of which 910,768 square kilometres is land and 13,000 square kilometres is water. The lower course of the River Niger flows south through the western part of the country into the Gulf of Guinea; swamps and mangrove forests border the southern coast, while inland lie hardwood forests. The rainforest region is arguably among the richest in Africa (Central Intelligence Agency, 2013).

***Geographical zones***

There are six main geographical regions in Nigeria established under a system introduced by the then-President Ibrahim Badamasi Babangida between 1985 and 1993 for the effective allocation of political and natural resources, namely the North Central, the North East, the North West, the South East, the South-South and the South West (Sanusi, 2010). The North Central, otherwise known as the middle belt, comprises seven states, namely Benue, Nasarawa, Kogi, Kwara, Niger, Plateau and the capital city Abuja. These states are situated around the confluence of the River Niger and the River Benue. Abuja became the capital city situated in the FCT in 1991. The FCT has largely grown since its inception as the home of the capital city of Nigeria and it is currently home to about 1.857 million inhabitants (Central Intelligence Agency, 2013). Abuja is home to the Presidential Villa and organs of government such as the National Assembly and the Supreme Court; as the seat of federal government, it is a politically influential place (Central Intelligence Agency, 2013). The regional segregation inherent in the state system has significantly influenced the political, economic and social development of the country, and it has shaped Nigerian politics by fuelling over the years many violent crises and identity rivalries (Omeje, 2006).

## 3.3 Political Context

In terms of political context, Nigeria's historical political structure has been characterised by rivalry, disintegration and violence.

***Political history and government structure***

Nigeria attained independence on 1st October 1960, barely six years after becoming a federation and ill-equipped to address the tasks of political, administrative, social, economic and cultural integration (Omeje, 2006). Since independence, Nigeria's political structure has been the locus of inter-ethnic rivalry, violence and instability because ethnic structures became a basis for national politics and behaviour (Omeje, 2006). A former British colony created by the controversial administrator Sir Frederick Lugard, Nigeria continued with the parliamentary system of government bestowed upon her by the colonial power after independence (Omeje, 2006). However, this political arrangement was disrupted in January 1966 by a military coup. The military ruled until 1979 when civilian rule was restored. However, in 1983, the military returned and ruled until 1999 when the current civilian dispensation commenced (Falola and Heaton, 2008); Nigeria is now experiencing its longest period of civilian rule since independence.

The country consists of 36 states carved out from the North Central, the North East, the North West, the South East, the South-South and the South West, plus the FCT. Each of the 36 states is led by a governor, with a state legislature known as the state House of Assembly and the state judiciary headed by the chief judge of the state. The states consist internally of local government areas (currently 774), which are led by chairpersons and legislative bodies known as the local government councils (Omeje, 2006). The federal government, in turn, consists of an executive arm led by the president, a federal judiciary and a national assembly. In view of the country's complex history of lingering regional conflicts and instability, the democratic government has progressively sought to address the challenging mission of neutralising potential conflicts, defusing ethnic and regional tensions, and disciplining potentially corrupt government officials (Osaghae and Suberu, 2005). So far, this has been achieved through more emphasis on the rule of law in accordance with constitutional rights and the use of participatory processes to seek wherever possible to minimise conflicts (Kolawole and Omobitan, 2014).

## 3.4 Social Context

The socio-cultural context in Nigeria, as discussed below, is complex and conditioned by the country's history.

### 3.4.1 Population and demography

With approximately 202 million inhabitants and one of the largest populations of youth in the world, Nigeria's population is the largest in Africa and is expected to exceed that of the USA by 2045 (Central Intelligence Agency, 2013; Worldbank, 2020). Populations of the major urban areas are as follows: Lagos 10.203 million, Kano 3.34 million, Ibadan 2.762 million, Abuja 1.857 million and Kaduna 1.519 million (Central Intelligence Agency, 2013).

### 3.4.2 Languages and ethnic groups

Being a former British colony, Nigeria adopted English as her official language. Despite this official recognition of English, other languages such as Hausa, Yoruba, Igbo and Fulani, plus over 500 additional indigenous dialects/languages, are also spoken, making Nigeria a multilingual country (Central Intelligence Agency, 2013; OPEC, 2020). In terms of ethnic groups, Nigeria houses more than 250 ethnic groups, of which three are dominant: the Hausas (predominantly from the northern part of the country), the Igbos (predominantly from the eastern part of the country) and the Yorubas (predominantly from the western part of the country) (Central Intelligence Agency, 2013). According to the McKinsey Global Institute Report (2014), the national population is composed of the most politically influential groups in each region as follows: Hausa and Fulani (29%), Yoruba (21%), Igbo (18%), Ijaw (10%), Kanuri (4%), Ibibio (3.5%), and Tiv (2.5%). As stated earlier, this regional/tribal diversity has fuelled many conflicts in Nigeria (Omeje, 2006), making it a critical subject for consideration in a study informed, like this one, by the institutional logics perspective.

### 3.4.3 Beliefs and values

There is no denying that religion, like ethnicity, plays a role in the construction of individuals' identities and behaviours in Nigeria, along the lines suggested by Friedland and Alford (1991) and Thornton et al. (2012). In fact, religion is deeply embedded in the Nigerian society and has contributed to major identity conflicts in the country since the amalgamation in 1914. The primary source of religious tension is between Christianity and Islam, which has caused several disruptive disputes (Ibrahim, 1991). A decade ago, the Nigerian population was estimated to comprise 42% Muslims, 40% Christians and 18% involved in other religious practices (Omeje, 2006). However, recent data suggests that the percentage of Muslims may have risen to 50% of the Nigerian population (Central Intelligence Agency, 2013). According to Osaghae and Suberu (2005), adherents of the Christian religion include Protestants (Anglican, Baptist, Methodist and Lutheran), Catholics, the Evangelical Church of West Africa, Seventh-day Adventists, the Celestial Church and Pentecostals; while in some remote parts where traditional religious practices are maintained, these include traditional masquerade activities and other forms of deity worship (Osaghae and Suberu, 2005). In turn, the Islamic religion consists of different sects, including Ahmadiya, Sanusiyya, Tijanniyya and Quadriyya. Unfortunately, following the Iranian Islamic revolution of the 1970s, there has been a surge in the operations of radical Islamic groups such as Boko Haram in the country (Osaghae and Suberu, 2005; Omeje, 2006).

## 3.5 Economic Context

Nigeria's historical economic context and reliance on crude oil – as discussed in the sections below – have significantly influenced the socio-political and economic development of the country.

### 3.5.1 Economic characteristics

The Nigerian economy is classified into three main sectors: the primary sector, comprising agriculture, mining and natural resources industries; the secondary sector, comprising processing and manufacturing industries; and the tertiary sector, comprising service industries such as financial institutions

(Sanusi, 2010). According to the former governor of the Central Bank of Nigeria (CBN) Sanusi Lamido Sanusi (2010), this classification is characterised by structural dualism, which entails a combination of multiple sub-sectors within a sector. Organizations operating within the Nigerian economy can be further classified as private sector organizations and public sector organizations (Kolawole and Omobitan, 2014; Schatz, 1984). Furthermore, Nigeria is currently categorised as a mixed economy and counts as an emerging market due to her ample supply of natural resources and well-developed communication and financial industries, compared to other countries in Africa (Effoduh, 2014). In 2012, Nigeria produced about 1.9 million barrels of oil per day from a proven estimated oil reserve of about 38 billion barrels and 5.11 trillion cubic meters of natural gas (Central Intelligence Agency, 2013). According to the Worldbank (2020), the Nigerian petroleum sector accounts for about 80% of the country's exports, which makes it a major driver of the Nigerian economy.

Nigeria joined the ranks of oil producers in 1958 following the discovery of crude oil in commercial quantities in the Oloibiri Niger Delta region in 1956 by Shell-BP. For over 50 years, the country's economy has hinged on the production and exportation of crude oil (Odularu, 2008). The oil boom of the 1970s led to the abandonment of other sectors of the economy and an unfortunate dependence by the country on crude oil (Omeje, 2006). However, owing to the decline in world oil prices and the decline in oil production, which resulted from unrest in the Niger Delta (where continued vandalisation of oil pipelines and theft of oil has prompted pipeline closures by the major oil companies), the country is beginning to expand other non-oil revenue-generating industries. These industries include communications, finance, agriculture, entertainment and technology, in an effort for stronger economic development (Osemeke, 2011). Despite the country's wealth, the Nigerian government has failed to distribute the country's vast revenue to displace the crushing poverty that affects more than 50% of its population. This is while a combination of poor governance, corruption, economic exploitation and a complex interplay of institutional challenges has continued to deny business the stable institutional environment that it requires (Kolawole and Omobitan, 2014; Central Intelligence Agency, 2013).

### 3.5.2 Economic reforms and development policies

Until 1990, the Nigerian economy witnessed some gains, which were associated with increased privatisation, deregulation and liberalisation in economic management (Odularu, 2008). However, at this point, the favourable trends in the main macroeconomic aggregates showed a reversal, thanks to policy slippages, delays and inconsistencies (Sanusi, 2010). In 1994, the federal government attempted to respond to alarming rates of inflation (48.8% in 1992 and 61.3% in 1993) by capping exchange rates and interest rates. As no clear strategy emerged over the rest of the decade, monetary policy implementation became ineffective and tax rates soared. However, in 1999 the scenario changed with the return of democracy (Effoduh, 2014). The democratic government introduced a series of reforms aimed at redressing distortions in the Nigerian institutional environment. Since then, continuing reforms have served as a catalyst for economic development and have moved towards providing a more stable environment for the private sector organizations that are perceived as the main drivers of the economy (Kolawole and Omobitan, 2014; Schatz, 1984). For example, according to the World Bank (2015), Nigeria was among the first countries to adopt and implement the Energy Industries Transparency Initiative (EITI) to improve governance in the oil and gas sector. A summary of the series of national economic development policies undertaken over time to stabilise the Nigerian institutional environment is provided in Table 6.

Despite the developmental challenges set by the Nigerian institutional environment, Nigeria has continued to experience strong economic growth in recent years as a result of the dynamism of the private sector (Effoduh, 2014; Kolawole and Omobitan, 2014). However, research suggests that the effectiveness and efficiency of private sector organizations may be influenced by multiple dominant institutional logics that form part of the Nigerian identity and should not be ignored (Omeje, 2006; Osemeke, 2011; Kolawole and Omobitan, 2014). Indeed, the economic development of Nigeria has been heavily undermined by the country's troubled history and complex ongoing institutional challenges (Falola and Heaton, 2008; Omeje, 2006). However, how dominant institutional logics may influence commercial hybrid organizations in the private sector is yet to be explored in the Nigerian context. Thus, this research attempts to fill this gap.

**Table 6: Economic Development Policies**

| Year | Policy | Function |
|---|---|---|
| 1962–1968: | First National Development Plan | Before 1986, a medium-term development plan was adopted as a major framework for developing and restructuring the Nigerian institutional environment. This plan gave priority to agriculture and industrial development, as well as the training of high-level and intermediate manpower (Sanusi, 2010). |
| 1970–1974: | Second National Development Plan | This plan gave priority to the reconstruction and rehabilitation of infrastructure damaged in the civil war, as well as improving the incomes of the people. |
| 1972 & 1974: | The Indigenisation Decrees | This plan aimed to put the management of the Nigerian economy in the hands of Nigerians within the context of a politics of nationalism. |
| 1975–1980: | Third National Development Plan | This plan was designed under favourable financial conditions of huge oil revenues that accrued to the nation from the mid-1970s. |
| 1981–1985: | Fourth National Development Plan | Like its predecessors, this plan was put in place for further development of the economy. However, the execution of this scheme was affected by the collapse of international oil prices. |
| 1982: | Economic Stabilisation Act | The government introduced this act as an immediate response to dwindling oil earnings and major external sector imbalances, with the purpose of reducing government expenditure and conserving foreign reserves to improve the country's balance sheet. |

| | | |
|---|---|---|
| 1986: | Structural Adjustment Program (SAP) | In 1986, the government accepted the International-Monetary-Fund-sponsored SAP aimed at removing cumbersome administrative controls and creating a more market-friendly environment, underpinned by measures and incentives that would encourage private enterprise and commercial organizations. However, the SAP failed to realise its goals of creating wealth and promoting sound economic development (Sanusi, 2010). |
| 1999: | Public Enterprise Act | Aimed at making policies on privatisation and commercialisation of public enterprises; ensuring that these organizations are managed on sound commercial principles, using prudent financial practices and managerial autonomy. |
| 2004: | National Economic Empowerment and Development Strategy (NEEDS) | Aimed at diversifying the economy away from oil and solid minerals, and privatising publicly owned industries to promote competition and wealth creation. |
| 2004: | Recapitalisation Policy | Designed to strengthen the Nigerian financial sector by setting the minimum paid capital at 25 billion naira. |
| 2010: | Nigerian Oil and Gas Industry Content Development Bill | Aimed at localising the management and control of the oil and gas industry. |
| 2012–2015: | Nigeria Agriculture Sector Development Policy | Developed to strengthen and enhance agricultural productivity, sector management and market access to farmers. |

## Section B: The Institutional Environment, Institutional Logics and Commercial Hybrid Organizations in Nigeria

Given the size of the Nigerian economy, it is unsurprising that the Nigerian institutional environment has proved hospitable to numerous businesses and initiatives aimed at dealing with the challenges associated with emerging markets (Central Intelligence Agency, 2013). Important relevant aspects of the institutional environment are discussed in the following sections.

## 3.6 The Institutional Environment

As stated earlier, the institutional environment in Nigeria is dominated by private sector organizations, all the more so as a result of extensive privatisation of public enterprises over the last decades (Osemeke, 2011; Okonjo-Iweala and Osafo-Kwaako, 2007). The private sector comprises large commercial organizations alongside small- and medium-scale businesses and self-employment of all kinds (Osemeke, 2011; Kolawole and Omobitan, 2014). According to Imaga (2003), a private sector organization possesses the following characteristics:

- It has freedom to own property
- It is subject to only limited control by government
- It is free to make profit, and
- It has freedom of choice when dealing with organizational resources.

This freedom of choice allows commercial hybrid organizations to explore alternative courses of action within complex institutional environments. In turn, it allows them to combine multiple logics to achieve multiple objectives and to secure legitimacy in multiple ways as hybrids (Imaga, 2003; Battilana et al., 2012; Ebrahim et al., 2014; Battilana and Lee, 2014).

### 3.6.1 Institutional logics at play in the Nigerian institutional environment

External pressure towards effectiveness and efficiency, on one hand, and endogenous factors that favour a balance between economic gains and social objectives, on the other, push many contemporary organizations towards hybridity. This enables them to be perceived as carriers of multiple institutional logics (DiMaggio, 1988; Battilana et al., 2012; Battilana and Lee, 2014; Currie and Spyridonidis, 2015). As discussed in Chapter 2, commercial hybrid organizations in Nigeria combine multiple institutional logics, which often may prescribe contradictory values for behaviours (Ebrahim et al., 2014). Such combinations may include, for example, banking logic and social value logic (Battilana and Dorado, 2010), banking logic and religion (Tracey, 2012), philanthropic logic and commercial logic (Alter, 2007), and social welfare logic and commercial logic (Battilana et al., 2012). However, to understand how multiple institutional logics manifest within commercial hybrid organizations in Nigeria, it is necessary to trace the dominant institutions that are embedded within the country's institutional environment (Greenwood et al., 2010). Drawing on the above discussion, various dominant institutions that prescribe logics that are likely to influence actors within the Nigerian institutional environment (see Section 2.4.2 Institutional logics and individuals' behaviours) are discussed next.

### 3.6.2 The capitalist market

The role of the capitalist market in the economic development and performance of Nigeria has long been widely recognised (Babalola and Adegbite, 2001; Kolapo and Adaramola, 2012). Nigeria, "like every other emerging economy adopted a private sector-led growth with emphasis on policies that will promote investment, capital and industrial development" (Osemeke, 2011:178). According to Osemeke (2011), this private sector-led initiative is often described as a market-driven system or capitalist system. This suggests that the capitalist market provides the fluid that keeps turning the wheel of the Nigerian economy (Falola and Heaton, 2008; Omeje, 2006). Indeed, "The capitalist market provides the impetus for the effective and efficient combination of factors of production to ensure sustainable economic growth" (Babalola and Adegbite, 2001:1). However, the country's political strategy for achieving its economic development goals is called "nurture-capitalism" (Schatz, 1984). Nurture-capitalism can be defined as an approach in which private enterprise is expected to foster the growth of the productive sector of the economy, while the government's role is to nurture the institutional environment generally and nationalistically to favour the indigenous enterprise in particular (Schatz, 1984). This implies that the main role of economic development falls primarily upon private sector organizations, while the government provides the framework, law and policies to guide the activities of these organizations (Schatz, 1984). The capitalist market has continued to play the role of influencing the mobilisation of medium- to long-term funds for economic development purposes through revenue generation, marketisation and commercialisation of resources in the Nigerian institutional environment

(Effoduh, 2014; Kolapo and Adaramola, 2012). In theory, the market is responsible for long-term growth, economic development and capital formation by issuing funds for long-term investment and ensuring the efficient and effective allocation of resources for the optimum benefit of the economy (Ekpung and Uchenna, 2013). This suggests that commercial hybrid organizations operating within the Nigerian institutional environment are likely to be constantly under pressure to pursue economic goals by efficiently and effectively harnessing their human and organizational resources.

### 3.6.3 The state/professions

Since the amalgamation of the Northern and Southern Protectorates by Frederick Lugard in 1914, the Nigerian institutional environment has been continuously at the mercy of the country's problematic political history and government policies (Osemeke, 2011). As discussed earlier, the Nigerian governance structure comprises three tiers of government: federal, state and local (Omeje, 2006). Through this structure, the government plays a major role in influencing, monitoring and controlling the goals and objectives of organizations and employees' behaviour. As suggested by Schatz (1984), the government exerts its influence by creating a conducive economic climate to assist and nurture businesses, which are regulated through an established framework of laws, rules and policies. Influence, which the government can bring to bear directly on private sector organizations, is limited, but the government does not remain an entirely inactive observer of the capital market and other key elements of the institutional environment (Osemeke, 2011). The government directly exerts its influence on the capital market through its agencies by providing frameworks and regulatory authorities established to oversee, regulate and govern the organizations operating within this institutional environment. Examples of these government agencies include the Federal Ministry of Finance, the Nigerian Stock Exchange (NSE), the Securities and Exchange Commission (SEC), and the CBN. However, the government may also indirectly exert its influence on actors' behaviours through established professional agencies such as the Nigerian Institute of Management. These agencies prescribe rules, guidelines, professional codes of conduct and regulations (which are often influenced by government policies) that govern members' behaviours and actions within the institutional environment. This provides support for the assertions of Friedland and Alford (1991) and Thornton et al. (2012) on the role of the state and the professions in influencing individual and organizational behaviour within those environments where they have a dominant position.

### 3.6.4 The community/family

In Nigeria, the basic units of the society such as family and tribes are closely organized around the community which is regarded as one of the most prominent institutions in which actors' behaviours and identities are formed (Ibrahim, 1991). A community has been defined as an important social unit derived from a particular ethnic group (Amnesty International, 2009). As an ethnically diverse country with more than 250 ethnic groups, regionalism and community have influenced the majority of economic, political and socio-cultural behaviours in Nigeria by providing impetus for the sharpening of individuals' identities through logics that they prescribe (Osaghae and Suberu, 2005; Thornton et al., 2012). In Nigeria, the attitudes and behaviours of individuals and groups reflect, to a large extent, a strong sense of loyalty to their family and community. In many cases, loyalty to the community's interests and affairs through philanthropic activities come before loyalty to organizations (Amnesty International, 2009). Thus, it comes as no surprise to read that "The Nigerian society is deeply organized along family, ethnic and community affiliation such that employers are more favourably disposed towards individuals of similar ethnic background" (Ituma and Simpson, 2009:740). Such observations suggest at the same time that individuals are likely to be biased against other individuals, qua members of a different community, with whom they do not share similar values. If this statement is true, the community is likely to influence the goals and objectives of commercial organizations and employees' behaviour within the Nigerian institutional environment. For now, this is only a conjecture and thus there is the need to empirically investigate this assertion for a better understanding of the influence of institutional logics on individuals' and organizations' behaviours.

### 3.6.5 Religion

As noted earlier, the Nigerian institutional environment is dominated by religion (Ibrahim, 1991). Literature shows that religion plays an important role in the identity of the majority of Nigerians, which enables it to form the basis for behaviour as suggested by Thornton et al. (2012) and Friedland and Alford (1991). Religion has been argued to play a dominant role in influencing the behaviours of individuals and organizations in Nigerian society (Omeje, 2006). As stated earlier, a recent study by PEW Research

Center in 2013 revealed that over 80% of Nigerians believe that religion plays an important role in their everyday lives (Gao, 2015). This may be because, as suggested by Tomes (1985) and Hoge et al. (1982), religion is part of the culture acquired during childhood in some societies. The self-perception of many religious individuals within the Nigerian institutional environment includes a belief that their corporate decisions and organizational goals are guided by their religious commitments (Nash, 1994). For this reason, most organizations in the Nigerian institutional environment are "religion accommodating organizations" (Mazumdar and Mazumdar, 2005). This suggests that religion is likely to influence the goals and objectives of commercial organizations and employees' behaviours within the Nigerian institutional environment. Thus, the subsequent section takes a closer look at how these dominant institutions, and the logics they prescribe, exert their influence within commercial organizations and the implications for employees' behaviour and trust in the organizations.

## 3.7 Case Study Organizations

An extensive review of the literature shows that the Nigerian institutional environment is highly pluralistic, with multiple institutional logics available to commercial hybrid organizations to combine while fulfilling organizational goals and objectives. Thus, this section takes a closer look at the two case studies selected for this research – ASL and BPL – to understand how they combine multiple logics to achieve organizational goals. At this juncture, it is imperative to state the justification for the selection of both organizations. Firstly, both organizations are private sector organizations, which have been argued to be the driving force of Nigeria's economy (Sanusi, 2010; Kolawole and Omobitan, 2014; Schatz, 1984). This suggests that the private sector organizations are likely to be constantly under pressure to continuously balance multiple interests. Secondly, both organizations fit into Besharov and Smith's (2014) framework. As stated earlier, the original intention of the current study was to select four different commercial hybrid organizations that fit into each of the criteria suggested by Besharov and Smith's (2014) framework. However, due to time limitations and delayed responses by the organizations, only two types of hybrid organizations are discussed in this study: the contested and dominant hybrid organizations. Also, it should be noted that the names of these organizations were changed for anonymity.

### 3.7.1 ASL

ASL was incorporated as an arm of a successful conglomerate operating in the Nigerian finance sector in 1993 and then commenced full operation in 1995. The organization is one of the leading members of the NSE and it is widely recognised for executing high volume transactions in the Nigerian finance sector. This sector comprises various institutions, markets, instruments and operators functioning within the Nigerian economy to provide financial services (Alade and Tule, 2017). At the core of the Nigerian finance sector are the commercial banks, which act as the major players in the capital market. The commercial banks are followed by institutional investors, such as pension funds, insurance companies and unit trusts, and non-bank financial institutions, such as finance companies, mortgage and securities specialists, micro-finance banks, and bureaux de change (Alade and Tule, 2017). At the apex of the institutional framework lies the CBN, which also serves as the principal regulator and governing body of the financial system. The CBN prescribes monetary policies, promotes both monetary stability and a sound financial system, and acts as a banker to the commercial banks and a financial advisor to the federal government as well as an issuer of legal tender.

The Ministry of Finance, on the other hand, is primarily in charge of the fiscal policy of the federal government; it influences monetary policy and acts as an advisor to the federal government. A step lower is the SEC, which sits as the apex regulatory body of the capital market. Its main role is to maintain surveillance over the market, to enhance effectiveness and efficiency and to protect the investing public. Its responsibilities include such matters as professional codes of conduct and matters of market regulation such as determining the prices of initial issues to the public, the volume of issues and the time at which company securities are sold. The body also registers all securities dealers to ensure the utmost professionalism in the sector. The NSE is the only securities exchange operating in Nigeria (Alade and Tule, 2017). Even though the CBN, SEC and Ministry of Finance appear to be the dominant governing bodies of the finance sector, other regulatory authorities contribute to ensuring the sector's efficiency. These authorities include the Nigeria Deposit Insurance Corporation, the National Insurance Commission, the Federal Mortgage Bank, and the National Board for Community Banks. Figure 9 illustrates the above discussion.

Figure 9: The Institutional Framework of the Nigerian Finance Sector

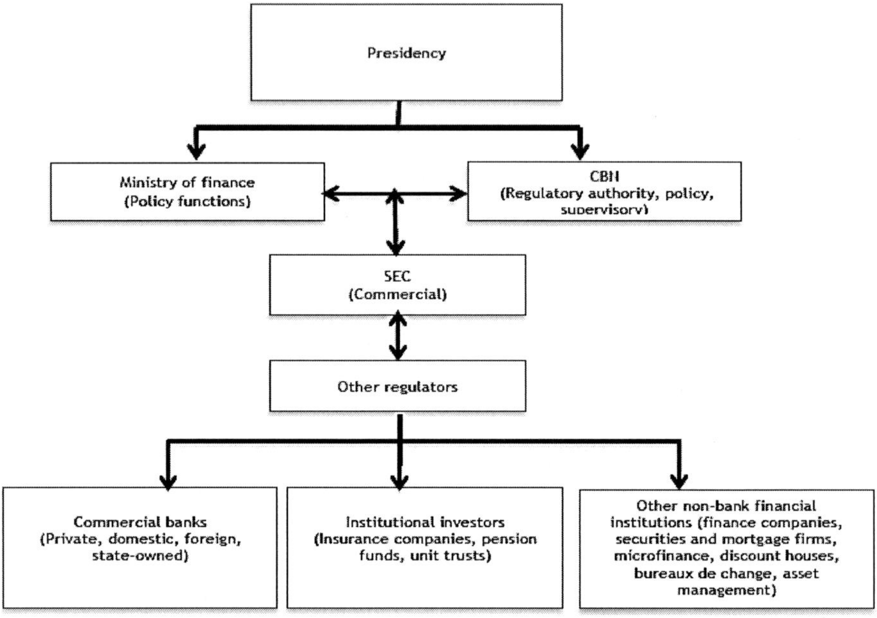


ASL stands as one of the leading stockbroking companies in Nigeria and sees itself as "well positioned to take advantage of the growing opportunities in the ever-changing market" (taken from the company's website; not shown here to maintain anonymity). The organization is currently registered as a broker/dealer with the SEC, as an issuing house and an active member of the NSE. Since its incorporation, ASL has expanded its retail activities and platform, and it has successfully maintained its position in the top five of the leading securities companies in terms of volume and value of securities traded on the stock exchange. As of today, the organization has has traded over $2.5 billion worth of transactions over the past five years.

### 3.7.1a The governance structure of ASL

ASL operates a formalised bureaucratic structure (Weber, 1947) that comprises the board of directors, the executive management team and the senior management team (taken from company's website). The governance structure includes the chief executive officer (CEO), the chairman and the executive directors at the board level. While the directors and group heads are at the executive-management level, the regional managers are at the management level. The governance structure of ASL allows for an independent chairman and CEO who are both members of the board of directors. The board of directors is charged with the responsibility for policymaking, decision-making, and monitoring and controlling the executive management team and the senior management team members. The executive management team reports to the board and is charged with the responsibility for implementing policies, procedures and strategies, and with making all strategic decisions in the organization. The management team is responsible for the day-to-day operations of the organization. This implies that power is centralised at the highest-level position and then trickles down to the bottom of the employment hierarchy (taken from company's website).

### 3.7.1b The corporate goals and objectives of ASL

According to the company's website, "Considering that capital actually drives the economy, creates jobs, facilitates growth and enables innovation, ASL's focus on excellence has helped in the growth and stability of the Nigerian economy." ASL has consistently maintained a strong position in an increasingly competitive market and has built a solid reputation as a highly professional investment banking and brokerage institution. The company prides itself on having some of the best brains in equity research in the Nigerian capital market. Furthermore, ASL "is committed to exercising the highest level of corporate governance, which reflects its core values in adherence to the provisions of the code of corporate governance in Nigeria as provided by the Securities and Exchange Commission (SEC) and global practice. Clear strategic goals, corporate values, transparency and accountability, are key elements of our corporate governance policy. Pursuant to our corporate governance objectives, members of our board of directors are chosen for the wealth of experience and unique perspectives they would bring to the board" (taken from company's website).

The above statements suggest that ASL's goals and objectives are strongly driven by the capitalist market and the need to make returns on shareholders' investments, which is viewed as being achieved through excellent professionalism. As a market-focused organization, ASL's core goal is heavily influenced by commercial logic, which drives the marketisation and commercialisation of the organization's resources. This is what would be expected on the basis of Day's (1998) argument in Chapter 2. However, as clearly shown above, ASL also stresses the need to achieve its organizational goals through professionalism and adherence to strict corporate governance codes of conduct prescribed by the governing authorities. In other words, to achieve core corporate goals and objectives, the company clearly embodies both commercial logics and professional logics as a hybrid, which is what the literature leads us to expect. This makes ASL a suitable case study for this research.

### 3.7.1c ASL: The hybrid type

As a commercial hybrid organization, ASL's core goals and objectives are heavily influenced by the capitalist market, which emphasises wealth creation through marketisation and commercialisation of organizational resources (Friedland and Alford, 1991). However, it is important to note here that although there are suggestions of other peripheral logics embodied by ASL, commercial and professional logics were the most prominent ones. Indeed, the dominance of market-orientated logics in ASL's core objectives cannot be overemphasised; it is made explicit in the organization's own statement of its core goals, objectives and values. For example, ASL's vision is "To champion wealth creation that makes a positive impact on society" (taken from company's website). At the same time, the organization's value statement also resolutely maintains the need to achieve these objectives using the maximum of professionalism, which involves emphasising strict corporate governance standards, codes of conduct, transparency and accountability in achieving its market-driven goals.

The emphasis on professionalism in the organization's core goals and objectives implies that professional logic is embodied as a peripheral logic to support the commercial logic. Indeed, commercial logic could be reinforced and supported by other institutional logics derived from institutional orders that prescribe consistent values, like a professional logic (Besharov and Smith, 2014). This is because professional logics shape the identity and values of actors according to their profession's norm, in this case emphasising unique strategic knowledge that is required for efficient allocation and management of corporate resources (Mangen and Brivot, 2014; Zajac and Westphal, 2004). More so, a professional logic exercises its influence over members' behaviour and actions through prescribed codes of conduct, norms and rules (Besharov and Smith, 2014). In this case, ASL's market-orientated goals are clearly reinforced by the codes, norms, values and rules prescribed by the SEC and NSE, which are believed to enable the organization to achieve its economic goals. Thus, commercial logic appears to be dominant in ASL's functioning, with professional logic acting as a peripheral logic that reinforces the commercial logic rather than contesting it; Figure 10 further illustrates this. Since this is the case, I argue that ASL is likely to be a dominant commercial hybrid organization, based on Besharov and Smith's (2014) typology.

Figure 10: ASL's Hybrid Type (Besharov and Smith, 2014)

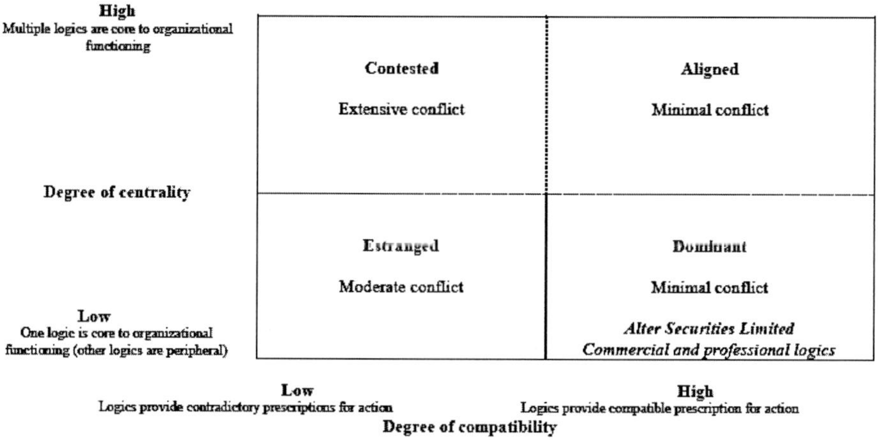


## 3.7.2 BPL

BPL is a family business that currently stands as one of the major suppliers of petroleum products to the African petroleum market (taken from company's website). The organization was created in 1994, before commencing full operations in 1995 as the subsidiary of a conglomerate with branches all over Africa and interests in manufacturing, trading and mining. BPL was incorporated as part of the Nigerian oil and gas sector, and specialises in both upstream and downstream petroleum manufacturing. Some of the products produced by the organization include kerosene, diesel, premium motor spirit (PMS), engine oil and brake fluid grease. The Nigerian oil and gas sector typically comprises three sub-sectors: upstream, downstream and gas. The upstream sub-sector comprises all exploitation and exploration of sweet crude oil resources, while the downstream sub-sector comprises the distribution of finished petroleum products to the consumers. The gas sub-sector, on the other hand, deals with all gas-related products, including liquified natural gas (LNG).

Over the past 50 years, the oil and gas sector has played a notable role in shaping the country's economic and social structure, providing substantial employment opportunities and making huge contributions to government revenues and the gross domestic product, including the supply of energy to the entire population (Odularu, 2008). However, no legislation was introduced to govern the oil and gas sector until the amalgamation of Nigeria in 1914, which led to the introduction of Oil Ordinance No. 17 (Amao, 2008). Government policy was not interventionist, limiting itself to a fairly minor regulatory role. However, the Nigerian oil and gas sector started to change post-1971 (Odularu, 2008). In 1977, Nigeria established her own government-owned national oil company, the Nigerian National Petroleum Company (NNPC), charged with, first, controlling the activities of the major players in both the upstream and downstream production of crude oil and, second, the development of the country's interest in crude oil production. The NNPC was created as a vehicle for the governmental rights and responsibilities of supervision, regulation and commercial activities in the sector, with secondary responsibilities for upstream and downstream developments.

The 1980s saw the establishment of a ministry charged with petroleum compliance, leases, permits, environmental standards and policy functions, and the regulatory responsibilities previously carried out by the NNPC; this is now known as the Department of Petroleum Resources (DPR) (Iledare, 2008). Despite the establishment of an additional regulatory body, the NNPC still traditionally carries out regulatory functions. Figure 11 shows a visual representation of the institutional framework of the Nigerian oil and gas sector, with clear indications of the governing bodies that prescribe rules and values for firms and other actors in the sector.

The majority of operations in the oil and gas sector are funded through joint ventures (JVs) between the NNPC and the oil companies, where the former remains the majority shareholder (NNPC, 2021). The rest of the contracts are managed through production sharing contracts (PSCs) and joint operating agreements (JOAs). The PSCs are part of the Nigerian fiscal regime, but do not always apply to deepwater projects; a PSC offers more attractive terms than a JV contract, while the JOA is the standard agreement between the NNPC and other operators such as Shell, Agip, Chevron, Texaco, Elf, Mobil. However, new initiatives, such as the Local Content Bill, have been passed into law to favour the participation of indigenous organizations in the oil and gas sector; BPL is such an organization. BPL continues to grow as it expands its business in many African coutries. The company is also currently involved in many philanthropic activities and seeks to engage its stakeholders by providing basic amenities such as hospitals, roads, pipe-borne water and scholarship funds; as of today, over

5,000 individuals from various local communities are claimed to have benefited from the philanthropic activities of BPL (taken from company's website).

Figure 11: The Institutional Framework of the Nigerian Oil and Gas Sector

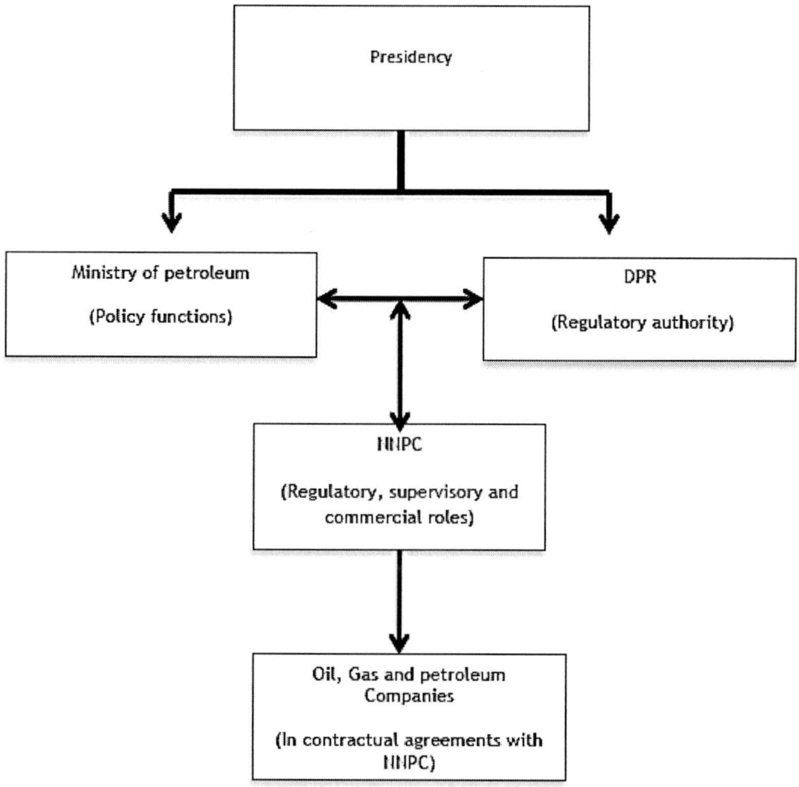


### 3.7.2a The governance structure of BPL

BPL operates a less bureaucratic structure than ASL. Its governance structure comprises two components: the board of directors and the executive management team. The board comprises the chairman – who is also the CEO and founder of the group – the managing director and the executive directors. The executive management team, however, comprises the group heads (a category that includes the general manager, the heads of internal control and exploration and production, the senior mining executive, the heads of information technology and other shared services, the financial controller, and the head of human resources). The chairman/CEO has the responsibility for overseeing the entire organization, including hiring, firing and compensating employees. The chairman/CEO is also a member of the board of directors, which has the responsibility for drawing up policies, making strategic decisions, and supervising, monitoring and controlling the executive management team. The executive management team, on the other hand, comprises executive members who are in charge of the day-to-day operations of the organization; they implement the policies and report to the board. This implies that power is centralised at the top and trickles down the employment hierarchy.

### 3.7.2b The corporate goals and objectives of BPL

According to the company's website, BPL aims to be a dynamic, vibrant and international organization that is far ahead of its competitors in delivering customer-focused goods and services profitably, and is capable of attracting some of the best human capital across the globe (taken from company's website). Furthermore, BPL's core objectives and policies are said to revolve around its mission, vision and core values, which foreground a business policy of integrity, performance, excellence, team spirit, reliability and trust towards its stakeholders and vice versa; with the mission to produce and market high-quality lubricants, adding value for customers through well-researched, innovative and efficient production methods. Even as a private initiative, BPL aims at fostering an integrated course of action that will contribute much to the growth and development of the lubricant sector (taken from company's website). This is supported by the organization's declared vision of becoming a leader in the lubricant sector, with a broad spectrum of brands to satisfy all lubrication needs in the country, the West Africa sub-region and beyond.

Like ASL, BPL's declared goals and objectives are primarily focused on making profits through commercialisation of organizational resources. However, the organization's emphasis on value creation for both internal and external stakeholders through philanthropy, reliability, integrity and trust cannot be ignored. This suggests that to achieve the company's core goals and objectives, BPL embodies both commercial logic and family logic (which informs the philanthropic business image of the organization). In its primary business and its philanthropic activities, BPL seeks to create social value, even though it is driven by market-orientated goals (Boyd et al., 2009). This makes BPL a suitable case study for this research.

### 3.7.2c BPL: The hybrid type

Although BPL appears to be influenced by the capitalist market, given its emphasis on commercialisation of organizational resources, its prominent emphasis on value creation for both internal and external stakeholders through philanthropy, reliability, integrity and trust puts it in a position where it can be argued to be a "market-orientated and common-good mission centred organization" as defined by Boyd et al. (2009). This implies that both goals are equally central to the organization's functioning (Besharov and Smith, 2014). According to the company's website, it "is focused on providing goods and services that meet international standards through innovative ideas and in the process create superior value for all stakeholders". In this way, the company can be seen as exemplifying the combination of multiple institutional logics, such as commercial, philanthropic and family logics, which may prescribe inconsistent values for goal-directed actions (Friedland and Alford, 1991; Battilana and Lee, 2014; Besharov and Smith, 2014). Research shows that organizations may combine market-orientated logics with non-market-orientated logics even though they may provide contradictory values for actions, such as banking logic and religion (Tracey, 2012), philanthropic logic and commercial logic (Alter, 2007), market logic and social activist logic (Mars and Lounsbury, 2008), as stated in Chapter 2. However, as both organizational goals appear to be highly central to the organization's functioning even though they may prescribe inconsistent values for action, I argue that BPL is likely to be a contested commercial hybrid organization, based on Besharov and Smith's (2014) typology, as shown in Figure 12.

Figure 12: BPL's Hybrid Type (Besharov and Smith, 2014)

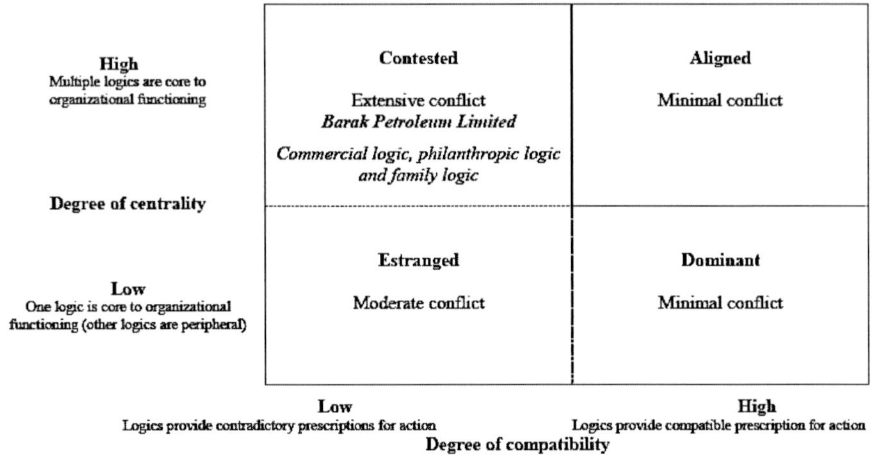


### 3.7.3 Summary of case studies

Drawing from the above discussion, it is evident that the Nigerian institutional environment is a highly pluralistic one infused with multiple institutional logics, frameworks, rules and laws prescribed by dominant institutions that guide and inform actors' behaviours. This gives both organizations – ASL and BPL – the liberty to draw values from multiple institutional logics available to them to achieve organizational goals and secure legitimacy, along the lines reflected in their core values. However, due to time restrictions, only the prominent logics are extensively discussed in this study. As commercial hybrid organizations, the market exerts a dominant influence on the activities of both organizations through the emphasis on marketisation and commercialisation of organizational resources. This enables the organizations to meet their economic objectives while both of them exercise their freedom of choice by drawing values from non-market-orientated logics, such as family and philanthropic logics, to achieve social objectives. However, whether or not there are implications related to the multiplicity of these logics for employees' trust in commercial hybrid organizations is yet to be established. Thus, further empirical evidence is required to legitimise any such claim specifically in the context of Nigeria. Table 7 summarises the profiles of both organizations.

**Table 7: Summary of Case Studies**

| Criteria | ASL | BPL |
|---|---|---|
| Form of ownership | Public limited company | Family business |
| Sector | Private | Private |
| Industry | Investment banking | Oil and gas |
| Listed on the NSE | Yes | No |
| Services provided | Financial services | Petroleum services |
| Institutions | The capitalist market and the profession | The capitalist market, the community and the family |
| Prominent logics | Commercial logic and professional logic | Commercial logic, philanthropic logic and family logic |
| Corporate vision | "To champion wealth creation that makes a positive impact on society" (taken from company's website) | "The company is focused on providing goods and to deliver services that meet international standards through innovative ideas and in the process create superior value for all stakeholders" (taken from company's website) |
| Corporate mission | "To actively seek the best opportunities to bring people and knowledge together to deliver greater than the sum of its parts… [ASL's] footprint is expanding with new products and services to match changing times and to complement the evolving business and investment character of our new clients" (taken from company's website) | "To be a dynamic, vibrant and international conglomerate that is far ahead of its competitors in delivering customer-focused goods and services, profitably and capable of attracting some of the best human capital across the globe" (taken from company's website) |

| | | |
|---|---|---|
| Company values | "Committed to exercising the highest level of corporate governance in adherence to the provisions of the code of corporate governance in Nigeria", in so doing it embraces the new opportunities, directions, growth and wealth creation (taken from company's website) | "Upholds a business policy of performance, excellence, team spirit, integrity, and trust towards its customers and business associates" (taken from company's website) |
| Governance structure | Board of directors, executive management team and senior management team (top-down approach) | Board of directors and executive management team (top-down approach) |

## Section C: Emerging Challenges of Organizational Hybridity in Nigeria

## 3.8 Implications of Organizational Hybridity for Commercial Hybrid Organizations in Nigeria

The above discussion draws attention to aspects of hybridity that are likely to restrict the efficiency and effectiveness of commercial hybrid organizations operating in the Nigerian institutional environment, especially when the logics combined prescribe inconsistent values for actors' behaviour and actions. According to research, these challenges could appear in the spheres of governance, creating organizational culture, creating leadership structure and behaviour. These challenges are discussed in turn next.

### 3.8.1 Governance challenges

One of the biggest challenges plaguing the Nigerian institutional environment is poor governance (Sanusi, 2010). The fundamental task of governance in organizations is to determine what kind of policies, control and leadership strategy are appropriate for the organizational context (Ebrahim et al., 2014). Poor governance, linked to weak institutions in the Nigerian economy and society (Sanusi, 2010; Iledare, 2008), has been held to be a major systematic problem of business in the country (Ezekwesili, 2011). According to Ezekwesili (2011), this deficiency in good governance leads to low efficiency, low effectiveness, poor competitiveness in the global market and reduced performance by commercial hybrid organizations. Unfortunately, as commercial hybrid organizations exercise their freedom of choice by combining multiple institutional logics, they may end up triggering internal tensions and contradictions as they try to cope with divergent interests and goals, as well as with practices engrained within the Nigerian institutional environment (Ezekwesili, 2011). Such internal tensions, reflecting incompatible values and norms espoused within the organization, may play an important role in shaping employees' perceptions of it (Sharkie, 2009).

Meanwhile, given that challenges inherent in the societal environment show no sign of being speedily addressed, commercial hybrid organizations may face challenges such as legitimacy issues. Indeed, commercial hybrid organizations in Nigeria could encounter problems surrounding the validity and authenticity of the organization, and the capability of those in leading positions in the organization to adopt effective governance mechanisms that would help it secure its legitimacy as well as achieve its organizational goals (Ebrahim et al., 2014). Furthermore, legitimacy issues could relate to balancing the organizational goals and objectives whilst making sure that organizations do not digress from their core objectives. This could be achieved by creating a management system that can withstand turbulent institutional pressure and ensure that the organization is run, as far as possible, in a way that does not subordinate legitimate objectives to personal interest (Jensen, 2001). Other issues could arise in the area of stakeholder engagement; more specifically, how the organizations involve and consider stakeholders' needs by incorporating social objectives into their market-orientated goals. These problems have emerged as the prominent governance issues likely to be faced by commercial hybrid organizations operating in the Nigerian institutional environment, and therefore they should be taken into consideration when exploring the tensions posed by hybridity in Nigeria.

### 3.8.2 Challenges of creating a leadership structure

As stated earlier, a leadership structure is the hierarchical arrangement of authority within an organization (Jensen and Meckling, 1992). Now, to maintain legitimacy as hybrid organizations, commercial hybrid organizations have to set up effective structures to check the misuse of power, and to ensure that the organizational goals and objectives are not distorted by personal interests. Unfortunately, this is likely to be a difficult task, based on Nigeria's long history of corruption (Ezekwesili, 2011). According to Gray et al. (1985), one major source of structural conflicts in organizations derives from imbalances of power. Furthermore, commercial hybrid organizations could face the challenge of addressing multiple objectives prescribed by multiple logics, in a situation where it is unclear who makes the important decisions (Battilana and Lee, 2014). This is because differences in employees' adherence to logics could affect the way they respond to problematic situations. This highlights a potential challenge for commercial hybrid organizations in Nigeria, as Nigerians are likely to be more favourably disposed towards the values of people from a similar background, as suggested by Ituma and Simpson (2009). Since this is the case, adopting a power and control structure may also be problematic if we accept the argument that Nigerians tend to be biased and are likely, for example, to cluster more readily around tribal commonalities of kinship and family than the class solidarities of the workplace. Thus, commercial hybrid organizations are faced with the challenge of setting up a bias-proof structure, with enough toughness built into it to defeat the temptation felt by whoever is in a position of power to enact a logic of favouritism towards one group or another, or indeed to interpret institutional logics in a way that is favourable to him/herself (Besharov and Smith, 2014).

### 3.8.3 Challenges of creating an organizational culture

An organizational culture shapes how employees interpret and manifest multiple logics available to them within the organization, and its development is embedded in the daily activities of the organization (Battilana and Lee, 2014). For this reason, the organizational culture is a critical means by which multiple logics and belief systems are communicated and maintained in an organization (Battilana et al., 2012). Since cultural assumptions within organizations may be influenced by multiple institutional logics from various backgrounds, commercial hybrid organizations may face the challenge of emphasising shared values that employees can identify with. For example, employees could question the legitimacy of an organization if it commercialises a product that is contrary to their cultural or religious values. This might lead, for example, to the manifestation of deviant behaviours due to incompatible prescriptions for actions generated by contradictory logics, which might well compromise overall organizational performance (Pache and Santos, 2013). One important mechanism by which institutional logics exert their influence on employees is through identification (Thornton and Ocasio, 2008; Ashforth et al., 2008; Weaver and Agle, 2002; Whetten, 2006). However, the process of identification may prove difficult in the Nigerian institutional environment, especially when it comes to logics prescribed by dominant institutions like religion and the community, as their motivational and interpretive power are historically the most grounded and persistent elements in Nigerian culture (Omeje, 2006).

Nevertheless, building employees' trust through clear communication and reinforcement of shared values could increase their acceptance of the organization's culture and make them keener to take risks for it (Thorgren and Wincent, 2011; Lewicki et al., 1998; Puusa and Tolvanen, 2006; Fukuyama, 1995; Dietz and Gillespie, 2012).

### 3.8.4 Behavioural challenges

As an intensely institutionalised dimension of an environment where major political, economic and social issues are contested along the lines of dominant institutions as discussed above, corruption appears to be known as the ultimate "Nigerian identity" (Osaghae and Suberu, 2005). "Corruption is the legacy of a long history of politics, state formation, economic exploitation and a complex interplay between indigenous and foreign understandings of appropriate governmental conduct" (Pierce, 2006:888). Corruption has been tied to most ethical and moral issues that have arisen in the country; it has been argued to result from the constant mismanagement and misappropriation of both financial and natural resources by opportunistic individuals in Nigerian society (Omeje, 2006). Such experience has inevitably increased the incentives for morally hazardous and opportunistic behaviour, as self-interest can be seen to guide actors' behaviour, inviting both imitation and complementary strategies of self-protection. As a consequence, individuals tend to adopt a winner-takes-all strategy and display unethical behaviours to achieve goals (Farrell and Knight, 2003).

By being exposed to multiple institutional logics, employees of commercial hybrid organizations are more aware of alternative courses of action, or of the possibilities inherent in any system of rules, to obey, alter, ignore or reject, in order to promote self-interest or to satisfy the requirements of their identity; all this is rich in the possibility of disruptive behavioural consequences (Omeje, 2006; Friedland and Alford, 1991). Thus, unethical behaviours, opportunism and distrust are likely to be common occurrences influenced by dominant institutional logics within commercial hybrid organizations in Nigeria (Osaghae and Suberu, 2005; Marquis and Lounsbury, 2007; Hardin, 2002; Pache and Santos, 2013). Moreover, the effective structural mechanism that would ideally have been applied to manage these challenges is good governance, which is in short supply for reasons systematically related to the Nigerian institutional environment. Thus, commercial hybrid organizations are likely to be faced with the tremendous challenge of managing these behavioural outcomes, which are liable to damage their effectiveness and overall performance.

## 3.9 Implications of Organizational Hybridity for Employees' Trust in Commercial Hybrid Organizations in Nigeria

The dominance of multiple institutional logics within the Nigerian institutional environment suggests that they may compete for dominance within organizations (Greenwood et al., 2011), as discussed earlier. In a context of such competition, I argue that actors who espouse contradictory values are likely to be discriminated against or treated with suspicion and distrust, while those who espouse similar values are likely to be perceived as trustworthy. According to Pache and Santos (2013), this would not be surprising, because actors' responses to competing institutional logics are likely to be driven by concerns related to social acceptance, status and identity. Moreover, the interpretation of trust may be connected to the actors understanding of the role of the institutional environment in which the business relations are embedded" (Bachmann, 2001).

Therefore, in the context of a highly institutionalised environment like Nigeria, getting employees to trust commercial hybrid organizations could help improve overall organizational performance (Dirks and Ferrin, 2001). When employees trust the organization, they are more willing to suspend doubts about it and carry out the tasks and objectives that they have been set, leading to greater effectiveness of organizational performance (Burke et al., 2007). Such a disposition on the part of employees represents "the willingness of a party to be vulnerable to the actions of another party based on the expectation that the other will perform a particular action important to the trustor, irrespective of the ability to monitor or control that other party" (Mayer et al., 1995:712). By the same token, distrust could undermine attempts to direct employees' attentions to specific goals (Mayer and Gavin, 2005; Searle and Ball, 2004; Kramer, 1999). Since this is the case, commercial hybrid organizations in Nigeria are likely to be faced with searching for effective ways of sustaining employees' trust, while exercising their freedom of choice by combining multiple logics as hybrids. For now, focusing on the theoretical and practical challenges of organizational hybridity is important, considering that organizations in developing countries tend to be poorly managed (Zoogah et al., 2015).

## 3.10 Gaps and Limitations of Organizational Hybridity in the Nigeria Context

The challenges highlighted in the above discussion reveal that there are similarities among researchers' assessments of the potential problems posed – against the background of an institutional logics perspective – by organizational hybridity, irrespective of the context. For example, the study by Battilana et al. (2012:51) highlighted various challenges that could be faced by hybrid organizations, and the authors argued that these issues could be observed in the legal structure and organizational culture of hybrid organizations. Similarly, Battilana and Lee's (2014:412) study highlighted organizational activities, design and culture. In brief, it is clear that organizational hybridity presents tensions and challenges, which may constrain the operational processes, goals, efficiency, effectiveness and productivity of the organization. However, what I find interesting in this chapter is that context, as well as the dominant institutions embedded within the context, could play a major role in the types of tensions and challenges experienced within commercial hybrid organizations. Thus, the challenges based on the Nigerian context are categorised by the following themes: governance, organizational culture, leadership structure, behaviour and trust.

## 3.11 Summary and Conclusions

In conclusion, an extensive review of the literature shows the pluralistic nature of the Nigerian institutional environment, which is infused with logics prescribed by dominant institutions such as the state, religion, community and market, influencing actors' behaviours and actions. Often, these institutional logics embedded in an organization are likely to generate incompatibilities and contradict each other as their host organization comes under pressure from the economic, legal and policy environment. A commercial organization that embodies multiple logics may be regarded as a hybrid and classified in terms of the apparatus introduced in Chapter 2. It seems to be the case, and I have given examples from the Nigerian institutional environment, that such a combination can exist for extended periods. Even though this is the case, hybridisation may create weaknesses or loopholes, which present organizations and employees with the opportunity to make strategic behavioural choices; some of the likely behavioural implications of situations where organizations change direction include distrust, as suggested by Pache and Santos (2013).

Hybridisation may have implications for employees' trust due to the failure of organizations to achieve clear and functional corporate objectives; such a failure has the effect of weakening governance, effectiveness, transparency, accountability and efficiency. More so, effective outcomes could vary depending on the contexts in which the organization operates (Freeman, 1984). Nevertheless, there is a general presumption that organizations have to be both ethical and profitable no matter the context – a presumption that supports the importance of building and sustaining employees' trust in commercial hybrid organizations as both capable of meeting the payroll and likely in most cases to do the right thing. The issues emerging in the preceding Chapter 2 have enabled the theoretical foundation of this study to be established and the research topic to be put in its context in this chapter. Thus, in the next chapter, I set out my methodology for addressing the research questions stated in Chapter 1.

# CHAPTER 4

# RESEARCH METHODOLOGY AND METHODS

## 4.1 Introduction

Figure 13: The Research Cycle (Phase 3)

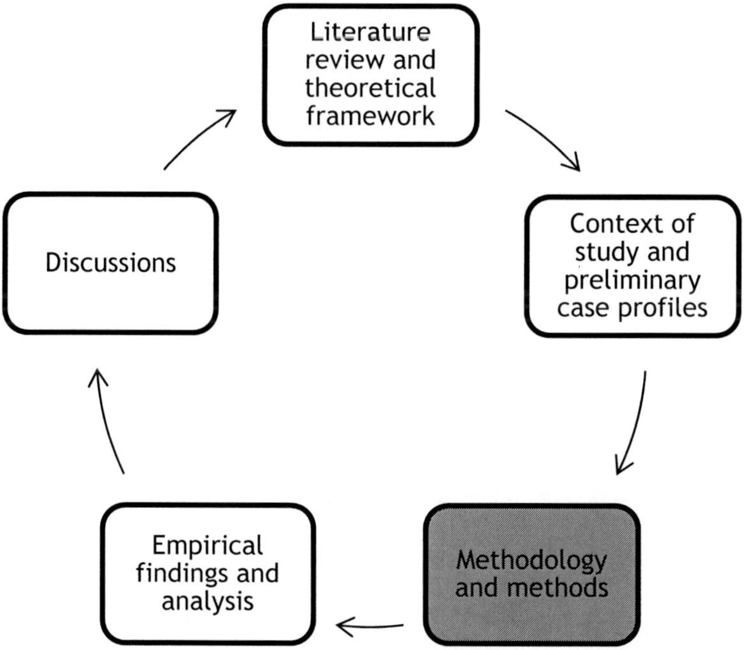


This chapter elaborates the research methodology and methods adopted for this study, as shown in Figure 13. The discussion begins with an overview of the research methodology and moves on to discuss approaches to developing the methodological framework for this study. The chapter consists of five main sections. The first section gives an overview of the development of the methodological framework used. It discusses the philosophical assumptions underpinning the study and positions it within the appropriate philosophical paradigm in terms of epistemology and ontology. The second and third sections discuss the research design and data collection process. The fourth section explains the data analysis procedures and the fifth section discusses ethical issues that arose in the context of the research. The chapter concludes with a summary.

## 4.2 Research Methodology: An Overview

The research methodology provides the basis for the definition of the topic of inquiry, critical analysis of the phenomena under investigation, and the preliminary approach for choosing the concepts, theories and techniques for collection and analysis of data (Bryman, 2004). Research methodologies and methods for social science researchers have evolved over the years; the stages of this evolution have been variously classified by different authors (Grix, 2010). Whichever account I followed, there is agreement among theoreticians that researchers can minimise bias and ensure congruence between their research approach and the original research problem if they are aware of their intrinsic beliefs, values and preferences (Miles and Huberman, 1994; Grix, 2010; Bryman, 2012; Bryman and Bell, 2011; Blaikie, 2009; Symon and Cassell, 2012). Such values and beliefs form a set of underlying philosophical assumptions relating to the nature of reality and how this reality is interpreted (Bryman, 2004).

Researchers cannot operate without adopting some sort of philosophical viewpoint. It is the variety of viewpoints in the community of researchers that has given rise to some of the different methodological approaches and choices adopted in this research, as illustrated in Figure 14, which will be referred to throughout the chapter. The main challenge for the researcher lies in the ability to understand and choose the appropriate approaches, design and methods to achieve the research objectives, with respect to the key issues to be researched, analysed and discussed, in particular in terms of the kinds of data being generated and whether the resultant approach is based on deduction, abduction or induction. The approaches to the development of the methodological framework for this study and how this study was positioned within the appropriate philosophical paradigm are discussed in the next sections.

Figure 14: Research Choices

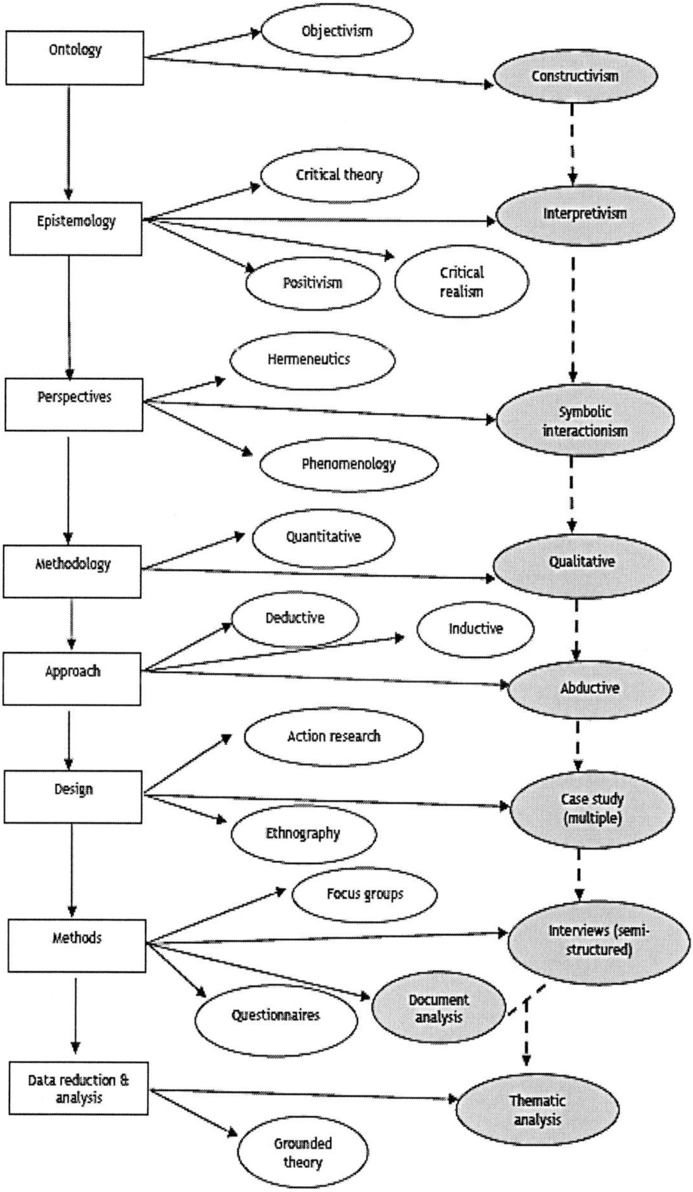

### 4.2.1 Developing the methodological framework

This study builds on previous research and in turn seeks to provide the foundation for future research. The overall aim of this research, as elaborated in Chapter 1, is: *To understand the implications of organizational hybridity for employees' trust in commercial hybrid organizations.*

To achieve the overall aim, this research seeks to do the following:

1. To explore the influence of organizational hybridity on specific organizational attributes, including governance, organizational culture, leadership and intra-organizational relations, in commercial hybrid organizations.
2. To understand the influence of non-market-orientated institutional logics on commercial hybrid organizations.
3. To shape an understanding of the implications of organizational hybridity for employees' trust in commercial hybrid organizations, with particular attention to those implications having a plausible relationship to organizational effectiveness.
4. To develop research-based recommendations for sustaining employees' trust in commercial hybrid organizations.

The study begins with the primary research question: *What are the implications of organizational hybridity for employees' trust in commercial hybrid organizations?* The supporting research questions are as follows:

1. To what extent does organizational hybridity influence specific attributes of commercial hybrid organizations?
2. What role does religion play in influencing employees' behaviour and shaping other organizational attributes of commercial hybrid organizations?
3. How does organizational hybridity affect the level of employees' trust in commercial hybrid organizations?
4. How can employees' trust in commercial hybrid organizations be sustained for improved effective organizational performance?

Given the diffuse nature of the above research aim, it appears inevitable that the nature and complexity of the knowledge required to answer the research questions will necessitate a holistic approach. A qualitative case-study design, employing abductive reasoning, was adopted for this study, as illustrated in Figure 14. The justifications for these research choices are discussed successively in this chapter. However, since the adequacy of the methodological approach is dependent on various assumptions regarding the nature of the knowledge sought (Yin, 1994), it was important to develop a set of questions (as shown in Table 8) at the preliminary stage of this research, to provide guidance in making the appropriate choices for this study.

**Table 8: Developing the Research Methodology Framework**

| Key questions |
|---|
| What are the sources of data available on organizational hybridity based on plurality of institutional logics and to what extent can this data be accessed? |
| What are the most appropriate ways of investigating and analysing the key dimensions of organizational hybridity? |
| What are the sources of data available on organizational trust and to what extent can this data be accessed? |
| What strategies can be used to explore, gain knowledge of and understand the implications of organizational hybridity for employees' trust in commercial hybrid organizations? |
| What is the most appropriate way of selecting the context of study? |

### 4.2.2 Epistemology and ontology: Positioning this study

Understanding the underlying philosophical assumptions that influence the research design is an essential foundation for social science researchers (Bryman, 2004; Grix, 2010; Berger and Luckmann, 1967). An important matter for deliberation when undertaking empirical research in the social sciences is the position of the researcher in terms of epistemology and ontology, which can influence the way the research is undertaken (Bryman, 2004). There is probably no justifiable way of stating that one philosophical paradigm is superior to the other in any absolute sense, but understanding the different paradigms and the relationships between them can help researchers to make better informed and thoughtful methodological choices (Bryman, 2004). Four paradigms are particularly prominent in contemporary social science research: positivism, critical realism, critical theory and interpretivism (Bryman, 2004, 2012; Bryman and Bell, 2011; Symon and Cassell, 2012). An extensive literature comparing and contrasting competing epistemological and ontological viewpoints is available to researchers. However, the purpose of this chapter is not to review this literature but rather to support and justify the methodological choices made in this study, since my beliefs about the nature and availability of knowledge inevitably helped to frame the methodological choices about how to approach this study and how data should be gathered, analysed and applied.

The central purpose of the study is to investigate the way employees relate to their employer organizations and such a focus naturally suggests an interpretive viewpoint. Interpretivism requires researchers to place themselves in the positions of those they are studying in order to achieve insights into observable social phenomena; insights which require a holistic approach that draws upon the subjective meanings of social actions. In other words, it precludes approaching the study of people in the way one might study inanimate objects (Bryman 2004; Bryman, 2012). Indeed, "people and their institutions [are] fundamentally different from that [i.e. the subject matter] of the natural sciences. The study of the social world, therefore, requires a different logic of research procedure, one that reflects the distinctiveness of humans as against the natural order" (Bryman, 2004:13). For this reason, interpretivism complemented this study as it recognises that the social world is subjective, socially constructed, full of meanings, context-rich and functions with sets of logics and individuals; a theoretical apparatus that best accommodates the research objective and my world view as a researcher (Jones, 1998; Bryman, 2004; Duberley et al., 2012). However, before positioning this study within interpretivism, I explored other alternatives, since it seems reasonable to suppose that consideration of different paradigms may offer insight into the strategy chosen (Bryman, 2004).

Positivism promotes an objective view of the world and seeks to assimilate as far as possible the natural and the social sciences. To position this study in that tradition did not appear to be an option, because the main purpose here is not to look for measurable cause and effect relationships, but rather to understand the implications of organizational hybridity for employees' trust in commercial hybrid organizations (Grix, 2010; Bryman, 2004). This requires understanding how employees construct social reality within commercial hybrid organizations and the meanings they assign to their own and others' actions (Berger and Luckmann, 1967; Bryman, 2004; Blumer, 1969). A positivistic perspective appeared unlikely, therefore, to accommodate the research aim and objectives.

Critical theory was unpromising for a different set of reasons. The strengths of critical theory lie in its power to generalise over forms of organization, technology, culture and power, and in its use of the idea of the dialectical nature of social reality to expose institutions as both liberating and dominating (Duberley et al., 2012:22). These concerns, however, seemed remote from the question at hand.

My attention then shifted to critical realism, which shows surface similarities to interpretivism, as both approaches take knowledge to be socially constructed. Critical realism acknowledges the reality of natural order, events and discourses of the social world, and argues that reality is that which exists regardless of whether we understand it or have experience of it. Its strengths lie, therefore, in the drive to expose hidden mechanisms that explain social phenomena (Grix, 2010; Bryman and Bell, 2011). Since my interest in this study is the phenomenon of trust, which is relatively well understood as a relationship between people and even between individuals and organizations, I expect little help from critical realism. I will be content to restrict myself to the subjective perceptions and views of the employees of commercial hybrid organizations, which mandates a broadly interpretivist approach. However, a variety of perspectives come under the banner of interpretivism, such as hermeneutics, phenomenology, symbolic interactionism and ethnomethodology (Flick et al., 2004), as demonstrated in Figure 14. The perspective taken in this study is discussed next.

### 4.2.3 Interpretivism: A symbolic interactionist perspective

Each of the different perspectives under the umbrella of interpretivism suggests different approaches to interpreting the social world, yet they all emphasise that the interpretation of reality is subjective, socially constructed and influenced by context (Bryman, 2004). For example, symbolic interactionism, derived from the work of George Herbert Mead, seeks to interpret human activity on the basis of those meanings that people project upon others, situations and things. In focusing on social actors' interpretation of reality, symbolic interactionists recognise that human beings act towards things by the meanings those things have for them (Blumer, 1969; Blumer, 1986). Since the conjecture underpinning this research holds that organizational hybridity may have implications for employees' trust in commercial hybrid organizations, a symbolic interactionist perspective presented the opportunity to conduct an in-depth study. This would probe the meanings attributed to the coexistence of multiple institutional logics within ASL and BPL, and the real consequences of organizational hybridity for employees' trust (Blumer, 1969).

In this way, understanding the relationship between institutional logics and organizational trust can be said to lend itself to symbolic interactionism (Thornton and Ocasio, 1999; Mayer et al., 1995; Jones and George, 1998;

Lewicki et al., 1998). Put another way, it appears that for the research objectives to be achieved, the taken-for-granted – the values, symbols, logics and beliefs of the subjects studied – need to be identified and considered, and the socially constructed meanings these subjects attach to practices and behaviours need to be critically analysed (Blumer, 1969; Blumer, 1986). Hence, a symbolic interactionist perspective allowed an exploration of the intangible meanings derived from relevant institutional logics embodied within the case organizations. This is as well as allowing an understanding to be gained of how employees select, suspend, check, transform, make sense of, interpret and respond to these meanings in the complex institutional environment in which they are embedded.

However, one of the major concerns about this research approach is the problem of bias (Blumer, 1969; Gioia et al., 2013; Bryman, 2004; Grix, 2010). As many interpretivists deny the possibility of bias in their views, it is arguably unavoidable and may get in the way of describing what is really happening (Gioia et al., 2013). However, while such concerns are real, the interpretivist position is self-reflexive and allows for changes in the research process as the study progresses (Bryman, 2004). Thus, throughout the study, I kept an open mind as much as possible, attempting to take into account the contextual issues and underlying assumptions that could influence data during the collection and analysis process. I identified as far as I could all sources of preconceptions in the preliminary stage of this study and kept a diary where I documented thoughts for daily reflection to avoid biased interpretation of the reality under investigation. Table 9 illustrates a comparative overview of the research paradigms discussed above and how they helped in positioning this study. The research design is discussed next.

**Table 9: A Comparative Representation of Research Paradigms**

(Adapted from Gioia and Pitre, 1990; Blaikie, 2009; Grix, 2010; Bryman, 2004; Bryman and Bell, 2011)

| **Research Paradigms** | *Research objective* | *Philosophical viewpoint* |
|---|---|---|
| **Positivism** | To explain causes and consequences in the social world. | Supports an objective world view and seeks to assimilate social science with natural science. |
| **Critical Realism** | To explain and understand the social world. | Based on the concept of historically changing reality, it recognises relatively enduring underlying structures and mechanisms constituting that reality. |
| **Critical Theory** | To act historically by encouraging an informed public, displacing ideology with scientific insights | A Marxian philosophy, which seeks to account for the historical role of values – social, economic, ethical, political, gender and cultural. |
| **Interpretivism from a symbolic interactionist perspective** | To understand the constructed world – in this case, employees' sense making and interpretations of multiple logics, and the implications of these for their trust in commercial hybrid organizations. | Reality is socially constructed, and its elements are subjective viewpoints and symbolic interpretations of things, people and behaviour. |

## 4.3 Research Design

The importance of research design stems from its role as a critical link between the theory and empirical argument that informed the research (Flick et al., 2004). This means that to achieve a research aim, the philosophical assumptions, methodology and methods employed must be appropriate for the research questions to be answered (Yin, 2003). Thus, my approach to the research design for this study involved two considerations: the theoretical and the empirical.

***Theoretical design***

The theoretical design is a major component of this study, as its main focus is to lead to a greater understanding of the phenomena under investigation based on research. The theoretical design was fundamental to formulating and developing the research aim, research questions and theoretical framework. The main objective of the theoretical design was to explore and acknowledge research on organizational hybridity, institutional logics and organizational trust to highlight gaps therein. So far, there is limited published research on organizational hybridity, especially from the institutional logics perspective. Moreover, the research that is available is predominantly on social enterprise organizations in contemporary Western society. So, I undertook an extensive literature review to inform the study. The theoretical research approach included an extensive literature review consisting of a computer-aided search of several databases of published and unpublished material, both in print and electronic, with particular reference to organizational hybridity, institutional logics, organizational trust and the Nigerian institutional environment. Theoretical propositions were made explicit during the conceptual framing of issues emerging from the literature, which then informed the empirical design (see Section 2.9 Research Propositions and Theoretical Framework for the Implications of Organizational Hybridity for Employees' Trust in Commercial Hybrid Organizations).

***Empirical design***

Choosing and evaluating the adequacy of the empirical design was dependent on various assumptions regarding the nature of the knowledge sought (Yin, 2003). To reiterate, the empirical design of this study was framed mostly by propositions emerging from a review of the literature, which guided the conduct of the fieldwork and other field-related aspects of the study. Based on the limited research linking organizational hybridity to organizational trust, a multiple case-study design, employing semi-structured interviews and document analysis techniques for data collection (see Section 4.4 Data Collection Methods), was employed for this study. This allowed the phenomena to be explored holistically, in depth, in context and through the viewpoints of the participants interviewed, while at the same time creating space for theory to emerge from the data (Bryman, 2004; Siggelkow, 2007). Moreover, the focal issues are along the lines of complex phenomena such as institutional logics and trust that are perceived rather than measured, and subjective rather than objective, depending essentially on an individual's perception.

### 4.3.1 The case-study design

This research uses a qualitative case-study design, as illustrated in Figure 14. A case study is an empirical inquiry that investigates a phenomenon in depth and within its real-life context, especially when the boundaries between phenomenon and context are not clearly evident (Yin, 2003). Various case-study designs are available to researchers. Yin (1994) distinguishes four types of case-study design, namely single (holistic), single (embedded), multiple (holistic) and multiple (embedded). There were, of course, links between the research design and topic of inquiry for this study, which is focused on understanding how commercial hybrid organizations embody logics and employees' responses to such situations. Considering the limitations highlighted in research, it was deemed appropriate to use a multiple (holistic) case-study approach rather than a single case-study design. This was because, unlike a single case-study design, a multiple case-study design presented the opportunity to make a holistic analysis of each case organization individually.

The design helped to gain an in-depth understanding of emerging themes and contradictions, as well as to compare and contrast the findings from both cases, which offered the prospect of informing theory (Bryman, 2012). By looking at a range of multiple similar or contrasting cases, a multiple case-study design helps to guard against the researcher's preconceptions and adds credibility to research findings (Symon and Cassell, 2012; Patton, 1999; Miles and Huberman, 1994). Adopting a multiple case-study design not only enabled the topic of inquiry to be explored holistically and in context, but it also helped to make a comprehensive analysis of the phenomena, taking social, cultural and institutional factors into consideration (Yin, 2003). Moreover, it contributed to theoretical clarification and theoretical reflection on the overall findings, and at the same time increased the dependability and credibility of the study's findings (Symon and

Cassell, 2012: Bryman and Bell, 2011; Patton, 1999).

However, there are perceived weaknesses of qualitative case-study designs, which include the dangers of selective reporting and lack of generalisability of findings (Yin, 1994). In fact, there are claims that a qualitative case-study approach depends heavily on the researcher's judgement and assumptions, and therefore it is not as accurate as the quantitative approach, where there are explicit guidelines for collecting and analysing data (Meyer, 2001). Moreover, the presence of the researcher is almost unavoidable and can affect the responses of the participants during data collection (Yin, 1994). Nevertheless, as Bell (2005) argued if a study makes no claims which cannot be corroborated, it may be well relatable in a way that will enable members of similar groups to recognise problems and see ways of solving similar problems in their own group. Therefore, to increase the credibility of this study, I strived to maintain an open mind and to be receptive to new ideas emerging from the data. Furthermore, I sought to identify the sources of preconceived assumptions and to minimise them by developing a case-study protocol (an overview of the case project, field procedures, questions and report guide), to which I made constant reference during the empirical data process. However, the main challenge encountered in this study was finding the research setting that matched the research aim and objectives. The research setting is discussed next.

### 4.3.2 The research setting for the data collection process

Informed by my practice-based experience, Nigeria was selected as the research setting because it provides a rich context for learning about trust, being a country that suffers from recurring trust issues. As stated earlier, Nigeria is a complex, pluralistic and highly institutionalised environment influenced by multiple dominant institutional logics constantly competing for legitimacy (see Section 3.6.1 Institutional logics at play in the Nigerian institutional environment). Thus, Nigeria was selected as the most appropriate setting for a study of organizational hybridity based on plurality of institutional logics, as it outstandingly exemplifies the contextual institutional elements implicit within the research purpose. Understanding the context in which the research is conducted is accepted to be crucial for case-study research (Saunders et al., 2007; Yin, 1994).

However, it is also true that achieving the greatest understanding of the context under investigation depends on selecting a suitable case(s) that will satisfy the research objectives (Yin, 2003). This is probably even more difficult where the goal, as here, is not just to capture and describe some pre-existing world but also to open up the underlying assumptions and subjective experiences of the individuals involved (Bryman, 2004; Duberley et al., 2012). Regarding this study, my life experience made it easy for me to relate to the situation of the interviewees and to feel empathy with their concerns. I developed a fairly profound and certainly detailed understanding of the uniqueness and complexity of the context and the cases.

### 4.3.3 Case selection process

Following the identification of the context, the next step was to choose the case organizations. According to Yin (2003), a case should be a representation of the phenomena under investigation, which in this case is the hybridisation of multiple institutional logics by commercial hybrid organizations. Hence, two commercial hybrid organizations operating in Nigeria were selected. Both organizations requested anonymity; therefore, pseudonyms are used (this expedient is further explained in Section 4.6.2). BPL and ASL were selected as the primary cases on which to base the current study, as they reflected the contextual elements inherent within the research purpose, being commercial hybrid organizations operating in Nigeria's private sector. Moreover, both organizations – which varied in contextual factors such as corporate objectives, governance and leadership structure/style – fit into Besharov and Smith's (2014) framework. As stated in Section 3.7, the original intention was to select four different commercial hybrid organizations that fit into each of the criteria suggested by Besharov and Smith's (2014) framework. However, this was not achieved due to time limitations and delayed responses from the selected organizations. Only two out of 10 commercial hybrid organizations that the letter of introduction was sent to granted access for the research. Therefore, for the purpose of this study, both organizations were discussed as the case organizations.

Organizations can be seen as frameworks from which individuals develop their actions, where structural features such as social systems, social roles and social stratification set conditions for these actions but do not determine them. As such, the environment of these organizations constituted a sort of laboratory for studying employees' responses to practices, gestures and situations, and the meanings they assigned to them (Blumer, 1969). In particular, a commercial hybrid organization is likely to be a favourable environment for studying institutional logics and its influence on employees' behaviour. The two case organizations varied in contextual factors, which could be expected to contribute to understanding the nature of hybridity by enabling comparative analysis of findings (Yin, 2003). However, undertaking a case-study research design could prove to be problematic, especially during the negotiation for access (Saunders, 2012). The next section discusses how access was negotiated for both case organizations.

### 4.3.4 Negotiating access

Access for this research was facilitated through a letter of introduction sent directly to 10 commercial hybrid organizations with their head offices in either Abuja or Lagos between 17th May 2013 and 20th December 2013. Only these two cities were chosen as possible research environments, after much consideration by the ethics committee, because of safety concerns arising from kidnapping and terrorist activities in other states in Nigeria. Before sending the letters, I undertook an investigation of the selected organizations, using public domain information from the companies' websites, to explore their status as hybrids using the Besharov and Smith's (2014) typology. I was invited on 26th and 27th August 2013 by two of the organizations located in Lagos to present an overview of the aim and objectives of this study, and to discuss what I intended to do with the data if access was granted. However, the requested access was denied by both organizations, as they were not comfortable with the area under investigation, especially regarding organizational trust.

On 9th September 2013, ASL and BPL, both located in Abuja (in the FCT), invited me to make a presentation highlighting the research objectives and this time access was granted. In return, I was asked to produce a short report with recommendations on how to improve trust within both organizations. Such a mutual exchange between research scholars and industry is not new. However, it is important for researchers to be realistic in their promises (Bryman, 2012). In this case, I am confident that realistic promises were made. The other six companies made no response. After access was granted, the next important thing to do was to select relevant participants. The sampling techniques I employed for this are discussed next.

### 4.3.5 Sampling technique

A crucial aspect of this study was identifying a sample of relevant participants who would contribute to the knowledge sought and to the research objectives. Sampling "is a small-scale representation of a larger grouping or population" (Hedged, 1978:57). It is the selection of a fraction of the total number of units that allows a conclusion to be drawn from that subgroup about the population to achieve the research objective (Saunders et al., 2007). Generally, in a case study, the sample is selected from people within the case setting (Yin, 1994). For this study, a mixed sampling technique was applied. Purposive and snowballing sampling techniques were employed, as they enabled the selection of participants relevant to this study.

The sampling was done in two phases. In the first phase, the participants were purposively selected, drawing a sample that was heterogeneous across different levels of the employment hierarchy from each of the case organizations, to allow the capture of various accounts of reality. Heterogeneous purposive sampling involves taking a diagonal slice through an organizational chart, ensuring that participants are included from all departments across all levels of the hierarchy (Saunders, 2012:42). These participants were then classified into three categories: top management executives, middle managers and employees.

The top management executives category comprises senior-level employees who are believed to have a wealth of experience and knowledge of organizational processes, corporate decision-making processes, management strategies, corporate objectives and human capital management within the selected organizations. The middle managers category comprises line managers, assistant line managers and supervisors with relevant knowledge of the organizational processes, procedures, policies and management strategies. These individuals are in charge of the day-to-day supervision and operations of the organization. The employees category is made up of workers engaged in the day-to-day operations of the organizations, often referred to as the foot soldiers. This categorisation provided the maximum variation of participants, as the study required (Saunders, 2012).

The second phase involved applying a snowballing technique afterwards to recruit participants within each category, which was achieved through referrals from existing participants. All participants were assured of their anonymity; therefore, all names, including references to other individuals, are fictitious. It is also important to note that there are no rules regarding the number of participants required in qualitative research (Yin, 1994); in this event, a total of 40 participants were recruited. There were 20 participants recruited from each case organization. A detailed representation of the sampling technique and process is illustrated in Figure 15.

Figure 15: Overview of Sampling Approach

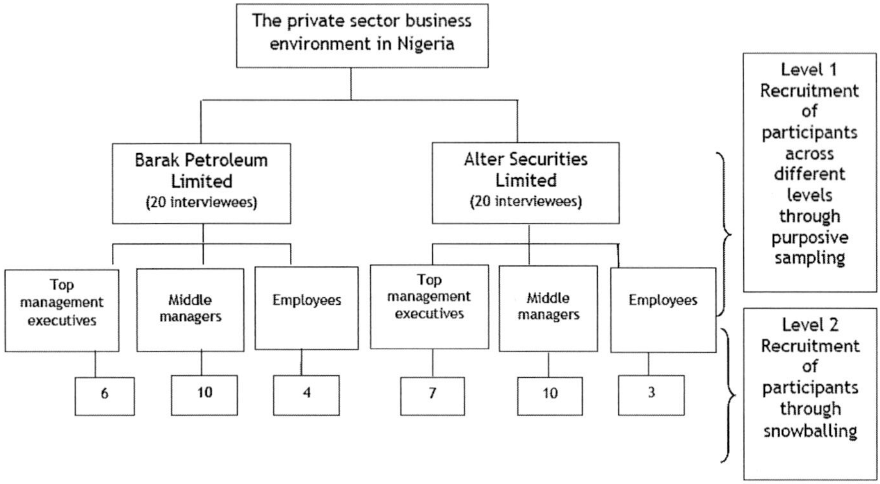


## 4.3.6 The sample size

The final sample size is made up of 13 top management executives, 20 middle managers and seven employees from both case organizations combined, as illustrated in Figure 15. However, more detailed illustrations of the interviewees' profiles for both organizations, and their age and length of service for each organization are shown in Table 10, Table 11, Table 12, Table 13 and Table 14, respectively. The research methods applied for data collection in this study are discussed next.

**Table 10: Interviewees' Profiles**

| Criteria | ASL | | | BPL | | |
|---|---|---|---|---|---|---|
| **Gender** | **Top management executives** | **Middle managers** | **Employees** | **Top management executives** | **Middle managers** | **Employees** |
| Male | 7 | 6 | 2 | 6 | 8 | 4 |
| Female | - | 4 | 1 | - | 2 | - |
| Total | 20 | | | 20 | | |

**Table 11: Interviewees' Age (ASL)**

| What is your age category? | | |
|---|---|---|
| Criteria | Gender | |
| Years | Men | Women |
| 25–35 years | 6 | 5 |
| 36–45 years | 8 | - |
| 46–55 years | 1 | - |
| 56–65 years | - | - |
| Total | 15 | 5 |

**Table 12: Interviewees' Length of Service (ASL)**

| How long have you been in this organization? | | |
|---|---|---|
| Criteria | Gender | |
| Years | Men | Women |
| Under 1 year | 4 | 1 |
| 1 to 5 years | 5 | 4 |
| 5 to 10 years | 5 | - |
| Over 10 years | 1 | - |
| Total | 15 | 5 |

**Table 13: Interviewees' Age (BPL)**

| What is your age category? | | |
|---|---|---|
| Criteria | Gender | |
| Years | Men | Women |
| 25–35 years | - | - |
| 36–45 years | 7 | 1 |
| 46–55 years | 11 | 1 |
| 56–65 years | - | - |
| Total | 18 | 2 |

**Table 14: Interviewees' Length of Service (BPL)**

| How long have you been in this organization? | | |
|---|---|---|
| Criteria | Gender | |
| Years | Men | Women |
| Under 1 year | 2 | - |
| 1 to 5 years | 8 | 1 |
| 5 to 10 years | 5 | 1 |
| Over 10 years | 3 | - |
| Total | 18 | 2 |

## 4.4 Data Collection Methods

While methodology addresses philosophical issues pertinent to undertaking research, methods refer to research techniques by which data is collected. According to Bell (2005), methods are selected because they will provide the data you require to produce a complete piece of research. Decisions have to be made about which methods are best for particular purposes and then data-collecting instruments must be designed to do the job." As stated earlier, this study drew upon a qualitative method approach that integrated semi-structured interviews and document analysis techniques (see Figure 14).

### 4.4.1 The semi-structured interview approach

The method employed for this study was primarily the semi-structured interview, as illustrated in Figure 14. This allowed the study to ground itself in the experiences of those involved (Saunders et al., 2007). However, to increase reliability and validity of the findings, additional data was collected: organizational documents were analysed and interviewees were asked questions aimed at verifying information obtained from this analysis.

Semi-structured interviews are open-ended and are particularly well adapted to exploratory research, where researchers do not have a vast knowledge of a topic and require a degree of flexibility to explore emerging issues (Bryman, 2004). Therefore, since the relationship between organizational hybridity involving multiple institutional logics and organizational trust is under-studied (Pache and Santos, 2013; Battilana and Lee, 2014; Karré, 2011), semi-structured interviews played such a role in this research. Not only did they further an in-depth understanding of the nature of hybridity within both ASL and BPL, they also allowed probing of the details of the interplay of institutional logics, as well as how institutional logics manifests and influences various organizational attributes, such as organizational culture, governance, leadership structure, intra-organizational relations and trust relations at the micro level of analysis. This enabled an exploration of a diversity of tensions and contradictions linked to organizational hybridity, making it possible to address the fundamental issues surrounding the topic of inquiry. Moreover, semi-structured interviews offered favourable conditions for the exploration of interviewees' various perceptions on complex and sometimes sensitive matters like trust. It provided interviewees with the opportunity to express their views in their own terms, and its flexibility allowed for probing and clarification of answers, while the set of themes developed around the theoretical frameworks was integrated into the topic guides.

Furthermore, using semi-structured interviews enabled the observation of the interviewees' body language, facial expressions and tone of voice during the interviews (Alvesson, 2011; Flick et al., 2004). In so doing, I was able to react appropriately by prompting interviewees for additional details so that misunderstandings could be clarified as they occurred and topics could also be changed when interviewees appeared distressed or uncomfortable (Bryman and Bell, 2011; Alvesson, 2011).

Having considered some of the limitations of interviewing (Saunders et al., 2007; Bryman and Bell, 2011), I took the following steps to avoid bias, misinterpretation and misrepresentation of interviewees' perceptions. Firstly, I refrained from asking multiple questions – e.g. questions joined by 'and' or 'or', or questions nested within questions – and interviewees were asked to clarify unclear answers. This latter step was taken to prevent confusion and also to avoid recording partial answers from the interviewees (Alvesson, 2011; Saunders et al., 2007). A follow-up email was used to seek clarification where an obscure response had been missed during the interview. Secondly, interviewees were informed at the outset that they were free to skip questions they were not comfortable answering. This step was taken to relieve them of any unnecessary pressure. The interview setting itself, of course, may influence the quality and mood of the dialogue between the interviewer and interviewee; this makes it an essential element for consideration when the interview technique is used (Lee and Cassell, 2013). The next section discusses how the interview was conducted.

### 4.4.2 Conducting the interviews

For the interviewees' convenience, the interviews were carried out within the office premises of both ASL and BPL over the course of 18 working days from 26th May to 18th June 2014 (see Appendix A: Interview Schedule for ASL and Appendix B: Interview Schedule for BPL). The rationale behind the occurrences of the interviews on the schedules relates to the varying degrees of available time and influence that interviewees had within the organization. Each interview lasted between 30 minutes and one hour depending on the interviewee and the time they had available.

The first few minutes of the interview were regarded as the icebreaker and this was not recorded since the time was spent summarising the purpose of the study, the research background and reading the plain language statement, as well as getting the formal consent of the interviewees. Interviewees were encouraged to ask any questions about the study at this point and also at any time during the interviews. After that, I asked the interviewees background questions about their current and previous roles in the organization. Thus, I asked the interviewees to introduce themselves briefly, stating their position in the organization, so as to gently introduce them to the topic of inquiry. Questions such as "How long have you been with this organization?" and "Can you describe the roles associated with your job and its function within the organization?" were asked, to help the interviewees relax and feel comfortable while starting off with familiar subject matter (Alvesson, 2011). At the same time, I hoped that my genuine interest at this stage would make interviewees feel valued, which would enable them to be open in their views especially concerning issues of trust in the organization.

After the interviewees had given their consent, the interviews were recorded using a digital recorder, with additional notes taken as I thought was necessary. Notes were taken in the first place in case the technology failed, but I also found that writing notes enabled me to document ideas and events that were likely to be forgotten and to create mind maps highlighting issues requiring further attention beyond the interview sessions (Alvesson, 2011). Recording the interviews, on the other hand, allowed me to concentrate and engage at an interpersonal level with the interviewees rather than being distracted by worrying about writing verbatim notes. Recording an interaction has been found to minimise infection through interpretation, which can occur when dealing with written field notes (Alvesson, 2011). However, using a recorder can also pose some challenges by adversely impacting the relationship between the interviewee and interviewer, as happens when there is an undue focus on the recorder (Alvesson, 2011). More so, it may inhibit some interviewees' responses, which could affect the reliability of data, if interviewees are unwilling to state something formally or further clarify a statement for the record (Saunders et al., 2007).

To overcome these challenges, I reassured the interviewees of their privacy and reminded them that the recorder would be switched off if they became uncomfortable at any point. The recorded interviews were stored in a computer database to be transcribed and analysed.

### 4.4.3 Transcribing the interviews

An important aspect of data collection is trying to minimise the effect of errors in the research (Alvesson, 2011). Thus, to minimise errors and to prevent interviews from piling up, interviews were manually transcribed verbatim shortly after the end of the interview sessions, using both the recorded conversations and the written notes, and any uncertainties identified were clarified with the interviewees. The transcription process was aided by the use of ExpressScribe, which is transcription software for professionals. Each interviewee was asked in a follow-up email to review any inconsistencies that had come to light in the recorded material and also to confirm quotations attributed to third parties. After transcribing the interviews, the audio data were cross-checked with transcripts to ensure that interpretations were accurate.

Despite the priority accorded to interview data as affording access to the perspectives of those involved, additional contextual materials were gathered through the analysis of relevant organizational documents, as stated earlier. These documents are discussed next.

### 4.4.4 Documents as data sources

Documents, according to Bryman (2004), are any materials that can be read, have not been produced specifically for research purposes, are preserved to become available for analysis and are relevant to the concerns of the social researcher. Organizations and their employees produce a multitude of documents for a diversity of purposes on a daily basis. There are documents that are public, such as annual reports, mission statements and public relations materials, and there are those that are private, such as minutes of meetings, internal/external correspondence, internal change programs and many financial documents (Bryman and Bell, 2011). Documents are frequently used as a source of qualitative data in case-study research, as they can be a rich source of information; contextually relevant and grounded in the contexts they embody (Lee and Cassell, 2013).

However, the first task regarding the use of documents as a source of data is to identify relevant documents and determine appropriate selection criteria. For this study, the difficulty of gaining access to the case organizations meant that I had to make do with the materials in the public domain of both ASL and BPL (Bryman, 2004). Even though this was the case, it was still important to ensure that the documents were authentic, free from errors and met other criteria of adequacy (Bowen, 2009).

The main documents that were analysed for this study included: annual reports, strategic reports, policy documents, governance and code of conduct reports, bulletins, news reports, periodical articles, and annual general meeting reports. Within these documents, the search focused on four main topics: (1) corporate goals, aims and objectives; (2) corporate governance; (3) corporate structure; and (4) corporate mission and value statements. This is because institutional logics are manifestations of organizational forms (Greenwood et al., 2010) and, as instances of practical rationality, they shape both habitual action and strategic decision; they can, therefore, shape, and their influences be traced in, organizational goals and objectives.

These documents, which were accessed through the organizations' websites, were analysed in terms of their authenticity, purpose, meaning and relevance to the study (Lee and Cassell, 2013; Bryman, 2004). As examples of the vocabularies of practice in use in the organizations, they provided an insight into the institutional logics in play, allowing the development of an informed view regarding the extent of hybridity within ASL and BPL, and also of the influences of the embodied multiple logics on the goals, governance, leadership structure, culture and intra-organizational attributes of both organizations. This was a necessary step to take, considering the nature of the investigation.

### 4.4.5 Analysing documents in context

The document analysis was undertaken before and during the intensive fieldwork stage of the research project. Document analysis can be used as a supplementary method to check the reliability of evidence given in interviews, just as it can function on its own as the primary method of research (Bowen, 2009). However, the analysis of pre-existing documents requires a different approach from that of self-generated texts such as interview transcripts. With self-generated texts, researchers can link the interview questions to the research focus. Therefore, when it comes to the analysis, they already have some direction. In contrast, researchers need to be flexible and open to change when using pre-existing materials (Bowen, 2009). Hence, for this study, documents were analysed and coded using a bespoke thematic coding frame. Analysing documents provided the opportunity to explore the topic of inquiry beyond the time scale of the interviews. Moreover, to overcome the challenge associated with selecting relevant documents and selective reading, I produced a file for the selected documents, recording descriptive details for each one including what it was written for and how the facts were presented if the factual presentation was its ostensible purpose (Symon and Cassell, 2012).

Combining this data with the rich data gathered from the semi-structured interviews provided a fuller picture of the complexity of organizational hybridity, specifically the complexities and tensions it presents within ASL and BPL. Table 15 illustrates how both methods were applied to achieve the aim and objectives of this study. The data analysis procedure for this study is discussed next.

**Table 15: Research Objectives and Methods**

| Research aims and objectives | Research methods | |
|---|---|---|
| | Semi-structured interviews | Document analysis |
| 1. To explore the influence of organizational hybridity on specific organizational attributes, including governance, organizational culture, leadership and intra-organizational relations of commercial hybrid organizations. | X | X |
| 2. To understand the influence of non-market-orientated institutional logics on commercial hybrid organizations. | X | X |
| 3. To shape an understanding of the implications of organizational hybridity for employees' trust in commercial hybrid organizations, with particular attention to those implications having a plausible relationship to organizational effectiveness. | X | X |
| 4. To develop research-based recommendations for sustaining employees' trust in commercial hybrid organizations. | X | X |

## 4.5 Data Analysis Procedure

A major issue for any qualitative research is deciding how the data should be transformed from an extensive assortment of raw materials into a concise and meaningful description of what was investigated (Bryman and Bell, 2011). This entails condensing highly complex information into a format that tells a story that is convincing to the reader. Thus, a reflexive interpretative position, employing thematic analysis, was adopted as the appropriate approach for analysing data for this study (Lee and Cassell, 2013). More so, since I wanted to avoid distancing myself from the data, I decided that the best way of gaining a deeper understanding was by following an abductive process, which typically involves immersing oneself into the social world of the actors to grasp their socially constructed meanings, as well as allowing themes to emerge from data (Blaikie, 2007).

### 4.5.1 A thematic analysis

Different approaches can be used for analysing qualitative data. Thematic analysis involves identifying patterns of meaning across the mass of qualitative data collected, which can thus be assembled into meaningful and related categories to provide an answer to the research questions being addressed (Saunders et al., 2007). The coding that emerges from this process essentially indexes the material, and allows it to be rearranged and analysed systematically and with rigour (Saunders et al., 2007; Pierre and Jackson, 2014). My coding strategy for this study is discussed in the subsequent section.

Analysing qualitative data comes with its challenges, which may arise out of the complexity of the data and the amount of time required for its analysis. A lack of clarity in the coding may also cause difficulties, as may problems inherent in the use of standardised analysis procedure (Bryman, 2004). There are computer-aided analytical tools such as Nvivo that could arguably be used to overcome these challenges, as well as making for better time management and reducing the biased selection of data in the analysis process. However, after much consideration on the pros and cons of using computer-aided tools in relation to this specific study and having considered the advice from peers and senior colleagues during conferences, workshops, colloquia and online reviews, I concluded that computer-aided approaches were less useful in terms of addressing issues that emerge during the data analysis process, because of the fluid way in which the themes emerged. More so, using computer-aided tools could have distanced me from the data (Bryman, 2004). Data analysis was carried out manually and emergent data were analysed with the theoretical propositions derived from the literature. This would ensure that non-verbal cues, such as silences, hesitations and the use of irony, not conveyed in the text transcriptions but evident in the interviews, were brought into consideration during the analysis process.

In an attempt to address issues such as lack of clarity, credibility and reliability often associated with the qualitative data analysis process, I thus took steps to organize, interpret and analyse the interview data (Saunders et al., 2007; Bryman, 2004; Gibbs, 2007). These steps enabled the interviews to be analysed in an abductive fashion. Such an approach has been argued to favour the development of new insights and theories from data without being overly influenced by past research (Blaikie, 2007). These steps include:

- Firstly, for the sake of good data management and to keep the task under control, interview transcripts were generated shortly after the interviews.
- Data was read and re-read so that I became familiar with the content by immersion.
- Initial summaries of the data were then generated, with a description of the research setting, and the meaning and objective impact of the phenomena observed (closely aligned to the interviewees' daily language).
- Noteworthy statements were listed, highlighted and categorised into similar themes. Knowledge of the literature, together with the initial summaries, allowed themes to be generated. Sections of the interviews were then categorised in relation to these themes. The first-order themes were generated.
- The data was then rearranged according to this categorisation and new summaries were produced. This involved looking at patterns or relationships, and identifying new themes or categories within the rearranged data. To minimise confusion, as changes were made the coding frame was updated, explanations were noted and previously coded materials were checked (second-order themes). Preliminary data analysis was then completed.
- Data was then interpreted more extensively to uncover a deeper understanding of the knowledge sought. This involved developing dimensions that determined the story line of each theme by capturing the differences and similarities in these accounts.
- The findings from each of the case studies were eventually tabulated for comparative analysis.
- Finally, analytic narrative and emergent theories were linked to the literature.

### 4.5.2 Coding strategy

To reiterate, the key element of thematic analysis is the generation and application of codes to the data. This involves grouping together different instances of datum under an overarching term to allow the description, exploration and analysis of the main themes within the data (Miles and Huberman, 1994). However, one of the most commonly mentioned criticisms of this approach is the possibility of losing the context of what was said in the interview through coding (Bryman, 2004). Moreover, the influence of existing theory is nearly impossible to escape and this could compromise the depth of the analysis (Bryman, 2012). Furthermore, several authors have argued that coding requires much time and there is a temptation for researchers to interfere with the information by filling in the blank space, which may result in data being incorrectly categorised (Gibbs, 2007). In the light of these criticisms, I endeavoured to maintain an open mind, being careful to note down preconceptions and assumptions, so as to resist the assumption that existing theory represented the final truth. I took pains to conduct the analysis with an eye on current literature and past research findings, so as to encourage an awareness of a conceptual dimension during the stages of theory generation (Bryman, 2012).

Following the data collection, I developed a thematic coding frame, which involved setting out the emerging themes along with descriptions of their content and a brief data example for reference (Gioia et al., 2013). More themes developed as I moved from one transcript to the next, so it turned out that most of the initial categories were descriptive, additional analytic themes being applied to the data after revisiting the literature and research questions. As coding is a reflexive process, the identification of categories and patterns helped to make sense of the data. It also helped to explore how different categories related to each other (Saunders et al., 2007; Gioia et al., 2013). As the analysis evolved, categories were refined, merged, split and related to each other, to produce a smaller, more concise set of themes and sub-themes that represented a more accurate picture of the data. After that, mind maps were created using boxes and arrows to provide an overview of the data and to assist in the sense-making process (Miles and Huberman, 1994; Gioia et al., 2013). The data display format (see Appendix C: Data Displa) was developed according to the information required to address the research problem, aim, objectives and questions. Table 16 summarises the data analysis procedure, while the ethical considerations raised in the course of this study are discussed next.

**Table 16: Data Analysis Procedure Summary**

| Procedure | Document analysis and semi-structured interviews |
|---|---|
| Description of the research setting and the unfolding event | The case studies, the setting and the meaning of the knowledge sought were described. |
| Data management | Interviews were recorded, transcribed and filed in a pre-specified filing system. |
| Coding | Initial codes were generated and key themes noted. Statements with similar meanings were identified and grouped into similar units. |
| Displaying, visualising and interpreting | The meaning of the codes, key themes and statements noted were visually displayed to make sense of interviewees' social reality and to derive the meaning of the problems at hand. |
| Conclusion | Patterns of themes were noted to build a logical chain of evidence and of limitations encountered during and after the research. |

## 4.6 Research Governance and Ethics

Ethical concerns arise in any human subject research and organizational research is no exception (Symon and Cassell, 2012). Thus, it is important for researchers to consider the implications of their research, so as to minimise the risks to participants and their environment (Bryman and Bell, 2011). When researching in an organizational context, researchers must remember that their presence is only temporary, whereas those who are being studied will still have to operate within the environment once the study is completed (Saunders et al., 2007). Such considerations meant that attention had to be paid to ethical research principles in the planning and realisation of this study.

### 4.6.1 Key ethical considerations

Given the importance of ethics for the conduct of research, it comes as no surprise that many universities have adopted specific codes relating to research ethics. Adhering to such codes can guide good practice and improve the credibility and reliability of the research in the eyes of participants (Symon and Cassell, 2012). There are a number of key interrelated areas of ethical controversy within social research, which include: voluntary participation, informed consent, research objectivity, data protection and retention, potential harm, and confidentiality and anonymity (Bryman, 2012; Saunders et al., 2007; Gibbs, 2007). Fundamental to many of these issues are the notions of privacy and personal integrity. Researchers should respect the privacy of both potential and actual participants, and should seek to avoid involving participants in doing things that they do not want to do or things that, on reflection, they might not approve of. This means being honest about the nature of the research, avoiding bias that may affect it, making it clear that the participant does not have to answer questions they feel uncomfortable with, keeping to promises, and managing the data in a way that observes anonymity and the confidentiality agreement.

Ensuring confidentiality and anonymity is especially important in this study, as allowing an organization or a participant to be described in a way that leads to easy identification may have severe consequences, ranging from embarrassment to psychological, economic or actual physical harm – which incidentally may make access difficult for future researchers (Saunders et al., 2007). Thus, for this study I adhered to the University of Glasgow's principles of ethical research and, before the fieldwork process commenced, ethical approval was obtained from the Adam Smith Business School's Ethics Committee, governed by the University of Glasgow's principles of ethical research.

### 4.6.2 Ethical access

Negotiating access for organizational research can create ethical challenges for researchers as a result of its academic and practical implications (Symon and Cassell, 2012). Researchers could be tempted into deceiving participants by being disingenuous about the actual purpose of the research. However, this would be not only contrary to the ethical guidelines discussed above, but also inimical to the development of any level of trust between researcher and participant. Gaining that trust and nurturing the relationship with participants inside the case organizations comes with its own set of challenges. Participation should be voluntary and researchers should gain informed consent from participants, which implies that participants should be fully informed about the nature of the research (Bryman, 2012; Saunders et al., 2007; Bryman, 2004; Gibbs, 2007).

Thus, for this study, access was managed through gatekeepers who were senior executive employees within both case organizations, and all participants were provided with an information sheet summarising the research aims and objectives before the interview sessions. I was honest regarding the purpose of the study, both with the people through whom access was negotiated and with the interviewees themselves. One of the conditions of access was that participants would be assured of confidentiality and anonymity. These promises were kept by disguising participants' identities, and by securely storing the transcripts, consent forms and audio recordings (Saunders et al., 2007). Legal considerations may sometimes make it difficult to maintain the assurances given to participants. However, even though this may be the case, researchers must make every effort to keep the promises they made while negotiating access. In this instance, interviewees were given the opportunity to review the interview transcripts and withdraw their consent at any point without providing any reason (Saunders et al., 2007).

### 4.6.3 Ethical data collection

Another practical consideration with ethical implications is the location and time of the interviews. It is important that interviews should be arranged at a time and place that is convenient and safe for interviewees, and the interviewer should aim to keep interviews within the prearranged timeframe (Alvesson, 2011). For this study, I ensured that the interviews were scheduled within the interviewees' office premises for their convenience. Furthermore, it was important to show interviewees respect by avoiding questions that were demeaning or overly sensitive. I reiterated during the interviews that the interviewees had the right to withdraw from the research at any time and also to decline to respond to any question if they felt threatened by it (Saunders et al., 2007). Despite these precautions, problems of an ethical complexion remained, including the following difficulties affecting the data collection process:

- The timing of the interviews coincided with the suppression of the insurgency (Boko Haram) in the FCT of Nigeria. The restrictions involved in this emergency made movement within the city difficult.
- Conducting the interviews within the workplace was very stressful for some of the lower-level employees, because of the nature of their jobs.

To address these problems, I developed strategies, which included:

- Pre-informing and prearranging the interview sessions a few days beforehand, followed by phone calls to the participants to confirm the meeting time, in order to minimise unnecessary journeys in the unsafe conditions of the city.
- Appropriate permission was obtained from line managers before engaging any subordinate or lower-level employees for interview. This permission meant that the employees were spared embarrassment and distraction while the interviews took place. Despite some interviewees initially being reluctant to participate in the interview, a good response was achieved.

## 4.7 Conclusions

This chapter has attempted to guide the reader through the interconnected theoretical approaches and methodological choices made for this study, as illustrated in Figure 14. Considering the alternative philosophical perspectives, it demonstrated that interpretivism from a symbolic interactionist perspective was suitable for this research, as it corresponded with both my world view as a researcher and the research aim and objectives. Moreover, it established that a multiple qualitative case-study approach was the most appropriate research design, as various participants' perceptions were required. Regarding the methods, semi-structured interviews were proposed as a suitable means of gathering the primary data and it was acknowledged that supplementary data from organizational documents in the public domain would provide useful background information relating to the research context. The case selection and sampling techniques were also reviewed, and an outline of the analysis process was provided.

In terms of ethical issues, steps were taken to minimise the potential for harm in the process of data collection, both for participants and for the organizations, which formed the research environment. I was open and honest about the research. Informed consent was obtained from interviewees at the outset, with each interviewee completing a consent form. The coding used during the gathering and processing of interview notes, recordings and transcripts was such as to anonymise the data. Moreover, data was stored and managed in a way that protected the confidentiality of the participants involved in the study, and undertakings were given that all source materials would be destroyed in the very near future. The subsequent chapters examine the findings of the study, which are grouped into two chapters (Chapter 5: ASL; and Chapter 6: BPL). Chapter 7 then discusses the findings in relation to the literature and considers the implications for the future of hybrid organizations. To conclude, Chapter 8 summarises the thesis, acknowledges its limitations and makes suggestions for future research.

# CHAPTER 5

# ORGANIZATIONAL HYBRIDITY IN PRACTICE: THE CASE STUDY OF ASL

## 5.1 Introduction

Figure 16: The Research Cycle (Phase 4)

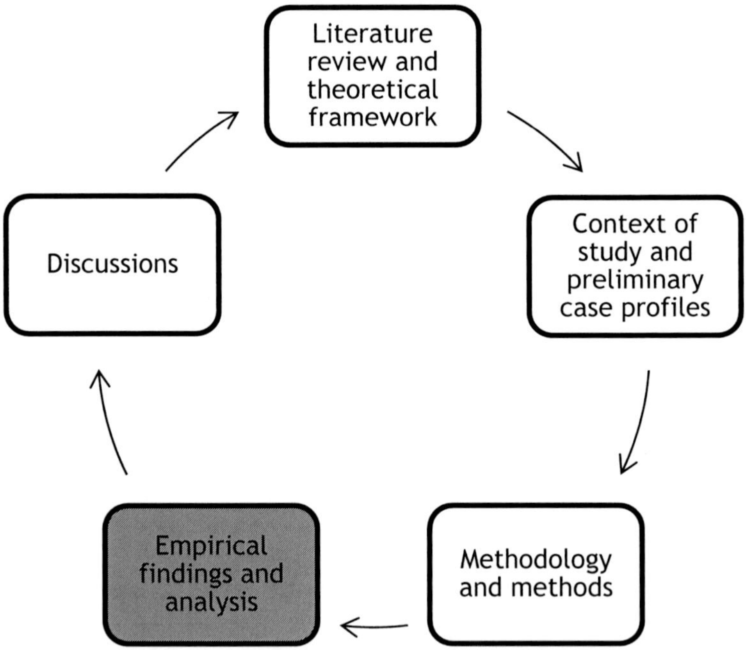


This chapter presents the data from interviews and document analysis carried out at ASL in Nigeria (see Figure 16). The data are analysed but not extensively discussed, within the framework of the research objectives, questions and propositions. The findings are discussed more extensively in Chapter 7. The present chapter comprises two main sections: A and B. Section A presents the data from the interviews and contains four main parts. The first contains profiles of the interviewees and explains the coding system used. The second part introduces the interviewees' views on organizational hybridity in practice, and the multiple institutional logics underpinning the goals and objectives of ASL. It also presents the interviewees' knowledge and experiences in relation to the governance, organizational culture, leadership style/structure and challenges presented by organizational hybridity at ASL. The third part presents interviewees' views on the tensions associated with organizational hybridity and describes employees' behavioural responses to these tensions. The fourth part presents the interviewees' views on trust and the implications of organizational hybridity for employees' trust in ASL. Section B, on the other hand, presents the data from the analysis of company documents. The chapter ends with a summary and concluding remarks.

## Section A: Findings from the Interviews

This section presents the data from the interviews involving 20 interviewees conducted at ASL. For the purpose of protecting the anonymity of the interviewees in this chapter and the subsequent chapters, they are referenced according to a code assigned as shown in Table 17. The top management executives are assigned codes AT1 to AT7, while the middle managers are assigned codes AM8 to AM17, and the employees are assigned codes AE18 to AE20.

**Table 17: Coding System for ASL**

| ASL | | | |
|---|---|---|---|
| **Level of the employment hierarchy** | Top management executives | Middle managers | Employees |
| **No. of interviewees** | 7 | 10 | 3 |
| **Assigned codes** | AT1–AT7 | AM8–AM17 | AE18–AE20 |
| **Total** | 20 | | |

## 5.2 Profiles of the Interviewees

Pertinent information about the interviewees was gathered by asking questions related to gender, age, native language and work experience, as discussed next.

### 5.2.1 Gender, age and native language of the interviewees

Interviewees were predominantly male, and exclusively aged between 25 and 55 years (see Table 11, which shows a summary of the interviewees' profiles including their age and gender). The language spoken within ASL is predominantly English, the official language of Nigeria, so interviews were conducted in English. However, the native languages spoken by the interviewees were mainly Hausa, Igbo and Yoruba. These findings are consistent with the discussion in Chapter 3 on the dominant tribes and language spoken in Nigeria.

### 5.2.2 Work experience in the organization

To obtain detailed information on the interviewees' work experience in the organization, the following information was solicited: previous job position, current job position and number of years in that position. The data show that the majority of the interviewees have up to 5 years' work experience (see Table 12). This highlights the possibility that those with relatively few years of work experience in the organization would likely have limited experience in interpreting, understanding and translating the vocabularies and narratives that represent one or other elements of the hybrid nature of ASL. The data gathered through the interviews supports this finding. The next section presents the findings associated with the research objective: exploring the influence of organizational hybridity on specific organizational attributes in commercial hybrid organizations.

## 5.3 Findings Associated with Exploring the Influence of Organizational Hybridity on Specific Organizational Attributes of ASL

**Proposition 1:** *The more extensive the tensions associated with organizational hybridity, the greater the likelihood of negative behavioural responses by employees.*

The data on organizational hybridity in practice and the tensions it presents were based on the interviewees' perceptions of the organizational attributes of ASL, in terms of: their experiences and knowledge of the organizational goals and objectives of the organization; the influence of multiple institutional logics in these goals; and their experiences and knowledge of the organizational culture, governance and leadership structure. These are discussed in turn. Exploration of this objective formed part of a strategy aimed at answering the overall research question as well as the supporting research question: *To what extent does organizational hybridity influence specific attributes of commercial hybrid organizations?*

### 5.3.1 Interviewees' experiences and knowledge of the goals and objectives of ASL

The data from interviews were based on the interviewees' perceptions of the corporate goals and objectives of the organization, the process of setting goals and objectives, and the involvement of employees in setting these goals. The data showed a strong consensus on commercial and professional goals as the core strategic agenda of ASL. Indeed, the strategic intent of ASL is perceived as focused not only on profit maximisation and commercialisation of resources as a financial organization but also on value creation, which is achieved by offering expert knowledge to customers. Thus, the core purpose of the organization is said to be to commercialise organizational resources by providing professional financial services to customers (AT3, AT1, AM10, AE17). Even though there was a strong acknowledgement of both agendas in the strategic intent of ASL, some interviewees perceived an imbalance in the degree to which each goal could be said to be core to organizational functioning.

Indeed, because of the business orientation of ASL and the sector of the economy in which it operates, the general feel and focus of the organization were interpreted as "money-making" by the majority of the interviewees (AT1, AM8, AE20, AE18). In particular, AT1 stated, "this is a money-making organization, we are profit making…the main focus is money and capital market assets". This indicates that the commercial goals are core to the organizational functioning. However, the data could also be interpreted as signalling a need to emphasise professionalism, which appears to have gained ground within the organization as an aftermath of the 2008 economic recession, aimed at developing "a value-packed experience for customers necessary within the financial industry" (AT7). According to some of the interviewees, the recession led to the strong emphasis on professionalism whereby customers were no longer solely viewed as tools to make money, but rather as individuals who should enjoy the services provided by the organization. Regarding this, AM8 stated, "As professionals, the main thing that we do here is to add value – if you are not adding core value to your client, then you are defeating the purpose of what you are doing." Overall, even though the interviews showed commercial goals as core to the organizational functioning of ASL in line with its commercial business orientation, there was an indication that professional goals are equally important, being a key element by which the organization's internal operations are directed and controlled.

***Influence of institutional logics in ASL's goals***

As predicted in Chapter 3, the interviewees' views reflected a commercial logic, which emphasises the commercialisation and marketisation of organizational resources, as the dominant logic with professional logic acting as the peripheral logic. Indeed, because of the market-orientated business model of ASL, commercial logic is not contested at the core of the organizational functioning, which makes it appear to be dominant with professional logic acting as a supporting logic. This is consistent with the data in Chapter 3 regarding the nature of ASL as a dominant commercial hybrid organization. There was an indication that the prescribed professional logic provides compatible values with the commercial logic, which permeate through the organization. Hence, it contributes to the financial success of the organization. For example, AM16, in particular, stated: "The core vision of this organization is to champion wealth creation that makes a positive impact on our customers and the society at large through our expertise and professional know-how." However, a common argument regarding the combination of both logics is that it is "beyond the organization's control" as the logics continue to "embrace new opportunities, direction and growth" (AT1, AM16, AE20). Thus, the coexistence of the two logics may be seen as having enabled a "growing sense of tension" within the organization (AT1).

### 5.3.2 Interviewees' experiences and knowledge of the governance of ASL

The data in this section were based on the interviewees' perceptions of the governance of the organization and the balance of power within it. Data showed that the organization operates a separation-of- ownership-and-control governance structure, where the office of the chairman is distinctively separate from the office of the CEO. The overall perception of governance at ASL is that it operates to maximise financial returns to increase value for shareholders, who constitute the dominant stakeholder group. More so, the ultimate responsibility for governance and strategic decision-making power lies with the board of directors, headed by the chairman, and the executive management team who are led by the CEO. AM8, in particular, stated, "I would say that governance is balanced between the executive management and the board because they are the ones that are managing the supposed guidelines with corporate governance…you know, the rules, guidelines that the company is run by, stakeholders interests and all the other people that are involved in a company's activity, their rights, and their interests." However, the data indicated that even though both groups are perceived to be in charge of making strategic decisions within the organization, the influence of the board of directors is rated as very high, and as such is held to play a profound role in influencing the executive management team and the management team to ensure they act in accordance with shareholders' interests. This is believed to have stimulated agency problems as well as contributed to the "sense of tension" within the organization.

The data showed that both the board of directors and senior management executives are seen to place emphasis on different logics and set employees' targets independent of the other party; a situation that sends conflicting messages to employees. For example, AT4, an executive management team member, stated: "After setting the corporate objectives, you have a management target Y, which is set by employees and the entire management team, you know, we sit down and discuss what we think we can make this year and also the board sits and they say, 'You know what, you guys know you can also meet X,' so usually the board's target is different from management target, which makes this whole thing so confusing."

In addition, while the board of directors emphasises commercial logic due to its profit-maximisation obligations, the executive management team's talk reflected a professional logic in line with the professional values and code of conduct of the financial sector. This is a situation that creates tensions and contradictions within the organization; under pressure to deliver on multiple expectations and without clear communication on how to meet them, employees are left "distressed". A majority of the interviewees associated these contradictions with the misalignment of multiple interests in the governance of ASL. AT6, for example, stated, "Like I said, it's unfortunate that even within a corporate structure there is always a problem between multiple goals and interests, in fact corporate interest and personal interest, I'm not saying that the organization shouldn't make money…they can do all of that but go about it in a way that it doesn't directly conflict with the other corporate objectives…if it does, it becomes a big issue."

Overall, two points emerged from the data. Firstly, in the governance of ASL, power rests between the board of directors and the senior executive management team. Secondly, there was a strong indication of a "growing sense of tensions" in the governance of ASL, which is generated as a result of misaligned multiple interests between the decision-making authorities, being the board of directors and the senior executive management.

### 5.3.3 Interviewees' experiences and knowledge of the leadership style/structure of ASL

The current leadership structure of ASL was explored. The data here were based on the interviewees' perceptions relating to the leadership structure, style and the balance of decision-making authority within the organization. The data showed that ASL operates a bureaucratic (top–bottom) leadership structure, where the chairman who is a member of the board sits at the apex of the organizational hierarchy, followed by the board of directors, the senior executive management and the management team. In fact, the ultimate power balance is seen to lie with the board of directors and senior executive management, as indicated above. According to AT3, "Looking at the organogram structure, it is like a top–bottom approach where information and every other thing about the organization trickles down."

There was a general perception that the organization operates a highly bureaucratic structure, where power is centralised with the board of directors and senior executive management who control the implementation of logics, strategies, objectives and guidelines. In so doing, strategic decisions are made in isolation from the other employees (AM15, AM16, AE18). However, there was a common perception among the middle managers that – just like the corporate goals and objectives – the leadership structure, power balance and ownership structure of ASL have evolved over the years, resulting in a much more "diluted ownership". According to these interviewees, the overall structure of the organization has considerably improved compared to where it was before 2008, as a response to external pressure that is "beyond the organization's control". For example, AM10 stated: "Prior to 2008, the largest owner was the chairman and it was close to a dictatorship, he was the almighty but with time from about 2008 till now we have seen a bit of a shift in that, because we have done things like diluted ownership so new owners have come to join the ownership so there is a dilution of ownership even though the control is still with the board, but what we have seen is that other people at management level are able to lend their voices."

The data showed that even though power is still centralised at the top with the chairman and the board of directors, the senior executive management team has a voice and contributes to the overall decision-making process within the organization. However, while this seems to be the case, there was an overall perception that the organization still lacked a comprehensive communication system to diffuse information beyond the board of directors and the senior executive management, to the management team and to the wider body of employees. In fact, some of the interviewees argued that the centralisation of power at the top of the employment hierarchy continued to contribute to the "contradictions" experienced within the organization, as necessary organizational decisions, including what goals and objectives to pursue, are made in isolation of the "foot soldiers". For example, AT3 stated, "I think these contradictions occur due to the bureaucratic organogram structure of the organization, which results in the organization disregarding employees' contributions." Thus, employees at the bottom of the hierarchy are left to interpret, understand and make sense of the organizational processes without any sense that their contribution is valued or appreciated by those at the top.

### 5.3.4 Interviewees' experiences and knowledge of the organizational culture of ASL

The data from the interviews were based on the interviewees' perceptions regarding the core values prescribed within the organization, its identity and what it stands for. Organizational culture, according to interviewees, should be about creating a single identity and unified purpose that captures what ASL is all about (AT1, AM11, AM17, AE19). But the reality is that decisions are made in isolation from the views of employees and they feel deeply a lack of involvement, which militates strongly against their desire to understand, make sense of or identify with the organization as it exists. A common view held by all the interviewees was that ASL has hitherto failed to achieve a common cultural fit that captures the core values of the organization. Specifically, the perceived cultural disjuncture within the organization occurs around the board of directors and the senior management team. It was felt that a more open, involving and inclusive culture was characteristic of the executive management team, more focused on providing value to customers, while a close and non-inclusive culture defined the board of directors who were more money focused. With regard to the "lack of common cultural fit" as suggested by AM12, some of the interviewees acknowledged that tensions were experienced during performance appraisals and policy implementation. Regarding policy implementation, tensions were said to arise because the prescription from leadership is not perfectly aligned and because policies on paper are different from what is practised within the organization. For example, AM8 stated: "You talk about bullying in your policies but you see it happening, even with the office cleaners. When someone is talking to them in an erratic way and you don't do anything, so it is conflicting because on paper you say this cannot happen, but it is happening in practice." These tensions and challenges are explored next.

One interpretation of these data is of interviewees appearing to suggest that, even though some of the values prescribed by the organization exist as words on paper, employees need to be more aware of those cultural values to understand what the organization stands for in practice. This is because a mismatch of values can produce ineffective actions and lead to "identity distress". For example, AM16 stated: "For everything like core values, honesty, integrity…it shouldn't be just on paper, it should be practical…it should be our culture, I believe. If I would suggest anything about balancing the organizational culture, I would say let these things leave paper and come to reality." However, despite the fact that a commercial logic predominantly influences the organizational culture of ASL, some interviewees maintained that the organization is continuously working towards creating an ideal cultural fit that will capture its hybrid nature both internally and externally. AM17, in particular, stated, "We learn every day; we learn from our past mistakes…the most important thing is to capture what makes us who we are in the process."

### 5.3.5 Interviewees' experiences and knowledge of tensions at ASL

The interviewees' views on tensions and contradictions associated with organizational hybridity were explored by questions regarding: times when they perceived that the organization was sending conflicting messages about expectations in terms of objectives; their responses to conflicting messages; and those occasions when they had to choose between their own personal values and what they were told to do within the organization. The interviewees were also asked to highlight some of the problematic aspects of organizational hybridity that in practice enhance the "growing sense of tensions" within the organization, as well as being asked to make suggestions on how to mitigate these problematic aspects. Three issues emerged from the data, which are broadly under the following points:

- *Lack of a clear and effective communication system.* Data showed that establishing a clear communication system that would enable the passage of undistorted information across the organization was seen as having the potential to increase the effectiveness and efficiency of the organization, by ensuring that employees are more aware of the organizational processes and goals, both on paper and in practice. Furthermore, the establishment of clear and effective communication channels and timelines was seen as something that would enable the clarification of the organizational goals to employees and thereby reduce conflicting messages. On this point, AT1, in particular, stated: "Information is very important for the organization to be able to improve. Information should not be distorted. The right information needs to be circulated amongst staff and also among clients." According to AM10, clear communication could be achieved by occasional multilevel strategy sessions, which would update employees on the status quo of the organization.
- *Lack of employee involvement in decision-making.* The data showed that allowing the employees to make inputs to the organizational strategic decision-making process was seen as something that would give them a "sense of belonging" and thereby increase their commitment to the organization (AM11). According to AM8, "Employees should be carried along; our type of business is employee friendly…so if we are not carried along, and we don't feel our interests are being covered or taken care of, you are not going to get the optimal best from us…yes, there is no way organizations will perform or exist in the first place without carrying along employees, yes, the involvement is needed, and it's important."
- *Lack of shared identification with the organization's hybrid nature.* The interviewees evinced perception of a need for a cultural reorientation, which could enable awareness of and identification with the organization's hybrid nature, and would hopefully thus help prevent misinterpretations of prescribed logics. Such a cultural shift can be achieved by giving employees a "significant role to play when setting strategic corporate objectives" (AM10). Indeed, "When you are part of a system, and you share a vision, an ideology you believe in, you want to defend it" (AT6). In other words, the involvement of

employees in strategy and the cultural realignment would automatically strengthen and bring to life employee commitment to the organization.

### 5.3.5a Organizational hybridity in relation to conflicting messages: commercial logic versus professional logic

The data pointed to the existence of extensive tensions experienced within ASL in the form of "conflicting expectations", triggered specifically by unclear communication and the lack of employee involvement in decision-making. According to some interviewees, these tensions are triggered by inconsistencies between policies on paper and what is practised within the organization, which comes as no surprise, given the interviewees' perceptions of the way the organization lacks a unified identity. Moreover, there were indications that these tensions and contradictions experienced within ASL are seen as common in modern-day organizations in their struggle for survival; ASL is not considered as an exception. For example, AM8 stated, "I don't think there is any organization that does not send conflicting messages to employees because when they come up with the objectives, they are written, they have not been tried, in practice they may not achieve what they want them to achieve, but you don't see them going back to change the objectives, so in practice it becomes conflicting."

However, contrary to this argument, some of the interviewees suggested that the tensions experienced within the organization occur as a result of the way employees interpret prescribed logics. For example, AM10 stated, "For me, conflicting messages leave a lot of room for interpretation…that is the first level of conflict you see." In trying to reconcile the multiple logics prescribed to employees so as to derive and determine what is expected from them, employees become distressed and conflicted. As one middle manager (AM10), in particular, put the point: "That's part of the main problem…you say you want to run by a certain form of objectives but all your actions show otherwise because you want to satisfy some other interests, that's the first level of conflict you see, and you as an employee is thinking but we are supposed to be X but all their actions as an organization depict Y…it's conflicting for me, and it makes me want to walk away."

One lesson that could be drawn here is that the organization would reap a positive impact in its overall performance if these challenges are adequately treated, but if disregarded, they will generate "further complications for employees, who are actually the bedrock of the organization" (AT3). Furthermore, within the overarching theme of the tensions at ASL, three domains emerged from the data. The first is the domain of *external influencers* as suggested above, which highlights the dominant institutional logics that play a role in prescribing values and generating internal contradictions and tensions within ASL. Regarding this domain, the interviewees' responses lent weight to the argument that the dominant institutions competing for legitimacy within Nigerian society require being brought to account in any attempt to address the challenges presented by organizational hybridity in commercial organizations in Nigeria. The second domain is of *identification*, which highlights the process by which the employees make sense of the multiple institutional logics operative within ASL. The third domain is of *behavioural responses*, which highlights interpretations and behavioural manifestations that can be seen to issue from the operation of the multiple institutional logics embedded within ASL. These domains are discussed in the subsequent sections.

### 5.3.5b Organizational hybridity in relation to identity distress

The data also showed that identity distress occurred as a result of the inability to identify with the prescribed logics or values within the organization. A majority of interviewees stated that they are often conflicted as a result of the multiple institutional logics prescribed within ASL, of which the dominant ones are commercial logic and professional logic as indicated above. According to the interviewees, since commercial and professional logics prescribe relatively different values, employees are often conflicted as to which one to follow in challenging situations. For example, AM10 stated, "A lot of times management has said something and done something else, it is a bit difficult dealing with that…I don't know if it is just me but I find myself conflicted." In so doing, employees often find themselves being dishonest to customers to achieve organizational goals, even though it may be against their own personal, spiritual or religious beliefs. According to AM8, "Every company goes through these challenges, but the impunity of the lying is what gets to me, like if I am to take money from a client from inception I already know I will have a problem to pay, so I lie to the customer…this makes me sad because I am a Christian and was not brought up to lie." Overall, there are indications that since organizational hybridity leaves a lot of room for interpretation within the organization, the inability of employees to identify with the institutional logics prescribed could lead them to display a variety of behavioural responses. Such responses are discussed next.

## 5.3.6 Behavioural responses to organizational hybridity

The data from the interviews showed various behavioural responses to organizational hybridity. The interviewees were keen to point out that these behavioural responses are very common within ASL; their variety is essentially reflecting the fact that employees are reacting, positively or negatively, to things they do not understand or comprehend. Four overarching themes emerged from the data as the employees' responses to organizational hybridity:

- Display of "insubordinate" behaviour
- Employee disengagement
- Resigning from the organization
- Display of synergic behaviour.

### 5.3.6a Display of "insubordinate" behaviour as employees' response to organizational hybridity

The data pointed to the display of "insubordinate" behaviour as one of the employees' responses to hybridity. According to the interviewees, insubordination involves the outright or subtle rejection of prescribed logics, rules or values by employees, which manifest as the disregard of rules and authority. For example, AT6 stated, "When you send mixed messages, especially when the criteria is not clear to everybody…if you are not careful, apart from demotivation, the staff will revolt subtly and become insubordinate." Consensus appeared to exist about the existence of this type of behavioural response, as many interviewees highlighted it. However, some interviewees argued that this sort of outright rejection is not common within the organization; rather than a direct confrontation with management, the most common way of rejecting prescribed logics and values within ASL is to vent one's anger to colleagues. AM8, in particular, stated, "You get angry, you vent to your colleagues, they listen to you. Who are you hurting? You are hurting yourself because it is a war you cannot end."

### 5.3.6b Employee disengagement as employees' response to organizational hybridity

There was general agreement among interviewees in the perception of employee disengagement as a common behavioural response; according to the data, in fact, it was the most common behavioural response within ASL. Interviewees recorded observable displays such as not paying attention to work, expressions of nonchalant attitudes and being negligent towards assigned duties. For example, AM11 stated, "Honestly, I am so lost in this company, but I have come to understand the people that I work with, you can recommend from now till tomorrow, they are who they are…so we have accepted it like that…so I do not even look at what they do anymore, I do not care, I will just do what I have been paid to do." Interviewees drew attention to further examples of employee disengagement in the form of "calling in sick", "coming late to work", "giving unnecessary excuses when given assignments" and "taking extended leave days" (AT4, AM12, AM11, AT6). AT4, in particular, stated, "You give the employees work to do and instead of delivering in 20 minutes they just do it for days. Some of them will start taking extended leave days, they call in sick, they just become very uncooperative."

Overall, the perception was that the manifestation of this behaviour signalled that the employees would end up resigning in the long run, which is consistent with the high employee turnover at ASL. Thus, interviewees suggested that the effective motivation of employees would increase employees' commitment to work, and thereby contribute to overall organizational effectiveness and performance. According to AM12, "Investing in the employees and understanding what makes the workplace conducive is important to organizational effectiveness and low employee turnover."

### 5.3.6c Resigning from the organization as employees' response to organizational hybridity

Resigning from work emerged as another behavioural response by employees. This was defined by the interviewees as an articulated intention to leave the organization. In fact, a majority of the interviewees associated organizational hybridity with high turnover within the organization. According to them, when employees are tired of being distressed and conflicted, they resign as a last resort. AT3 put it this way: "Well, a lot of people resign, you know, because of this modern day, if you are not being heard or if you are being told to do what you feel is wrong, you go somewhere else where you know you will be heard. There is no way you are going to move forward when you keep on being mandated to do stuff." The interview findings showed that when employees are faced with conflicting messages and contradictions, they become "distressed", "disgruntled", "insubordinate", and start to show "a nonchalant attitude towards assigned work" and "eventually walk away". This suggests a behavioural response cycle, which is extensively discussed in Chapter 7. AM10, in particular, expressed this idea: "Because of the conflicting messages, a lot of people have resigned, people are beginning to look for other jobs, the morale is low because there is this sense that these guys are not serious…so a lot of people are not happy with this. People are disgruntled and are beginning to have second thoughts."

On the other hand, a few of the interviewees affirmed that some employees return after being offered higher positions and given huge financial incentives. Regarding this, AT7 added, "I have been here for five months now but I worked for this organization for four years, so this is like a second coming…I got a more senior role, better pay and a management appointment."

### 5.3.6d Display of synergic behaviour as employees' response to organizational hybridity

Contrary to the negative connotation of the above responses, synergic behaviour emerged as a peculiar type of response. This is a situation that occurs, according to the interviewees, when employees reach the maximum point of awareness of the multiple expectations of the organization, which they can then interpret in ways that make sense to them (AM10, AM12, AM14, AM17, AM11). In fact, these employees are acutely aware of what is expected of them. However, they interpret this in a way that makes sense to them and respond accordingly. For example, AM10 stated: "I will be honest with you…the business at times requires some diplomacy and tact. Knowing what is expected from you and how to achieve that, no matter what, is one of the skills one has to develop to survive in this organization." This behavioural response was highlighted by a majority of the middle managers. In these interviewees' views, the multiple institutional logics prescribed within ASL are not necessarily oppositions or causes of conflicts all the time; rather, they do necessarily sometimes go together. Data showed that this type of response could manifest in two ways:

- Firstly, employees who respond in this manner are aware of, and have the full knowledge of, what is expected from them; they interpret the information in a way that makes sense to them by following the rules "by the book" to achieve organizational objectives. For example, AM14 stated, "At times I get conflicting messages, but I just try to do what I feel is right by the book and it's been working for me."
- Secondly, employees who respond in this manner are also aware of, and have the full knowledge of, what is expected from them. However, they interpret the information, find loopholes and, instead

of following the rules "by the book", they take advantage of the loopholes by becoming opportunistic. For example, AM9 stated, "Those who understand the system take advantage of the situation since lining their pockets motivates them more than achieving the organization's objectives."

Overall, the majority of the interviewees (mostly middle managers) favoured taking advantage of the loopholes within the organization, since they did not identify with its culture or values. Moreover, the questionable integrity of the organization made them cautious about taking risks for it. Despite their reservations about the organization, a few of the interviewees, mostly top management executives, argued that they would rather follow the rules in favour of the organization than take advantage of the situation (AM14, AT4, AT2, AT5). This indicates that the hierarchical arrangement, more specifically the power balance within the organization, could be a factor influencing the employees' identification process and possibly a response to hybridity. The next section presents the data associated with understanding the implications of organizational hybridity for employees' trust in ASL.

## 5.4 Findings Associated with Understanding the Implications of Organizational Hybridity for Employees' Trust in ASL

**Proposition 2:** *The greater the tensions produced by multiple logics, the less likely it becomes that employees of commercial hybrid organizations will trust their employers.*

Interviewees' views on trust were explored by asking questions on their perceptions of it and specifically on how well they trust the organization. Regarding interviewees' perceptions of trust, the data showed that interviewees' definitions of trust fell under three themes: "competence", "integrity" and "security". These themes, therefore, are presented as the most important dimensions of trust for employees at ASL. Exploration of this objective formed part of a strategy aimed at answering the overall research question as well as the supporting research question: *How does organizational hybridity affect the level of employees' trust in commercial hybrid organizations?*

### 5.4.1 Integrity as a dimension of trust

Integrity emerged from the data as an important dimension of trust in ASL. A majority of the interviewees agreed that an organization is perceived as trustworthy when it is "open", "honest" and "fulfils promises made". According to the interviewees, even if the organization is not 100% competent, fulfilling promises and being honest are important dimensions of trust, which should not be ignored. AM10 put it this way: "I think what makes an organization trustworthy is simple, open and honest communication." The interviewees stated that an organization could be perceived as trustworthy when management say what they do and do what they say. At the same time, some interviewees pointed out that ASL had failed to fulfil certain promises, constituting a reason why there is high employee turnover in the organization. AT4, in particular, stated: "For integrity…I expect that every point in time management should be open…I think integrity is when you say it is morning, everybody should go outside and say it's morning, so to that extent management should always come with open arms…unfortunately, it is not always the case, especially for the board." Overall, there was a view that when an organization has open and honest communication systems – bearing in mind that employees do not trust what they do not understand – employees are more committed and more willing to take risks for the organization.

### 5.4.2 Competence as a dimension of trust

In common with Mayer et al. (1995), competence emerged as an essential element in the interviewees' interpretation of trust in ASL. Regarding competence, some interviewees argued that the organization had demonstrated competence, especially on the issue of remuneration since it has never defaulted on any payments. On this basis, the organization is perceived as trustworthy regarding its ability to fulfil financial obligations to employees. According to AM13, "If you pay my salary, you have satisfied me at the end of the month so I think it is also a function of individuals and the different layers of what you consider to mean satisfaction or trust." However, some interviewees related the overall competence of the organization to the employees' collective skills. According to these interviewees, the organization employs very competent employees, who do their best to ensure that it continues to carry on its business activities effectively; it is, therefore, these people who drive the competence of the organization in the first place. AT4 stated, "For competence, I mean in Alter Securities we have a number of competent people that can run the show, I mean some have been here for 15–18 years, I have been here for 14 years, and my experience spans across asset management, securities trading back office, so we have the experience."

### 5.4.3 Job security as a dimension of trust

The final dimension, highlighted by six of the interviewees, is job security. The interviewees argued that an organization that offers job security and safety for employees is perceived as trustworthy. According to these interviewees, ASL has offered them just that, so the issue of trust in the company is to that extent settled. AM15 put it like this: "Trust is about feeling safe both financially and physically…I think it's just basically for the employees to feel safe in the environment and to be reassured that whatever happens they've got your back." The importance of this dimension is obvious, given the instabilities that affect the Nigerian institutional environment. Overall, therefore, the data supports the view that employees' understanding of trust in ASL is based on perceptions of the organization's position along the dimensions of:

- Integrity (open and honest communication)
- Competence (payment of salaries and remuneration)
- Security (feeling safe financially and physically).

Some of these perceived dimensional characteristics were evaluated as defective. Thus, interviewees suggested the need to develop more strategies and lines of communication to improve the organization's integrity, in terms of relationships with employees and also with clients (AM11, AM17, AM10, AM8, AM12).

### 5.4.4 Employees' trust in ASL

The interviewees' trust in the organization was explored. Regarding the question of "How well do you trust the organization?", the data showed that a majority of the interviewees do not trust the organization in all three dimensions highlighted above. A majority of the interviewees affirmed that they trust the organization in terms of competence but do not trust it in terms of integrity. For example, AE18 stated, "If I cannot trust you to act the way you said you are going to act, which is for the best interest of the organization, then it means the answer is no. I think we suffer that in ASL, people do not trust the organization because they [the organization] do not deliver on their promises." A majority of the interviewees affirmed that this is because the board and the executive management have not dealt openly with employees or involved them in the decision-making process; therefore, they feel that the organization does not have their interests at heart. AM11 put it this way: “I don’t trust them because they have not shown me any level of integrity…with the experiences we have had here, there is no integrity.” Interviewees took the view that when an organization tries to be open and gives employees some access to definite information, this gives them confidence that they are in safe hands (AM11, AM15).

However, these conditions are not met at ASL, where a lack of trust in terms of the organization’s integrity has sapped employees’ commitment to work and in the long run it encourages high levels of employee turnover. AM17 powerfully expresses this mood: “When there is a breach of trust, it affects my morale as an employee and most times I say to myself, what’s the point really?” According to interviewees, employees who cannot stomach integrity issues tend to resign after a while. AM12 added, “It is the basic logic of life – you get what you put in.”

Furthermore, the data also pointed to the perception that involving employees in decision-making, as well as clearly communicating core organizational objectives to employees, will show that the organization is concerned about employees’ welfare, giving them a sense of belonging so that they are more committed to the organization. For example, AM11 suggested, “Ensuring that the governance structure and objectives of the organization is made clear can help build trust, because you can’t force trust on somebody but you can get the person to trust you through how you behave towards them.” Other measures suggested by interviewees to improve trust include the implementation of an open and honest communication system, the involvement of employees in the organizational decision-making process, procedural devices to favour fulfilment of promises and measures to encourage employees’ identification with the values prescribed within the organization.

According to the interviewees, building employees’ trust and acknowledging the effort they put into the organization could help mitigate the possible tensions generated by conflicting values. Ideally, such acknowledgement would take the opportunity to reinforce understanding of the organization’s values, goals and objectives, because, without a good knowledge of the organizational goals and objectives, employees are less likely to trust the organization. Overall, even though some of the interviewees perceived ASL as competent in terms of remuneration and financial incentives, a majority revealed that they do not trust the organization due to the lack of openness and integrity. This suggests an urgent need to rebuild employees' trust in ASL.

### 5.4.5 The implications of organizational hybridity for employees' trust in ASL

Regarding the implications of hybridity for employees' trust in the organization, the following question was asked: Do you think these conflicting messages can influence your trust in this organization? The data showed that organizational hybridity had negative implications for employees' trust in ASL. AM11 summed it up this way: "Definitely…when you bring such conflicting things at a point in time it is glaring…the employees will begin to say that the company has lost it, there is a problem in the organization. So, my level of trust begins to drop, that means that there is a problem in the organization. These are the possible problems so it's for me to have a plan B." The data showed that the contradictions and tensions presented by organizational hybridity at ASL created conditions for trust to diminish, as employees are distressed and conflicted due to multiple expectations. In support of AM11's statement, AT1 added, "To be honest, these contradictions do not bring trust…they bring a lot of distrust, so these are the things the organization needs to correct."

The inability of employees to come to grips with the hybrid nature of the organization results in diminished trust. This is because employees do not trust what they do not understand, and attempting to interpret the multiple directions in which the organization expects them to perform gives rise to these tensions and contradictions in the first place. AM16 put it in a nutshell: "My trust in the organization has retrogressed instead of progressing because of these conflicting messages sent to the employees." However, some of the top management executives portrayed this point slightly differently. They argued that the behavioural responses highlighted above are the result of diminished trust in the first place, and if trust were fixed from the top, then the behavioural responses would be different. AT5, in particular, stated, "I think these behavioural responses are obviously a result of lack of trust in the first place, so I think if we take it the other way round…if, from the top, trust was going to be fixed, then I think the reactions will be different…I think people will react differently…it will also be foolish for management to recognise these responses and not do anything about it."

Overall, the data pointed to the possibility that employees experience identity distress due to conflicting messages and multiple expectations.

Furthermore, their trust diminishes due to the lack of identification, they become insubordinate and disengaged from work, and in the long run they leave the company. This is extensively discussed in Chapter 7. The next section explores the findings associated with understanding the influence of non-market-orientated logics at ASL.

## 5.5 Findings Associated with Understanding the Influence of Non-Market-Orientated Logics at ASL

**Proposition 4:** *The stronger employees' affiliations to religious logics, the greater the influence of such logics on employees' behaviour and trust in commercial hybrid organizations.*

The data showed that ASL operates within an institutional environment infused with market-orientated and non-market-orientated institutional logics prescribed by the dominant institutions in Nigerian society. These dominant institutions prescribe the values that form part of ASL's hybrid nature, just as they influence the employees' behaviour within the organization. Thus, with Nigeria being an intensely religious country that drives its economy using nurtured capitalism as discussed in Chapter 3, it was not surprising that all the interviewees' highlighted religion and the capitalist market as the two dominant institutions that prescribe values for ASL, as well as for the employees. Although the capitalist market prescribes logics that are classified as market orientated in this research, its influence on ASL cannot be overlooked owing to the operation of the organization within the financial sector of the Nigerian economy. These dominant institutions are discussed in turn next. Exploration of this objective formed part of a strategy aimed at answering the overall research question as well as the supporting research question: *What role does religion play in influencing employees' behaviour and shaping other organizational attributes of commercial hybrid organizations?*

### 5.5.1 The influence of the capitalist market at ASL

There was a general perception of the capitalist market as a major institution that influences the identity, goals and objectives of ASL. The organization operates within the financial sector of the Nigerian economy and its main operations in banking and financial services are oriented to one or another of a set of interrelated markets. This by itself suggests that the organization is strongly influenced by values prescribed by the capitalist market. For example, AT4 stated, "This is still a capitalist structure. Capitalism will always reign in this organization." The data pointed to a general awareness that the capitalist market prescribes logics and values that emphasise the marketisation and commercialisation of resources, such as market and commercial logics (see Section 2.5 Contemporary Commercial Organizations as Carriers of Multiple Institutional Logics).

However, the pressure to achieve both internal and external financial targets contributes to the tensions experienced by employees working within ASL, especially since they are not involved in the decision-making process. For example, AM11 stated, "The Nigerian financial sector puts us in a difficult position where we have to meet both internal and external financial targets. But if you ask me, I would say that the problem is from the organization, trying to make money by all means and not considering how the employees feel about it or how they can even meet these targets." According to the interviewees, this non-involvement in decision-making encourages employees to seek alternative means of action, even to the extent of embracing unethical behaviours such as bribery, corrupt practices and dishonesty, to achieve multiple organizational goals and objectives. According to the interviewees, this occurs because corruption has become endemic in some sectors of Nigerian capitalism and is thus accepted as "the Nigerian culture".

Regarding the endemic nature of "corruption" in Nigeria, AM8 stated, "It's just like saying you are fighting corruption in Nigeria, or you are fighting corruption in the ministries, you cannot even do anything so you just go with the flow and hopefully pray that God phases those people out." Thus, employees working within ASL who are required to achieve multiple objectives, as well as meet both internal and external financial targets, are exposed to situations where they must adopt unethical behaviours, even when it is against their own personal or inherent values (AM10, AT7, AM8, AE20). As AT7, in particular, put the matter, "Getting government contracts involve a lot of kickbacks, I will say a lot of people have that personal thing not to give bribe or take bribe, but once you find yourself working in this environment you have to…so I go to the ministry, I try to bribe people, it goes against my personal values but I have to do it…it is more of a national problem than an organizational problem."

Furthermore, the data pointed to the perceptions that in the process of satisfying the external pressure, organizations try to "window dress" and "misrepresent" themselves unethically (AM8) and that in the process of misrepresenting themselves they send conflicting messages to their employees (AT6, AM16). For example, AM9 stated, "I used to write research reports at some point and a researcher to an extent is unbiased, straightforward, which is part of our values…you write a report which is your honest opinion and the MD says, sorry, this report can't fly because it's going to damage his relationship with my people and business partners, the only way it could go is when you change it a bit. So what will you do? You tell white lies to make the image look good."

Overall, there was a consensus that external pressure mediated by the capitalist market results in the "acceptance of unethical behaviour" by employees of ASL, contributing both to the tensions experienced by employees and the perceived "questionable integrity" of the organization. Thus, some of the interviewees suggested that there is a need to restructure the rules, regulations and practices governing the Nigerian institutional environment in a broad sense to mitigate the negative influence of the capitalist market and the logics it prescribes.

### 5.5.2 The influence of religion at ASL

The data were replete with allusions to religion as a further dominant institution that plays a role in influencing organizational and employees' behaviour, and many of the interviews included references to "God", "spiritual values" and "religious values". For example, regarding the challenges posed by the Nigerian institutional environment, AM8 stated, "In Nigeria, we are used to the phrase it is OK, it has already happened, God will sort it out for us." However, although a majority of the interviewees made the point that religion plays a dominant role in their personal lives, as it forms part of individual's identity in the Nigerian society as a whole, there was a strong indication that religion played no direct role in influencing the corporate objectives of ASL.

On the other hand, the data revealed that when faced with difficult situations within the organization, employees used religion as a coping mechanism because of its embedded influence in their lives. This would typically consist in referring the problem to God. For example, AM11 said, "I have had a situation where a retired lady gave me her savings, and there am I telling her we are working on paying her, which I obviously know it's a lie, we are having issues with the bank, but I am trying to protect ASL – that's against my personal values…I have a conscience, there is always something I say, there is a God above in all of what we do, there is a God above capitalism…they call it managing here…it is not managing; it is pure wickedness". Interviewees argued that such reference to God is an unavoidable coping strategy, a way of dealing with unethical behaviour in a country where unfettered capitalism reigns. The only way around it is to accept it as a way of life, since there is nothing anyone can do to stop corruption except to "pray to God" for divine intervention. Such thoughts are deeply rooted in the Nigerian society (AM8).

In addition to being used as a coping mechanism, the data showed that religion could also foster dysfunctional behavioural consequences, generating further tensions for employees, especially when the organization embeds values that are contrary to those of the employees' religious beliefs. AM8, in particular, put the matter this way: "If the payment of a client is being delayed, I say I am not lying anymore, I want to go to heaven, you are making us lie, and I do not have any lie anymore…but at the end of the day, I still lie to the client because there is nothing more I can do."

Overall, the data showed employees of ASL engaging in unethical behaviours to achieve organizational objectives, even though it was against their religious beliefs. However, when employees perceive that the prescribed values of the organization are contrary to their own religious beliefs, they use religion as a coping mechanism, referring the problem to God. Even though the capitalist market (that prescribes market-orientated logics, as discussed in Chapter 2) influences the behaviour of employees and objectives of ASL as an organization operating within the financial sector of the Nigerian economy, employees' behaviours are deeply influenced by the religion that forms part of the Nigerian identity, which thus directly or indirectly influences overall organizational performance. This makes religion a factor that cannot be ignored in addressing the tensions experienced by employees in commercial hybrid organizations.

### 5.5.3 The importance of identification at ASL

Identification emerged as another domain of tensions experienced by employees in relation to organizational hybridity. Some interviewees proposed that establishing a shared identity with ASL would reinforce a "sense of oneness". AT3, in particular, stated, "It is important that employees are reminded who we are occasionally because the employees are a set of people that will really drive the company, they are the people you entrust most of your daily activities." Among the interviewees, identifying with the organizational culture was seen as very important as it will determine how employees understand and respond to the multiple logics prescribed within the organization, especially when they prescribe contradictory values for behaviour and actions. This is because understanding the organization means that employees have come to terms with the hybrid organizational processes. AM12, in particular, stated, "Identification with the organizational culture kind of says I know who we are and what is expected of me as an employee…and this affects employees' behaviour." Shared identification helps employees make sense of the organization and what is expected from them. However, interviewees argued that as a result of the lack of cultural fit, employees are unable to understand properly, interpret and make sense of what is expected from them. In other terms, when employees are not able to identify with multiple logics prescribed to them within the organization, they begin to experience identity distress, which shows in their attitude to work and the way they behave (AT4, AM10, AT1, AT2, AT5, AM15, AE20).

Overall, a majority of the interviewees suggested a cultural reorientation of the organizational values and norms of ASL so as to create a unique cultural fit. According to AM10, this reorientation should go "from the corporate strategy section down to a management strategy section, down to an entire organization strategy section where the new message, the new intent, the new drive, is passed on to the entire organization". The next section presents the data associated with developing research-based recommendations for improving employees' trust in ASL.

## 5.6 Findings Relevant to Developing Research-Based Recommendations for Sustaining Employees' Trust in ASL

**Proposition 3:** *The greater the employees' trust in commercial hybrid organizations, the more effective the organizational performance.*

Regarding the importance of employees' trust for organizational hybridity, the following question was asked: Do you think employees' trust can influence the performance of hybrid organizations? The data pointed to the perception that building employees' trust could minimise the above negative behavioural responses, and thus increase the overall organizational effectiveness and efficiency of ASL. Indeed, AM13 stated, "If trust is managed well, the employees are not going to see the organizational goals as conflicting." Thus, a majority of the interviewees suggested that building employees' trust would improve the organizational identification, effectiveness and performance. Exploration of this objective formed part of a strategy aimed at answering the overall research question as well as the supporting research question: *How can employees' trust in commercial hybrid organizations be sustained for improved effective organizational performance?*

### 5.6.1 Improved organizational identification

The data showed that gaining employees' trust would enable a clearer understanding and identification by them of the prescribed logics, and thus neutralise conflicts and inconsistencies. In other words, developing strategies that will enhance employees' trust in the organization will not only enable the clearer understanding of the logics prescribed within ASL but also facilitate employees' perceptions of themselves as one with the organization. AM10, in particular, stated, "Employees can make or mar you…I think that as much as we are paid to work, we are very important in the organization, you know, when you carry your employees along and make them understand what you are doing as an organization, it will increase their loyalty in all fairness." According to a majority of the interviewees, if the employees trust the organization, it shows in their productivity because they will put in more effort to achieve the assigned goals. For example, AE20 stated, "When a company can be trusted by its employees, it builds the employees' loyalty, job satisfaction and commitment to the set goals of the organization." However, if the employees feel that the organization is not keeping to its obligations, this brings disloyalty, lack of commitment and employees will no longer be willing to take risks for the organization.

### 5.6.2 Improved organizational effectiveness and performance

Furthermore, the data also showed that employees' trust in the organization enhances relationships within the organization, which in turn improves its overall performance and effectiveness. According to AE18, "Trust improves organizational effectiveness because it enhances my relationship with other employees…when the relationship is enhanced, it improves trust flow, which also improves organizational effectiveness. If you trust your employer, you will work very effectively with others because you feel like there is no backbiting, but even if there is, you are sure the organization will not be unjust when dealing with the issue because they have your back." Moreover, if employees trust the organization, they will be more likely to be comfortable and a lot happier when working with others, which should reflect in their performance (AM13, AE20, AE19, AE18). Once again, the need is underlined to develop strategies that could help to regain employees' trust in ASL so as to improve overall organizational performance. The next section presents the data from the analysis of company documents.

## Section B: Findings from the Document Analysis

To support the interviews, a range of documents were gathered for analysis. Documents were collected based on their availability on ASL's website and their relevance to the topic of inquiry, as discussed in Chapter 4. These documents included strategic reports, policy documents, governance and code of conduct reports, bulletins, annual general meeting reports, news reports and periodicals.

## 5.7 Profiles of Analysed Documents

Document analysis was used to evaluate, support and validate the argument made by the interviewees regarding the evidence of organizational hybridity in practice and the underlying institutional logics that prescribe values at ASL in Section A. Pertinent information was gathered by analysing the documents based on their relation to the topic of inquiry. Table 18 summarises the documents that were collected and used for this research.

**Table 18: Documents Collected and Used**

| Document title | Year of publication | Purpose of publication | Reason for use in this study |
|---|---|---|---|
| Strategic reports | 2014 | To provide shareholders and clients with the opportunity to assess the performance of the directors. | To analyse the organizational culture, corporate goals and objectives, underlying institutional logics, and the strategic intent for achieving the objectives of ASL. |
| Policy documents and capability brochure | 2014 | To inform shareholders on policies that drive governance and decision-making, and the implementation of decisions made. | To analyse the core values, governance and leadership structure of the organization. |
| Governance and code of conduct report | 2014 | To inform shareholders and employees of the values, norms, rules and regulations governing behaviour and actions. | To analyse the organizational culture, leadership structure, power balance and implementation of organizational policies. |
| Annual general meeting reports | 2012–2014 | To inform shareholders of annual financial performance. | To analyse the organizational performance and core strategic intent that drives the organization. |
| Bulletin, news reports and periodicals | 2010–2015 | For stakeholder engagement and investor relations. | To analyse communication principles and employees' awareness of organizational processes. |

## 5.8 Findings Associated with Exploring the Influence of Organizational Hybridity on Specific Organizational Attributes of ASL

**Proposition 1:** *The more extensive the tensions associated with organizational hybridity, the greater the likelihood of negative behavioural responses by employees.*

The overall data provided support to the hybridity of ASL as a commercial hybrid organization that embodies both commercial and professional agendas for effective performance and to maintain legitimacy in the ever-changing Nigerian institutional environment. The hybrid nature of the organization is clearly stated as its strategic intent. For example, according to the organization's strategic report, "the product + professional expertise = greater value to customers". This is consistent with the data from interviews above. However, to further understand organizational hybridity in practice, the corporate goals, leadership structure, organizational culture and governance were explored. This exploration formed part of a strategy aimed at answering the overall research question as well as the supporting research question: *To what extent does organizational hybridity influence specific attributes of commercial hybrid organizations?*

### 5.8.1 Organizational hybridity in relation to goals and objectives of ASL

The data showed that the core business goal of ASL is to expand the organization through the commercialisation of new products and services to match changing times, and to complement the evolving business and investment requirements of customers. According to the company's website, "the primary goal of ASL is to champion wealth creation that makes a positive impact on society". Also, ASL's goal includes a commitment to customers, and adequately and accurately keeping all stakeholders informed. For example, "we are committed to providing unrivalled service to our clients" (taken from company's website). Furthermore, the data confirmed that even though ASL incorporates multiple objectives in its operations to achieve the core organizational goals, the financial goal appears to be the dominant one that influences most of the services the organization provides to customers, such as inventory advice, equity trading, financial product distribution and high-frequency trading. This is the result of its business orientation as a financial organization operating commercially in a number of markets and facing resource prices that are more or less set by competition. Nevertheless, professional goals are incorporated within the organization to achieve its long-term financial objectives. For example, according to the organization's capability brochure, "we place much emphasis on the professional development of all our people". This is consistent with the interview data.

***Influence of institutional logics in ASL's goals***

The data pointed to ASL's embodiment of professional and commercial logics to fulfil its corporate goals and objectives within the Nigerian institutional environment in which it operates. However, ASL's goal is not only to make a profit but also to deliver added value to stakeholders through professionalism, as suggested above. This is portrayed in the corporate strategic report, which states, "At ASL, we have consistently maintained a strong position in an increasingly competitive market, and have built a solid reputation as a highly professional Investment Banking and Brokerage Institution. We equally pride ourselves as having some of the best hands in equity research in the Nigerian Capital Market. Considering that capital actually drives the economy, creates jobs, facilitates growth and enables innovation, ASL's focus on excellence has helped in the growth and stability of the Nigerian economy."

Furthermore, the data showed that ASL aims to "inculcate professionalism", which forms a "critical part of its culture as a behavioural practice for all employees". ASL prides itself in actively seeking the best opportunities to bring people and knowledge together to deliver value greater than the sum of its parts. This finding is in agreement with the data from the interviews about the emphasis on both commercial and professional logics within the organization, as discussed in Section A.

## 5.8.2 Organizational hybridity in relation to governance of ASL

Regarding the governance of ASL, the data showed that the organization adopts a separation-of-ownership-and-control governance structure, where the CEO is separate from the chairman. In fact, the organization operates a three-tier governance structure and is committed to adhering to the highest level of corporate governance codes – a commitment that is reflected in its statement of core and professional values. According to the governance and code of conduct reports, "ASL is committed to exercising the highest level of corporate governance in adherence to the provisions of the code of corporate governance in Nigeria as provided by the Securities and Exchange Commission (SEC) and global practice. Clear strategic goals, corporate values, transparency and accountability are key elements of our corporate governance policy. Pursuant to our corporate governance objectives, members of our board of directors are chosen for wealth of experience and unique perspectives they would bring to the board." The first part of this statement suggests that the organization has clear goals, corporate values, transparency and accountability, which goes contrary to what the interviewees have argued in Section A. However, the latter part of the statement regarding the organization's competence is very consistent with the interviewees' arguments in Section A. Furthermore, the documentary data showed that the ultimate responsibility of governance and strategic decision-making power lies mostly with the board of directors, which includes the CEO. This provides support for the findings from the interviews.

### 5.8.3 Organizational hybridity in relation to leadership style/structure of ASL

The data showed that ASL operates a bureaucratic leadership structure, where the highest level of leadership rests with the board of directors. The leadership structure comprises the board of directors, the senior executive management team and the management team. The board of directors is the highest on the power ladder, and is charged with the responsibility for monitoring and controlling the senior management team and the management team members. The board is headed by a chairman while the executive management team is led by the CEO. The executive management team reports to the board, and is charged with the responsibility for implementing policies, procedures and strategies, and making all strategic decisions in the organization. The management team, on the other hand, is in charge of the day-to-day operations of the organization. This structure is consistent with the interviewees' statements in Section A. However, data showed that the structure of the organization was changed as a response to the 2008 recession, which led to the reassignment of certain powers from the board to the senior executive management team. This was not displayed on the organization's website but was highlighted by the interviewees. Nevertheless, the overall data indicate a consistent line of argument.

### 5.8.4 Organizational hybridity in relation to organizational culture of ASL

The data showed that the organizational culture of ASL revolves around three themes: "growth", "financial strength" and "customer service" (taken from strategic reports, capability brochure and policy document). Growing the organization to meet the ever-changing and unstable financial market is important to the organization as a business; growth is achieved by embracing new approaches, directions and opportunities for wealth creation. The data showed that the culture of the organization is mostly tailored around maintaining a strong financial presence on the NSE and in the challenging financial services market by delivering value to customers through professional services. This indicates that the organization is faced with multiple pressures to grow, to perform and to meet both internal and external financial targets, which they expect the employees to achieve. This was highlighted in the data from the interviews. Therefore, it is not unlikely that the organization would be faced with challenges of securing a unique cultural fit that represents its hybrid nature, which employees could identify with. Overall, empirical findings indicate a situation consistent with the documentary data reviewed.

### 5.8.5 Organizational hybridity in relation to tensions at ASL

The document analysis showed that tensions at ASL are triggered by an emphasis on multiple logics incorporated within the organization. For example, in terms of how the organization views itself as a financial services organization, the organization showed an emphasis on "innovation". ASL uses innovative, creative and dynamic ways to improve the services offered to clients in accordance with the corporate governance code of conduct for the financial sector, as is clearly stated on the company's website. This may require employees to achieve financial targets by offering professional services in creative ways. In other words, employees are mandated to pursue multiple objectives without being given clear guidelines on how to achieve them, as they are expected to be creative. This could easily be conjectured to underly the "growing sense of tension" revealed in the interview findings.

However, the data also indicated that the organization is aware of these challenges. For example, according to the company's website, "Challenge enables us to be better. We embrace the unknown with the understanding that mastering new spaces makes our services more valuable to you, and we are working towards the future focused and determined, we continue to develop our services to match the changing times." Even though this seems to be the case, exactly how these challenges will be addressed was not revealed. In particular, there was no hint of a general approach to ensuring that intellectual novelties – new financial products, say – do not generate situations where logics conflict and operating staff are put in a bind.

### 5.8.6 Organizational hybridity in relation to employees' behavioural response at ASL

The overall data showed no indication of employees' behavioural responses to organizational hybridity. However, there were indications regarding the organization's multiple behavioural expectations for employees, like "professional development", which forms a critical part of the organization's culture. This indicates that employees could be constantly under pressure to perform, which could trigger some type of behavioural response. This is consistent with the interview data.

## 5.9 Findings Associated with Understanding the Implications of Organizational Hybridity for Employees' Trust in ASL

**Proposition 2:** *The greater the tensions produced by multiple logics, the less likely it becomes that employees of commercial hybrid organizations will trust their employers.*

While the goals, objectives, culture and leadership structure of the organization have been investigated, the data showed no evidence of the implications of organizational hybridity for employees' trust in the organization. The exploration of this objective formed part of a strategy aimed at answering the overall research question as well as the supporting research question: *How does organizational hybridity affect the level of employees' trust in commercial hybrid organizations?*

## 5.10 Findings Associated with Understanding the Influence of Non-Market-Orientated Logics at ASL

**Proposition 4:** *The stronger employees' affiliations to religious logics, the greater the influence of such logics on employees' behaviour and trust in commercial hybrid organizations.*

An extensive analysis of company documents showed no direct support for the influence of religion at ASL. However, the data pointed to religious ritualistic activities that were taken for granted, such as "opening prayers" during the annual general meeting, as the possible influence of religion on individuals' behaviours within ASL. The exploration of this objective formed part of a strategy aimed at answering the overall research question as well as the supporting research question: *What role does religion play in influencing employees' behaviour and shaping other organizational attributes of commercial hybrid organizations?*

## 5.11 Findings Relevant to Developing Research-Based Recommendations for Sustaining Employees' Trust in ASL

**Proposition 3:** *The greater the employees' trust in commercial hybrid organizations, the more effective the organizational performance.*

There was no indication of trust or strategies for improving employees' trust in the organization. Moreover, the interviewees argued that the organization has not shown them any reason to trust it. Nevertheless, taken all together, this suggests that employees' trust may need to be developed so as to improve the overall organizational efficiency and effectiveness of ASL. This is consistent with the argument in Section A. The exploration of this objective formed part of a strategy aimed at answering the overall research question as well as the supporting research question: *How can employees' trust in commercial hybrid organizations be sustained for improved effective organizational performance?*

## 5.12 Summary and Conclusions

The overall empirical findings in this chapter have provided further insights into the experiences of the interviewees and their views on organizational hybridity in practice. Section A descriptively analysed the perception and views provided by the different interviewees as relevant to this study. Section B analysed the relevant documents, which provides support for the findings from Section A. The overall empirical findings, as well as the key themes that emerged from the data as illustrated in Table 19, are discussed extensively in Chapter 7.

The findings in this chapter are summarised as follows. Firstly, ASL operates as a dominant commercial hybrid organization by incorporating commercial logic as the dominant logic, with professional logic acting peripherally. The market-orientated commercial business model of ASL enables the dominant influence of the capitalist market. Even though this seems to be the case, other non-market-orientated institutions such as religion appear to play a role in influencing the behaviours and actions of the employees of ASL.

Secondly, ASL operates a highly bureaucratic leadership structure, where the decision-making power is centralised at the top of the organizational hierarchy and decisions are made without the participation of lower-level employees. The governance structure of ASL indicates a clear "separation of ownership and control". However, as a dominant commercial hybrid organization, the tensions experienced within ASL appear to be extensive, which contributes to the lack of identification with the values prescribed by the organization. This seems to be as a result of the leadership/governance structure of ASL, which encourages the isolation of employees, and thus leads to unclear communication and conflicting expectations.

Thirdly, organizational hybridity has fostered both positive and dysfunctional employee behaviours at ASL, which has allowed employees' trust to retrogress instead of progress. Finally, the data pointed to the need to regain employees' trust in the organization through their involvement, the establishment of clear communication channels and a cultural reorientation, so as to enable employees' identification with the values prescribed at ASL, which could help to foster employees' commitment.

In conclusion, the overall findings in this chapter point to recommendations on how to address the tensions posed by organizational hybridity. They also provide evidence that will contribute towards filling the identified gaps in current knowledge on establishing a relationship between organizational hybridity and organizational trust.

**Table 19: Summary of Emerging Themes**

| Research objectives | Research propositions | Emerging issues |
|---|---|---|
| *Objective 1* | *Proposition 1* | |
| To explore the influence of organizational hybridity on specific organizational attributes, including governance, organizational culture, leadership and intra-organizational relations of commercial hybrid organizations. | The more extensive the tensions associated with organizational hybridity, the greater the likelihood of negative behavioural responses by employees. | • Identity distress<br>• Employee disengagement<br>• Resigning from the organization<br>• Insubordinate behaviour<br>• Opportunistic behaviour |
| *Objective 2* | *Proposition 2* | • Value disjuncture<br>• Lack of identification<br>• Distrust |
| To shape an understanding of the implications of organizational hybridity for employees' trust in commercial hybrid organizations, with particular attention to those implications having a plausible relationship to organizational effectiveness. | The greater the tensions produced by multiple logics, the less likely it becomes that employees of commercial hybrid organizations will trust their employers. | |
| *Objective 3* | *Proposition 3* | • Communication gap<br>• Improved organizational effectiveness and performance<br>• Improved organizational identification |
| To develop research-based recommendations for sustaining employees' trust in the commercial hybrid organizations. | The greater the employees' trust in commercial hybrid organizations, the more effective the organizational performance. | |
| *Objective 4* | *Proposition 4* | • Honest behaviour<br>• Unethical behaviour |
| To understand the influence of non-market-orientated institutional logics on commercial hybrid organizations. | The stronger employees' affiliations to religious logics, the greater the influence of such logics on employees' behaviour and trust in commercial hybrid organizations. | |

# CHAPTER 6

# ORGANIZATIONAL HYBRIDITY IN PRACTICE: THE CASE STUDY OF BPL

## 6.1 Introduction

This chapter presents the data from the interviews and document analysis carried out at BPL in Nigeria (see Figure 16 above). The data are analysed but not extensively discussed within the framework of research objectives, questions and propositions. The overall empirical findings are discussed more extensively in Chapter 7. This chapter comprises two main sections: A and B. Section A presents the data from the interviews and contains four main parts. Firstly, it presents the profiles of the interviewees and describes the coding system used. The second part presents the interviewees' views on organizational hybridity in practice, and the multiple institutional logics underpinning the goals and objectives of BPL. Furthermore, this part presents the interviewees' perceptions and experiences in relation to the governance, organizational culture, leadership style/structure, and challenges presented by organizational hybridity at BPL. The third part presents the interviewees' views on the tensions associated with organizational hybridity and employees' behavioural responses to these tensions. The fourth part presents the interviewees' views on trust and the implications of organizational hybridity for employees' trust in BPL. Section B presents the data from the analysis of company documents. The chapter ends with a summary and concluding remarks.

## Section A: Findings from the Interviews

This section presents data from interviews involving 20 interviewees conducted at BPL. For the purpose of protecting the anonymity of the interviewees in this chapter and the subsequent chapter, they are referenced according to their assigned code as shown in Table 20. The top management executives are assigned codes BT1 to BT6, while the middle managers are assigned codes BM7 to BM16, and the employees are assigned codes BE17 to BE20.

**Table 20: Coding System for BPL**

| BPL | | | |
|---|---|---|---|
| **Level of the employment hierarchy** | Top management executives | Middle managers | Employees |
| **No. of interviewees** | 6 | 10 | 4 |
| **Assigned codes** | BT1–BT6 | BM7–BM16 | BE17–BE20 |
| **Total** | 20 | | |

## 6.2 Profiles of the Interviewees

Pertinent information about the interviewees was gathered by asking questions related to gender, age, native language and work experience, as discussed next.

### 6.2.1 Gender, age and native language of the interviewees

Interviewees were predominantly male, and exclusively aged between 36 and 55 years (see Table 13, which shows a summary of the interviewees' profiles including their age and gender). The language spoken within BPL is predominantly English, the official language of Nigeria, so interviews were conducted in English. However, the native languages spoken by the interviewees were mainly Igbo and Yoruba. These findings are consistent with the discussion in Chapter 3 on the dominant tribes and languages spoken in Nigeria.

### 6.2.2 Work experience in the organization

To obtain detailed information on the interviewees' work experience in the organization, the following information was solicited: previous job position, current job position and number of years in that position. The data show that the majority of the interviewees have up to 5 years' work experience (see

Table 14), and it is likely that those with relatively few years of work experience in the organization would have limited experience in interpreting, understanding and translating the vocabularies and narratives that somehow represent the hybridity of BPL. The data gathered through the interviews supports this finding. The next section presents the findings associated with exploring the influence of organizational hybridity on specific organizational attributes of BPL.

## 6.3 Findings Associated with Exploring the Influence of Organizational Hybridity on Specific Organizational Attributes of BPL

**Proposition 1:** *The more extensive the tensions associated with organizational hybridity, the greater the likelihood of negative behavioural responses by employees.*

The data on organizational hybridity in practice and the tensions it presents were based on the interviewees' perceptions of the organizational attributes of BPL, in terms of: their views, experiences and knowledge of the organizational goals and objectives of the organization; the influence of multiple institutional logics on these goals; and their experiences and knowledge of the organizational culture, governance and leadership style/structure. These are discussed in turn. Exploration of this objective formed part of a strategy aimed at answering the overall research question as well as the supporting research question: *To what extent does organizational hybridity influence specific attributes of commercial hybrid organizations?*

### 6.3.1 Interviewees' experiences and knowledge of the goals and objectives of BPL

The data were based on the interviewees' perceptions of the corporate goals and objectives of the organization, the process of setting goals and objectives, and the involvement of employees in setting these goals. The data showed a strong emphasis on family, commercial and philanthropic goals as the core strategic objectives of BPL. As a commercial organization, BPL's focus is not only on profit maximisation and commercialisation of petroleum resources through innovative processes but also in the creation of "superior value for stakeholders at large". As interviewee BT4 put the matter, "The core purpose of this organization is to create something new, create value for customers and also make profit in the process." The data also showed an inclination to promote family goals as equally paramount to the organizational functioning. A majority of the interviewees expressed the view that the factor making the organization successful was the chairman's determination to leave a legacy that will be able to stand the "test of time". BT1 put it this way: "This company is the chairman's legacy."

Furthermore, the data showed that the "superior stakeholder value" referred to is mostly represented by philanthropic support to the wider community. According to a majority of the interviewees, this includes providing healthcare services, scholarships and pipe-borne water to the communities where the organization operates. The interviewees argued that these core goals are evident in the organization's corporate values and vision statements. Overall, the data showed that even though BPL's goal is focused on marketisation and commercialisation of petroleum resources due to its business orientation, there was a strong perception of philanthropic and family goals and objectives as being equally core to the organizational functioning of BPL.

### *Influence of institutional logics in BPL's goals*

The influence of institutional logics on the organizational goals of BPL was explored. As expected, the data showed commercial logic that emphasises the commercialisation and marketisation of organizational resources, and family logic that emphasises traditional values passed from generation to generation within a family unit, as the dominant logics that are core to the organizational functioning of BPL. The influence of the community as an institutional order that emphasises social development for the community emerged in the form of philanthropic logic, which is embodied as a peripheral logic at BPL (see Section 2.5 Contemporary Commercial Organizations as Carriers of Multiple Institutional Logics). Furthermore, the data also pointed towards the presence of religious logics at BPL.

However, the general perception of the interviewees is that the dominant family logic may have enabled the peripheral philanthropic logic and religious logic, as a result of the embeddedness of religion in Nigeria. These orientations sometimes hid behind formulaic responses. For example, BT4 stated, "This organization is out to make profit by producing high-quality lubricants and adding value to stakeholders." However, perhaps because of an awareness of the family-owned business model of BPL, family logic was identified by the interviewees as being equally core within the organization. For example, BT3 stated, "This is a family business, we are one big family." However, there was an indication that family and commercial logics provided contradictory values for employees' behaviours since they emphasise different values. According to a majority of the top management executives, these logics often conflict leading to "misalignment" of the core organizational goals as a result of the contradictory values prescribed. Referring to such a situation, BT3 remarked, "It will take us time to realign these various goals to the central objectives." This provides support for the findings in Chapter 3 regarding the nature of BPL as a contested hybrid organization, which is further discussed in Chapter 7.

### 6.3.2 Interviewees' experiences and knowledge of the governance of BPL

The current governance structure of the organization was explored. The data were based on the interviewees' perceptions of the governance structure of the organization and of the locus and balance of power in that structure. The data showed that BPL operates a dual ownership and control governance structure, where the chairman is also the CEO. The data indicated that power is centralised solely with the chairman/CEO who is a member of the board of directors. It comes as no surprise, and data bore this out, that the influence of the chairman/CEO is very high, as he is the founder of the organization. Therefore, even though the governance structure comprises the board and management team, the chairman/CEO alone has the power to make final decisions. BT5 put it this way: "The power and decision-making ability lies with the chairman, he is in the centre and every other thing revolves around him, so he is the main man. Without him a lot of things will go bad."

The interviewees stated that the outlook of the organization is organic and unstructured, which has enabled easy communication and accessibility to leadership. Moreover, there was a strong consensus among a majority of the middle managers and employees that this structure fostered employees' trust in the organization, thanks to the easy accessibility to leadership. For example, BT6 stated: "This organization uses organic structure in its business, meaning that the hierarchy and roles are not prescribed as in bureaucratic organizations. So this ensures that the people on the lower level can communicate with the chief executive and in this sense, a level of trust is inherent in the people in the organization."

While this may be the case, data showed that the organization is also working towards having a global outlook and coloration, where the international best governance practices can be brought into the organization. According to BM10, "We are making concerted effort to move the organization away from being a one-man-dominated business into a conglomerate that embraces structures, divisions, a fusion of power – proper division and structuring that exemplifies a concept of corporate governance in its totality." On the other hand, it would be fair to say that there was a strong perception in the organization at the moment that its organic governance structure enhanced employees' trust and easy accessibility to leadership, which in turn promotes quicker decision-making and achievement of set goals. Thus, a majority of the middle managers and employees argued that they would like to see power remain with the chairman/CEO.

### 6.3.3 Interviewees' experiences and knowledge of the leadership style/structure of BPL

The current leadership structure of BPL was explored. The data here were based on the interviewees' perceptions relating to the balance of power, leadership and decision-making authority within the organization. This showed that BPL operates a less bureaucratic structure than ASL, since the chairman – who is also the CEO and a member of the board – sits at the apex of the employment hierarchy and structure, followed by the board of directors and executive management. The interviewees' reported that the board of directors has the traditional responsibilities of drawing up policies, making strategic decisions, supervising, monitoring and controlling the executive management team. The executive management team, on the other hand, comprises executive members who are in charge of the day-to-day operations of the organization; they implement the policies and report to the board. However, there was general agreement that these responsibilities are only on paper, as the chairman/CEO has the full responsibility for overseeing the entire organization, including hiring, firing and compensating employees. The leadership structure is thus a highly centralised one.

While this seems to be the case, there was a perception that the CEO operates an open-door system, which makes him accessible to all the employees as well as enabling his leadership style to have a servant leadership appearance (see Section 7.3.2 The influence of organizational hybridity on the leadership style/structure of commercial hybrid organizations). BT6, in particular, stated, "We have breakfast with the CEO every morning; he is open for discussions freely." Against this, some interviewees – especially the top management executives – took the view that the present leadership structure contributes to "growing concern" within the organization. According to the majority of the top management executives, the concentration of power with the chairman/CEO causes some of the tensions experienced within the organization, since "organizational processes" are often "contradicted" in an anxiety to get quick results and meet organizational obligations. BM7 gave an example of how this could happen: "Sometimes, when it is necessary, you can bypass all the people involved in a transaction process to the person you need, it happens sometimes because if you try to follow process, quick decisions will not be made so sometimes you have to bypass some processes to make sure that you get results."

Overall, the interviewees' opinions seem to differ regarding the leadership structure of BPL, with a majority of the top management executive seeing it as a source of tensions and contradictions, while the majority of middle managers and employees appeared to experience minimal tension with the structure.

### 6.3.4 Interviewees' experiences and knowledge of the organizational culture of BPL

The data were based on the interviewees' perceptions of the values prescribed within the organization and what it stands for. Some interviewees defined organizational culture as the history and legacy of the organization, which gives the organization and employees a shared sense of purpose (BT2, BT6, BE18, BM10). The data showed that the organizational culture of BPL revolves around three core themes: "legacy", "performance" and "trust". According to the interviewees, these basic themes are reflected in the mission statement of the organization. Interviewees took the core themes seriously, observing that they were based on the organization's "genuine interest to build trust" and "add value to stakeholders based on mutual benefit" (BE20, BE18). They felt that the organization reflected an open and inclusive culture that generated a sense of trust and belonging among the employees.

However, a few of the top management executives took a different view. According to these interviewees, there is still a communication gap in the management processes that needs to be addressed, arising out of the coexistence of multiple logics such as the commercial, philanthropic and family logics that prescribe contradictory values for behaviour, and thus create tension within the organization. While the organization – with its proud traditions and interest in local people – mediates multiple values to its employees, the need to achieve other organizational goals can communicate different messages. However, even though there were tensions and disagreements surrounding the leadership and communication channels at BPL, there was no perception of a struggle to maintain a cultural fit that embodied the hybrid nature of the organization.

Overall, there were indications of the existence of a unique organizational culture that captures the hybridity of BPL. The challenges and tensions that were perceived to exist are explored next.

### 6.3.5 Interviewees' experiences and knowledge of tensions at BPL

The interviewees' views on tensions and contradictions associated with organizational hybridity were explored by questions regarding: times when they perceived that the organization was sending conflicting messages about expectations through set objectives; their responses to conflicting messages; and occasions when they had to choose between their own personal values and what they were told to do in the organization. The interviewees were also asked to highlight some of the challenges that create tensions within the organization in relation to organizational hybridity in practice, as well as being asked to make suggestions on how to mitigate these challenges. One main challenge emerged from the data, which is broadly along the following lines:

- *Lack of a clear communication system.* Some of the interviewees argued that due to the contradictory values prescribed by the embodied logics, employees at BPL are subjected to expectations that are unclear. According to these interviewees, communication channels may be compromised by the lack of separation of ownership and control, which allows the chairman/CEO to use his power to bypass standard organizational processes. Situations like this often arise where employees are left "distressed" and "confused" due to "multiple unclear expectations" stemming from their immediate supervisors, on the one hand, and the chairman/CEO, on the other. According to the interviewees, the current structure has generated "communication gaps" in the management processes of BPL. BM9, in particular, stated, "We have conflict of duties in the sense that we do not know who is responsible for the particular thing. In fact, the organizational structure is not properly defined because we have the chairman sending people to do different things at different times." Some interviewees suggested that when there is a "weak structure and control system, good people could become bad" (BT3). There is a perception that there could be behavioural consequences displayed by employees who are faced with this challenge. Thus, the data indicated that there is a need to restructure the leadership model of BPL to reduce contradictions and thus increase effectiveness, as employees will have a definite idea of what is expected from them. At the same time, clear and open communication across all levels of the employment hierarchy, using properly structured channels that are respected by those in authority, will enable the employees to understand new challenges faced by the organization (BT3, BM9).

### 6.3.5a Organizational hybridity in relation to conflicting messages: commercial logic versus family logic

The data showed that minimal tension is experienced within BPL. Despite this, however, a few interviewees – especially the top management executives – seemed to suggest that the present leadership structure of BPL lay at the root of tensions experienced within it (BT2, BM9). According to these interviewees, the centralisation of power with the chairman/CEO caused many cases of communications being ignored or misunderstood, and proper processes being neglected or failing to show a result, since he has the power to make decisions independent of the board and executive management team. For example, BT6, in particular, stated, "You see the CEO is an astute businessman and a purpose-driven man, he has the power to do anything here…sometimes he bypasses the team leaders who already have their interpretation of how to achieve financial and philanthropic targets with their team and communicates directly with the team members regarding how to achieve the same targets using his own ways. So, before expectations are communicated depending on what the other party knows, there is already conflict in the information flow, and it becomes conflicting for the employees."

There were indications that, beyond the lack of clear separation of leadership and control, the chairman/CEO's decisions concerning the organization could be influenced by other values that may or may not be prescribed within the organization, which is a situation that generates further conflicts. For example, "achieving the targets using his own ways" could suggest that he draws upon values not accommodated within standard organizational processes, which is a behaviour likely to "enable unclear interpretation of expectations from employees" (BT4). According to BT2, "There were times when challenges surfaced concerning whom we should channel certain information to and take instructions from; the roles were not clearly defined. We had HR giving us some instructions and then the chairman introduced a department called OSS giving out certain instructions, which caused a lot of confusion."

However, contrary to the perceptions of the top management executives, the majority of the middle managers and employees argued that tensions of this sort are part of the challenges faced by contemporary commercial organizations as they struggle for legitimacy. According to BM13, "There is no organization that does not experience conflicting messages; the most important thing is learning how to manage the conflicts as they occur." The data pointed to the perception that "the management-by-conflict approach" is often purposely applied by the chairman/CEO to achieve quicker results.

However, it is important to know how to manage the tensions, which may not be foreseen, arising from these interventions. BM9 gave a telling example: "You know there is something called management by conflict, sending one person against the other by sending conflicting messages to get the truth out of a situation. An example is that sometimes the chairman can designate a duty to you through your boss and then come directly to you to find out the results, knowing full well that you have not communicated with your boss, and then when he gets the information, he calls your boss to find out what's happening and then your boss calls you, so it becomes conflicting because the organizational process has been distorted." Even though this approach could be advantageous as it leads to quicker decision-making and turnaround time, the data showed that it could generate confusion and damage employees' morale.

Furthermore, within the overarching theme of the tensions experienced at BPL, three domains emerged from the data. The first is the domain of *external influencers*, which highlights the dominant institutional logics that play a role in prescribing values and influencing internal contradictions and tensions within BPL. Regarding this domain, the interviewees' responses were such as to lend plausibility to the view that the dominant institutions competing for legitimacy within Nigerian society should be taken into account when addressing the challenges presented by organizational hybridity in commercial organizations operating there. The second domain is of *identification*, which highlights the process regarding how the employees at BPL make sense of the multiple institutional logics operating there. The third domain is of *behavioural responses*, which highlights interpretations and behavioural manifestations that can be seen to issue from the operations of the multiple institutional logics embedded within BPL. These domains are discussed next.

### 6.3.5b Organizational hybridity in relation to identity distress

Identity distress emerged from the data as the result of the inability to comprehend or identify with the prescribed logics within the organization. Some of the interviewees revealed that they are often conflicted, when faced with the multiple requirements of institutional logics embedded in the organization. For example, BM7 stated, “There were times when we were having challenges concerning what goals to pursue as the expectations were not clearly defined…It was confusing, really.” These interviewees argued that the experience resulted in multiple problems for the organization, as employees struggled to interpret organizational processes and understand what is expected of them. Others took the view that however contradictory the values prescribed by multiple logics embedded in the organization, minimal tensions are generated within it due to its leadership structure. According to these interviewees, having the chairman/CEO as the highest level of authority enables an uncontested single line of authority, which does not give room for multiple opinions. Overall, there seems to be a preponderant view that regards organizational hybridity as encouraging various behavioural responses. The behavioural responses are discussed next.

## 6.3.6 Behavioural responses to organizational hybridity

Various behavioural responses to organizational hybridity emerged from the data. Interviewees were keen to point out that these behavioural responses are very common within BPL, as employees are likely to react positively or negatively to things they do not understand or comprehend. The data pointed to three overarching themes highlighted by the interviewees as characterising employees’ responses to organizational hybridity, namely:

- Display of “insubordinate” behaviour
- Employee disengagement
- Display of synergic behaviour.

### 6.3.6a Display of “Insubordinate” behaviour as employees’ response to organizational hybridity

According to the interviewees, “insubordinate” behaviour involves the outright or subtle rejection of prescribed logics, rules or values by employees. This often manifests in employees’ behaviour as the disregard for rules. The data unveiled the display of insubordinate behaviour as quite a common behavioural manifestation, especially when employees are not happy. Particularly revealing here were comments by interviewees reviewing their tendencies towards insubordination. As one middle manager (BM16) put it: "I am stubborn. Whenever I am asked to do something, I challenge the instruction, then the issue of insubordination comes up." BM15 added, "If you want me to do something, and you cannot communicate to me the clear terms of what you want me to do or the desired results you want to achieve…how do you expect me to do what you want? Automatically, I will not want to take instructions from you."

However, interviewees maintained that problems of insubordination tend to be quickly resolved since the organization operates an open-door policy. This means that "unhappy employees" have the chance to express their disappointments to management (BM11). Interviewees suggested that clearly communicating and defining intended outcomes of management directives and commands could help to mitigate insubordination within the organization (BT5, BT6, BM9).

#### 6.3.6b Employee disengagement as employees' response to organizational hybridity

There seemed to be a consensus in the perception of employee disengagement as a common behavioural response. In fact, the data suggested it to be the most common behavioural response within BPL to issues plausibly related to organizational hybridity. According to the interviewees, this entails observable displays such as not paying attention to work, expressing nonchalant attitudes and being negligent towards assigned duties. One middle manager (BM10) described the syndrome: "When messages conflict, it shows in the attitude to work – the employees become lackadaisical, that drive for excellence to do the needful will not be there, all types of funny excuses will begin to crop up. It does affect the attitude to work, it is common in human nature." Interviewees suggested multiple examples of attitudes triggered by employee disengagement: making excuses, avoiding work, being late to work, lying, stealing and being disgruntled (BM17, BM11, BE20).

Overall, there was a perception that disengagement signalled that employees are demotivated within the organization. Thus, several interviewees suggested that creating an effective system for motivation could help boost employees' attitude towards work (BM8, BM7, BM17, BT2).

### 6.3.6c Display of synergic behaviour as employees' response to organizational hybridity

Contrary to the above behavioural responses, synergic behaviour emerged as a peculiar type of response. This response was identified and emphasised by some of the middle managers, who explained it as a situation where employees reach a point of awareness of organizational expectations, which they are then able to interpret in a way that makes sense to them (BT2, BM15, BM9). Synergic behaviour is manifested when employees can understand and interpret information, rules and values in their own way, but also in the interest of achieving core organizational goals. Interviewees emphasised that synergic behaviour entails being aware of the available corporate rules, values and norms prescribed within the organization, since it is only through this awareness that employees can interpret and make sense of expectations, using their own discretion when problems arise. A senior executive (BT2) put it this way: "When faced with a difficult challenge, I use my discretion, absolutely, because the desire is to achieve results and that is where the issue of personal sacrifice has to come in."

There were some dissenting voices: some interviewees took the view that employees can take advantage of their situation, and especially when they are very aware of the applicable rules, values and expectations. In other words, employees who are very knowledgeable about rules and values can, by the same token, find loopholes to take advantage of it. As one middle manager (BM9) put it: "Sometimes you just have to do what you have to do to be successful in Nigeria, it's a common practice…you have to be smart or else they will outsmart you." But this view was a minority one, with most of the interviewees arguing for the positive side of synergism, which proposes that employees follow the rules for the common good of the organization. The perception is that employees may take this positive approach because, since they trust BPL and believe the organization has their interests at heart, they are more concerned with achieving the collective organizational goals. In so far as this happens, employees faced with conflicting messages and competing values can separate their own personal values and goals from work so as to achieve the organizational objectives (BM17, BT4, BT3, BM16). The data gathered through the interviews supports this finding. The next section presents the data associated with exploring the implications of organizational hybridity for employees' trust in BPL.

## 6.4 Findings Associated with Understanding the Implications of Organizational Hybridity for Employees' Trust in BPL

**Proposition 2:** *The greater the tensions produced by multiple logics, the less likely it becomes that employees of commercial hybrid organizations will trust their employers.*

The interviewees' views on trust were explored by asking questions on their perceptions of it in general and how well they trust the organization in particular. Regarding interviewees' perceptions of trust, in common with Mayer et al. (1995), the interviewee's definition of trust fell under three themes: "competence", "integrity" and "benevolence". These themes, therefore, are presented as the important dimensions of trust for employees at BPL. Exploration of this objective formed part of a strategy aimed at answering the overall research question as well as the supporting research question: *How does organizational hybridity affect the level of employees' trust in commercial hybrid organizations?*

### 6.4.1 Integrity as a dimension of trust

Integrity emerged as an important dimension of trust at BPL. A majority of the interviewees agreed that an organization is perceived as trustworthy when it is "open" and "fulfils promises made" (BE19). BM7, in particular, stated, "For an organization to be trustworthy, you look out for the vision and the mission statement as well as the ability to be open, to be honest in their operations and to have core values that can deliver on promises and objectivity in the operation." More so, trust is about "making sure you keep to all your promises, your integrity and your reputation" (BE19). Interviewees agreed that trust is about openness and transparency; honesty and respect for integrity were repeatedly identified as characteristics that engender trust in any organization, and these characteristics in particular were fundamental to employees' confidence in BPL (BM11, BM12, BT1, BT3, BM17, BE20).

Overall there was a perception that when an organization has an open and honest communication system – bearing in mind that people do not trust what they do not understand – employees are more committed and more willing to take risks for the organization. When an organization has integrity, employees can air their views and communicate freely with management, which makes them more effective (BT3). Thus, there is a need to promote honest and open communication, the free flow of information, and transparency within the organization as these things encourage employees' trust (BE20, BM14, BM8, BM7, BT4, BE18, BT3, BE16).

### 6.4.2 Competence as a dimension of trust

Competence emerged as another important dimension of trust at BPL. Regarding competence, interviewees proposed that an organization should be able to meet its obligations, and achieve its goals and objectives, to be considered trustworthy (BT2). BE20, in particular, stated, "The organization has to be able to deliver unparalleled services in the sense that they have to live up to their stakeholder expectations and capability." In this view, the conditions of trustworthiness included just-in-time delivery and quality products delivery. Other interviewees argued that for an organization to be considered trustworthy, it has to deliver value to both internal and external customers, to be capable of meeting obligations to its customers and be ready to accept responsibility for any failure to meet those obligations (BT1, BM13, BM16). In the words of one middle manager (BM8), "When it comes to service delivery, if the organization says they are giving you a particular product, it should be what they said and nothing else." Regarding trust in BPL, there appeared to be a consensus that competence was fundamental. This was exemplified by the ability of the organization to continue to deliver high-quality products, services and value to both external and internal stakeholders (BM12, BT4, BT3, BT5, BM13).

### 6.4.3 Benevolence as a dimension of trust

The final dimension of trust that emerged from the data is benevolence. There was a consensus that an organization that shows goodwill towards employees, and a degree of care and interest in their welfare, can be perceived as trustworthy. For example, B15 stated, "An organization can be trustworthy when they are fair to employees, their welfare staff packages have impact on the staff when they consider the years of work, when they consider input and appreciation." Interviewees proposed that active benevolence reflects that the organization cares about its employees, who try to reciprocate by being more committed and productive at work (BM11, BM14, BM16, BT3, BE19). BM10, in particular, stated, "Showing love and goodwill to employees are contagious – when you show love, the employees will reciprocate and show love back to you, that is how it works, the laws of nature." The reverse of this relationship was also important: interviewees took the view that where employees feel that the organization does not care about them, problems tend to follow as employees actively display their dissatisfaction through their behaviours.

### 6.4.4 Employees' trust in BPL

The interviewees' trust in the organization was explored. Regarding the question of "How well do you trust the organization?", the data showed that a majority of the interviewees trust the organization in all three dimensions highlighted above. A majority of the interviewees affirmed that they trust the organization in terms of all three dimensions, as the organization has given them every reason to trust it. Many spoke in glowing terms: "I trust the organization 100% because it's a wonderful system, I have been here for 13 years…this is a system that started with one man and is growing larger; I believe we are going higher" (BM8). Others were more circumspect but just as positive: "I don't think I would have stayed this long here if I don't trust the organization, I would have moved on to another, so I trust and so much believe in their aims and objectives so that's why I am here" (BT5).

The data showed that the employees trust the organization on the basis of a shared identity with the values it prescribes. However, the data also showed another angle to why employees trust the organization. According to interviewees, the chairman/CEO plays a unique role in influencing employees' trust in the organization. As one middle manager (BM9) put it, "I don't trust them collectively, I trust them individually…I believe they are all competent in their core areas. I have dealt with the chairman and he has high integrity, but I cannot generally say for sure that all of them have integrity."

In fact, the chairman/CEO appears to be the main reason why the majority of the interviewees indicated that they trust the organization. As one of the senior management team (BT5) put it, "It has a lot to do with the person that has the vision, the chairman. It has to do with his personal integrity, his charisma and his aura. I have been with this company for 10 years and I have had the privilege to work with the chief executive since I report to him as regards to operations, and his word is his bond – if he gives you his word he keeps to his word." Interviewees argued that trust starts with leadership and in this case the leader, who is the chairman and is trustworthy. BT1, in particular, stated, "I trust the board because the board has the chairman who has the power…I am personalising the chairman because he is a father figure and a trustworthy individual." Moreover, the CEO is a "near-perfect gentleman that we can trust" (BT2).

However, a few interviewees argued that even though the organization is trustworthy, there is still room for improvement. BM7 put it this way: "As per trust, I give the organization 80%, it is a trusted organization, but there is a need for improvement in some of the processes." There are signs of lapses in the effectiveness of organizational processes, which were highlighted by a majority of the top management employees. They alluded to a "communication gap" and a "leadership gap". These interviewees suggested that the organization needs to put proper structural mechanisms in place that will reduce contradictions and power misuse, and increase effectiveness (BT6). BT3 agreed that processes needed to be redesigned: "When you set up a system, it will be difficult for people to beat that system when there are proper processes and procedures in place…if the process is bulletproof, it will be difficult for powerful members to do otherwise."

In general, interviewees suggested that for the organization to continue to maintain the high level of employees' trust, it has to continue to employ competent employees irrespective of religion or culture (BT2). More so, there was a perception that continuous employee involvement in the decision-making process will enable the organization to reap the benefits of trust (BM17, BE19, BE18, BT3, BM13). And most importantly, there was the view that BPL should adopt the leadership/organizational structure of organizations that are doing better than it is in the sector in which it operates, establishing a proper governance structure that encourages open, clear and honest communication so that employees understand the challenges that management is facing at any time (BT2, BM12).

### 6.4.5 The implications of organizational hybridity for employees' trust in BPL

Regarding the implications of hybridity for employees' trust in the organization, the following question was asked: Do you think these conflicting messages can influence your trust in this organization? The data suggested that organizational hybridity had a negative effect on employees' trust in BPL. One middle manager (BM7) agreed: "I think so, it will definitely influence trust because if messages are conflicting, we are no longer working towards achieving the same objective…so it distorts trust." More so, interviewees argued that conflicting messages will lead to confusion among employees as to what is expected of them, and this is bound to cause them to trust the organization less; trust is, after all, a matter of reciprocal expectations and how does an employee know whether they are fulfilling their side of the bargain? (BM15, BE19, BE20). BM15 put it this way: "If messages are conflicting, trust will be marred…it cannot improve trust…because everything we do here has targets. It will never improve, rather it will diminish trust." The data pointed to the perception that the contradictions and tensions presented in BPL, though minimal, create room for trust to diminish, as employees sense the conflict of the multiple logics embedded within the organization. For some interviewees, this link between conflicting values and the deterioration of trust was a piece of management wisdom: "Conflicting values cannot improve the trust…it will never improve, rather it will affect the trust" (BM12).

Overall, even though the interviewees reported having high trust in BPL, there was a perception that employees' trust in the organization was liable to be damaged due to some of the implications of organizational hybridity. This was often put as a piece of folksy wisdom: employees do not trust what they do not understand, and, therefore, if tensions arise due to conflicting messages and employees are unable to identify with/understand the prescribed values, their trust in the organization is likely to diminish (BE18). The next section explores the influence of non-market-orientated logics at BPL.

## 6.5 Findings Associated with Understanding the Influence of Non-Market-Orientated Logics at BPL

**Proposition 4:** *The stronger employees' affiliations to religious logics, the greater the influence of such logics on employees' behaviour and trust in commercial hybrid organizations.*

The data showed that BPL operates within an institutional environment infused with market-orientated and non-market-orientated institutional logics prescribed by the dominant institutions in Nigerian society. These dominant institutions prescribe the values that form part of BPL's hybrid nature, just as they influence the employees' behaviour within the organization. Thus, since Nigeria is an intensely religious country shaped by multiple ethnic groups and it drives its economy using nurtured capitalism as discussed in Chapter 3, it was not surprising that all of the interviewees highlighted the capitalist market, religion and family as the three dominant institutions that prescribe values for BPL, as well as for the employees. The interviewees were clear in maintaining that these factors are beyond the organization's control and must, therefore, be brought into consideration as given realities when addressing organizational challenges. They are discussed in turn next. Exploration of this objective formed part of a strategy aimed at answering the overall research question as well as the supporting research question: *What role does religion play in influencing employees' behaviour and shaping other organizational attributes of commercial hybrid organizations?*

### 6.5.1 The influence of the capitalist market at BPL

There seems to be a consensus regarding the capitalist market as a major institution that influences the identity, goals and objectives of BPL. It is clear that the commercial logic that emphasises the marketisation and commercialisation of BPL's petroleum resources is a direct application of the logic of the capitalist market. BE17 put the point clearly: "The company is all about profit making, it is a capitalist society." However, findings revealed that external pressure to achieve financial objectives contributes to the challenges experienced by employees within the organization. For example, BE19 stated, "The environment we are operating in has a huge influence on our values and organizational culture. Working within an unstructured society where external pressures have the upper hand on your belief system is very challenging. We struggle to maintain our individual and company values but external forces most times overwhelm us." The data indicated that the organizational processes of BPL are continuously subject to change driven by external pressures from the politico-economic environment of Nigeria and that this accounts for many of the tensions experienced within the organization.

According to the interviewees, while trying to keep up with external pressure, the organization is prone in most circumstances to give up on its values, which includes giving into the "acceptance of unethical behaviour" (BE19, BE20, BT3, BT5, BM9). BM13, in particular, stated, "Moral values and ethical values are very important but at times other imperative political, social and economic factors influence those morals and ethical values, which could result in unethical behaviours." Reflecting a perception that capitalism, as the unrestricted pursuit of financial gain, is at the root of ethical misbehaviour, some of the interviewees argued that Nigerian society "is so corrupt that it has become a culture of the people so people see it as a lifestyle" (BM17). Moreover, the issue of corruption was perceived by the interviewees as one of the most problematic factors that hinders employees' trust in organizations (BT1). Thus, employees working within BPL, who are required to achieve multiple objectives as well as meet both internal and external targets, are likely to tolerate unethical behaviours even when this is against their own personal values (BM17, BE18, BE20, BT1). Again, BM17 stated: "I once had to give a bribe because management approved of it, meanwhile it's against my personal values. I also had to separate my values from work by following the rules of the company; it is a terrible situation but unavoidable."

Overall, there was a consensus regarding the influence of the capitalist market as a source of unethical behaviour in Nigerian society as well as within BPL. Thus, some of the interviewees suggested a need to restructure the Nigerian institutional environment to mitigate the negative influence of the capitalist market and the logics it prescribes.

### 6.5.2 The influence of family at BPL

The family emerged as another dominant institution that plays a role in influencing organizational and employees' behaviour. In fact, there was a consensus regarding the influence of family within the organization. "Family values" were frequently mentioned during the interviews, along with "community values" and "cultural values". The family is important in Nigeria, but so is community and ethnicity. As BM12 put it, "Our community values influence our daily operations…Nigeria is a bizarre environment; things that wouldn't happen in sane economies happen here." According to some interviewees, the influence of family values undergirds the perception that all employees are regarded as equally important within the organization, irrespective of their cultural backgrounds. These respondents saw the religious and philanthropic logics apparently supporting such a generous attitude towards diversity as underpinned by the dominant family logic since they form a part of the CEO's personal identity. The same would go for the logic of community development. "As a Christian, he is a visionary and emphatic leader, a philanthropist" (BM11). Others pointed to what appears to be economic rationality undergirding liberal views on cultural difference: "The organization needs to continue to employ competent hands, irrespective of the tribe" (BT2).

According to the majority of the interviewees, the family business model of BPL lies at the heart of the organization's philanthropic activities and support for the community (BE19, BT3, BM17). BM17 reflected on the cultural importance of patriarchy at the heart of the Nigerian family model, when he summed up the basis of the organization's community focus: "The chairman is an Igbo man. If you look well, you will see that we are trying to develop the livelihood of our people and in Igbo land it is a taboo to question the authority of an older man, so we just have to do what he says." According to other interviewees, the determining factor is that the chairman/CEO, who embodies the dual role of ownership and control, has the sole power to shape organizational activities. Overall, there seemed to be a perception that the chairman/CEO's family values are reflected in his leadership style, conditioning the adoption of a philanthropic logic by the organization.

### 6.5.3 The influence of religion at BPL

Religion emerged as a dominant institution that plays a role in influencing organizational and employees' behaviour in the Nigerian institutional environment. Several interviewees mentioned "God", "Christianity", "spiritual values" and "personal values", and a majority of the interviewees saw religion playing a role in influencing behaviour in the Nigerian society that BPL and its employees are part of. There was a widespread belief that the organizational goals and objectives of BPL were influenced by religious values since power is centralised with the chairman/CEO, who is a religious man. Interviewees maintained that his personal conviction influenced his religiously motivated behaviour and that this was widely recognised outside the organization: "Every government and organization want to deal with the chairman of BPL because he keeps to his agreements and does not cut corners, which is only made possible because he believes in God so much" (BT1). The data showed the perception that the chairman acts out his religious beliefs to such an extent that it reflects in his decision-making and leadership style, marked by many characteristics of the servant leader in a way that is seen as very positive: "The values prescribed to us are inherent in our chairman but God forbid he resigns today. I don't know what will happen here, a lot of people might not be interested in working here anymore" (BT6).

Furthermore, there was a perception among some interviewees that the influence of religion could manifest in two ways: positive but also negative. Regarding the positive influence of religion, BM8 stated, "For me at all times, I will have to tell the truth as a Christian and also coming from my own background truth is always the best." This suggests that employees who identify with the chairman/CEO's religious values are likely to show honest behaviours. However, this may not always be so. There was also a strong indication that religion is often used as a coping mechanism, especially when dealing with situations that are "beyond the employees' control" (BT1, BT2). For example, concerning giving bribes, BT2 stated, "There are areas where I had to do the needful to get results and those areas I go philosophical, God is the rewarder." According to the interviewees, this generates "identity distress" for employees, especially when employees are expected to perform tasks that are "contrary to their religious beliefs" (BT6).

Despite such problems, interviewees maintained that the values prescribed by religion are part of what makes their organization trustworthy. Moreover, here it can be said that, although religious logics are not evidently determinative of the organizational goals of BPL, there seems to be a strong perception of the operation of religious logics within the organization, especially in peripheral forms and in areas of particular concern to the leadership of the organization. Moreover, there seems to be another strong line of argument that would maintain the impossibility of separating religious values from personal or family values, since religion is deeply embedded in Nigerian society. This suggests again that the dominant family logic may have encouraged the embedding of peripheral philanthropic and religious logics in the organization. Overall, the data showed that the capitalist market, religion and the family are three dominant institutions that prescribe values for BPL and its employees.

### 6.5.4 The importance of identification at BPL

The data pointed to "identification" as another domain to consider while addressing the tensions experienced by employees in organizational hybridity. There was an indication that the sustained involvement of the employees encourages a shared identification with the prescribed logics and a "sense of belonging" within BPL (BM15). BM10, in particular, stated, "When you have a corporate dream, and you incorporate both the senior and the junior staff into the dream, mission and core values, collectively it becomes everybody's dream, everybody knows they have a role to play – there will be more commitment." Interviewees argued that identifying with the values prescribed within the organization is crucial as it helps employees to understand, make sense of and respond to these values accordingly. Sharing in the organization's dream, in this view, means that employees have come to perceive their values to be aligned with those of the organization.

Shared identity helps employees make sense of the organization and what is expected from them, and when employees identify with the organization, they are more committed and willing to take risks for it. As one of the middle managers (BM12) put it, "When an organization has shared values with employees, it increases organizational effectiveness because the employees trust the organization, and when you trust an organization, you become more committed to work.". However, when they are unable to identify with the requirements of multiple logics embedded in the organization, they begin to experience identity distress, with consequences for their attitude to work and the way they behave (BT1, BM11, BT5, BE20).

Overall, interviewees took the view that, for employees to be able to share in the organization's identity, continued efforts must be made to calibrate and, where necessary, reorient the organization's value system. The data gathered through the interviews support this finding. The next section presents the findings associated with developing research-based recommendations for sustaining employees' trust in BPL.

## 6.6 Findings Relevant to Developing Research-Based Recommendations for Sustaining Employees' Trust in BPL

**Proposition 3:** *The greater the employees' trust in commercial hybrid organizations, the more effective the organizational performance.*

Regarding the importance of employees' trust for organizational hybridity, the data indicated that building this could minimise conflicts associated with hybridity and the negative behavioural responses discussed above, as well as increasing the overall organizational effectiveness and efficiency of BPL. Indeed, "When employees understand what is expected from them through an undistorted, open and honest information channel, they feel a sense of belonging and in that way they become more productive. However, if they do not, it becomes a problem, as they will no longer trust the organization to keep the promises made to employees" (BM17). Thus, interviewees suggested that building employees' trust would improve the organizational identification, effectiveness and performance. These are discussed in turn next. Exploration of this objective formed part of a strategy aimed at answering the overall research question as well as the supporting research question: *How can employees' trust in commercial hybrid organizations be sustained for improved effective organizational performance?*

### 6.6.1 Improved organizational identification

The interviewees affirmed that gaining employees' trust will promote a clearer understanding of, and easier identification with, the prescribed logics within the organization. Trust may be based on the feeling that one is, to some extent, in control; this may underlie the idea that having a role in setting objectives makes employees "feel part of" (i.e. trust) an organization: "When employees contribute in setting objectives, they feel like they are part of the organization because they clearly understand what is expected of them and therefore respond positively knowing they set the objectives" (BM17). Interviewees took the view that to be able to understand the values of the organization, trust was not only beneficial but also essential. The benefits of employees' trust are thus seen to be substantial: while neutralising conflicts and inconsistencies through shared identification of values, trust will cause employees to be willing to take risks for the organization, which will increase overall organizational productivity in the long run (BM9, BM13, BM12). BM9, in particular, stated, "Trust really improves the activities of every company in the sense that if you trust a company, you will do everything possible as an employee to see there is less waste, you will do everything possible to see there is high productivity, you will do everything possible to even protect the company with your last drop of blood until you leave that place."

Overall, the data unveiled the perception that if the employees trust the organization, they will do everything possible to make sure it achieves its goals and objectives, even when the values prescribed run contrary to their own personal values. Therefore, trust should be sustained by adopting strategies that facilitate employees' identification with values prescribed within BPL.

### 6.6.2 Improved organizational effectiveness and performance

Furthermore, the data also showed that employees' trust in the organization is felt to enhance relationships within it, which in turn improves its overall performance and effectiveness. For example, BT3 stated, "When there is trust, people will be able to relate well with each other and share their knowledge, thus, making trust compatible with organizational effectiveness." The data revealed that an environment where there is trust is perceived to provide a conducive work environment for employees, enabling them to share valuable information and knowledge, which increases overall organizational performance. According to BT6, "Trust is coherent with organizational improvement. The fact that I feel like I trust my boss gives me the confidence to work in a productive way because I owe him that performance and I feel like I am part of something good, which I believe in so I will strive to be as outstanding as I can be."

In fact, the general perception of the interviewees is that "overall organizational productivity will be high where there is trust, labour turnover will reduce where there is trust" (BM12) and there will also be significant innovation where there is trust. More so, the perception that the organization has employees' best interests at heart will influence their level of commitment, which benefits the organization directly and also translates into employees' satisfaction with the job. This, in turn, promotes improved organizational effectiveness in the long run. This indicates that trust addresses the social aspect of governance; with trust, there is a better understanding of goals and objectives between management and employees. Even when the goals are conflicting, employees are confident that the organization has their best interests at heart. Thus, there is the need to develop strategies that will help to sustain employees' trust in the organization (BT3, BT6, BM9, BM10, BM15, BM16, BM11, BM17, BE18). The next section presents the data from the analysis of company documents.

## Section B: Findings from the Document Analysis

To support the interviews, a range of documents were gathered and analysed. Documents were collected based on their availability on BPL's website and their relevance to the topic of inquiry, as discussed in Chapter 4. These documents included strategic reports, policy documents, governance and code of conduct reports, bulletins, general meeting reports, news reports and periodicals.

## 6.7 Profiles of Analysed Documents

Document analysis was used to evaluate, support and validate the argument made by the interviewees regarding the evidence of organizational hybridity in practice and the underlying institutional logics that prescribe values at BPL in Section A. Pertinent information was gathered by analysing the documents based on their relation to the topic of inquiry. Table 21 illustrates a summary of the documents that were collected and used for this study.

**Table 21: Documents Collected and Used**

| Document title | Year of publication | Purpose of publication | Reason for use in this study |
|---|---|---|---|
| Strategic reports | 2014–2015 | To provide stakeholders the opportunity to assess the performance and strategic intent of the organization. | To analyse the organizational strategic intents, culture, corporate goals and objectives, underlying institutional logics, and the strategic intent for achieving the objectives of BPL. |
| Policy documents | 2013–2015 | To inform stakeholders of policies that drive governance and decision-making. | To analyse the goals, values, mission, culture and vision of the organization. |
| Governance and code of conduct report | 2009 | To inform stakeholders and employees of the values, norms, rules and regulations governing behaviour and actions. | To analyse the organizational leadership structure, power balance and implementation of organizational policies. |
| General meeting reports | 2014 | To inform stakeholders of the overall performance of the organization. | To analyse the overall performance of the organization. |
| Bulletin, news reports and periodicals | 2015 | For stakeholder engagement and philanthropic activities. | To analyse communication principles and employees' awareness of organizational processes. |

## 6.8 Findings Associated with Exploring the Influence of Organizational Hybridity on Specific Organizational Attributes of BPL

**Proposition 1***: The more extensive the tensions associated with organizational hybridity, the greater the likelihood of negative behavioural responses by employees.*

The overall data showed that, as a family business, BPL combines commercial and family goals to achieve its legacy and to maintain legitimacy in the ever-changing Nigerian institutional environment. The hybridity of the organization is clearly stated as the organization's strategic intent. For example, according to the organization's policy report: "As a private family initiative, BPL aims at consistently providing goods and profitable services that meet international standards by creating superior value for all stakeholders." This is consistent with the findings from interviews in Section 6.3. However, to further understand organizational hybridity in practice, the corporate goals, leadership structure, organizational culture and governance were explored. The exploration of this objective formed part of a strategy aimed at answering the overall research question as well as the supporting research question: *To what extent does organizational hybridity influence specific attributes of commercial hybrid organizations?*

### 6.8.1 Organizational hybridity in relation to goals and objectives of BPL

The data showed that the core corporate objective of BPL is not only to make profit through the commercialisation of innovative products and services but also to provide value to stakeholders. This also emerged in the data from the interviews. In fact, the organization's strategic goals are centred on three themes: "community development", "value creation" and "profit maximisation" (from the policy document). The organization provides basic amenities to improve the lives of some of its stakeholders, while producing quality services for customers and thus reaping financial benefits in return. This is summarised on the company's website: "The primary strategic goal of the organization is to offer exceptional combination of superior quality and value…achieved through well researched, innovative and efficient production methods." Thus, growing the family business through profit maximisation and value creation appear to be the core objectives that equally influence the organization's activities, which include both upstream and downstream oil and gas activities. The prominence of the family agenda is stated in the organization's value statement: "We are one big family" (taken from company's website). BPL's vision is to become a leader with a broad spectrum of brands in the lubricant industry, to satisfy all lubricant needs in the country, the West Africa sub-region and beyond. This finding is consistent with the interview data in Section A.

***Influence of institutional logics in BPL's goals***

The data showed that BPL combines family and commercial logics to achieve its corporate goals and objectives within the Nigerian institutional environment in which it operates, while philanthropic logic plays a peripheral role. Statements such as "we are one big family" and "as a family initiative" reveal the importance of the family legacy within the organization. This is clearly reflected in the organization's value and mission statements, as well as in the policy documents. Moreover, the organization's goal is not only to make profit through the commercialisation of its products but also to provide value to stakeholders through philanthropic activities; a combination that reflects both commercial and philanthropic logics.

Regarding philanthropic logic, the organization is engaged in various projects to provide value to its stakeholders. For example, "Since the inception of the organization, Barak Petroleum has embarked on community social services, such as road construction, pipe-borne water supply, basic healthcare, and scholarships" (taken from policy document). Regarding commercial logic, BPL consistently provides goods and profitable services (taken from policy document). This is in agreement with the data on interviewees' perceptions of the emphasis on commercial, family and philanthropic logics within the organization, as discussed in Section A.

## 6.8.2 Organizational hybridity in relation to governance of BPL

The data showed that BPL adopts a dual ownership and control governance structure, where the chairman is also the CEO. In fact, the organization operates a two-tier governance structure, which includes the board of directors and the executive management. The two groups are accountable for the overall effectiveness of the organization and the welfare of the wider group of employees. More specifically, the two groups are: the board of directors, which is headed by the chairman, and the executive management team, which has the responsibility for making strategic decisions for the organization as well as monitoring and controlling the employees. The data showed that the organization strives to operate effective corporate governance that ensures the alignment of the business goals and outcomes over time, which helps the organization to sustain its promised delivery of value to stakeholders. For example, BPL adopts a "very hands-on approach for efficiency in management as well as effective corporate governance" (taken from policy document). Moreover, governance mechanisms and guidance, which include the governance policies, corporate social responsibility policies and authority specifications, are designed and adopted by the organization to nurture intra-organizational trust and ensure effective alignment of the organizational culture.

However, even though there is a broad correspondence regarding the governance of BPL between the interview data and data from the document analysis, there are also large inconsistencies, arising out of the fact that the governance style that exists on paper does not reflect the reality in practice, since the final decision-making authority rests solely with the chairman who is also the CEO.

### 6.8.3 Organizational hybridity in relation to leadership style/structure of BPL

The data analysis showed that BPL operates an organic leadership structure, where the highest level of leadership authority rests with the board of directors. The two-tier leadership structure comprises the board of directors and the executive management team. The board of directors comprises the chairman/CEO, one managing director, five executive directors and seven directors. The board has the responsibility for drawing up policies, making strategic decisions and supervising the executive management team. The executive management team, on the other hand, comprises four executive members who report to the board and are also monitored by the board. The executive management team is in charge of the day-to-day operations of the organization. This is quite consistent with the interviewees' statements in Section A.

However, one contradiction to this finding is the argument that the highest level of leadership authority rests with the board of directors, instead of solely with the chairman/CEO as suggested by the interviewees. Nevertheless, the overall findings indicate a line of argument regarding the leadership structure of BPL that is consistent between the documentary sources and the interview data.

### 6.8.4 Organizational hybridity in relation to organizational culture of BPL

The organizational culture of BPL revolves around three themes that emerged from the data: “performance”, “team spirit” and “trust” (taken from policy document). The organization upholds a business policy of trust, integrity and reliability towards its internal and external stakeholders, which is achieved by producing high-quality lubricants and products that add value for customers. The culture of the organization is tailored around “team spirit” and “performance”, which emphasises a collective culture towards achieving a single goal of optimum organizational performance.

Furthermore, there was an indication that the organizational culture of “trust” and “team spirit” is deeply influenced by religious logic. For example, the data showed that “prayers” are said collectively every morning, as well as before and after each annual meeting held within the organization. This is consistent with the data from the interviews, as a majority of the interviewees perceived a personal commitment by the chairman/CEO to a religious logic, which, by virtue of his position and active involvement in the affairs of the organization, influences the organizational goals and processes. Even though religious values are not paraded among the core organizational goals of BPL, there are strong indications that, because of its deeply embedded status in Nigerian society, religious logic functions as a peripheral logic within the organization. Overall, the documentary data indicate a consistent line of argument with the interview data.

### 6.8.5 Organizational hybridity in relation to tensions at BPL

Consistent with data from interviews discussed previously, the data showed that even though BPL embodies multiple logics that prescribe contradictory values for action (e.g. commercial logic and philanthropic logic), minimum tension is experienced by employees as they can identify with the existing culture of trust, team spirit and philanthropy, which the organization exemplifies. For example, in terms of how it views itself, the organization revealed three themes – “integrity”, “trust” and “philanthropy” – as its image of identification, all of which are clearly stated on the company’s website. These are represented with statements such as “we deliver on our promises, our word is our bond” (taken from company’s website).

However, the data indicated that a downplay of financial values might not mean that profit maximisation is not paramount to the organization. Such a de-emphasis on the financial aspect depends on broadly political factors in the organization and how it chooses to portray itself. There are indications that, as a family business, the organization prefers to portray itself as a philanthropic-commercial organization rather than a commercial-philanthropic organization, which may be the reason why employees experience minimal tension as they can identify with the non-market-orientated identity rather than the market-orientated identity.

### 6.8.6 Organizational hybridity in relation to employees' behavioural responses at BPL

The overall data yielded no specific indication of employees' behavioural responses to organizational hybridity. However, there were indications of the organization's multiple behavioural expectations for employees, regarding "stakeholder value maximisation" and "profit maximisation"; this duality reflects the hybridity of the organization. This suggests the likelihood of conflicting messages since the two objectives prescribe contradictory values for action. This is consistent with the interview data.

## 6.9 Findings Associated with Understanding the Implications of Organizational Hybridity for Employees' Trust in BPL

**Proposition 2:** *The greater the tensions produced by multiple logics, the less likely it becomes that employees of commercial hybrid organizations will trust their employers.*

In the course of a wide-ranging investigation, which has looked at the goals, objectives, culture and leadership structure of the organization, the data has shown the explicit awareness of trust as an issue within BPL. The organization emphasises trust and integrity in its values statement, and to the extent to which this statement forms part of, and gives expression to, the organization's culture, employees are likely to experience high trust in the organization. This is consistent with the argument in Section A. Exploration of this objective formed part of a strategy aimed at answering the overall research question as well as the supporting research question: *How does organizational hybridity affect the level of employees' trust in commercial hybrid organizations?*

## 6.10 Findings Associated with Understanding the Influence of Non-Market-Orientated Logics at BPL

**Proposition 4:** *The stronger employees' affiliations to religious logics, the greater the influence of such logics on employees' behaviour and trust in commercial hybrid organizations.*

Although the data showed no direct influence of religion on the leadership and governance of BPL from the analysis of company documents, rituals that are taken for granted – such as "morning devotions" and "opening prayers" during daily office meetings and annual general meetings – emerged as markers of the possible influence of religion on the organizational culture and behaviours of employees. This is consistent with the data from the interviews. The exploration of this objective formed part of a strategy aimed at answering the overall research question as well as the supporting research question: *What role does religion play a role in influencing employees' behaviour and shaping other organizational attributes of commercial hybrid organizations?*

## 6.11 Findings Relevant to Developing Research-Based Recommendations for Sustaining Employees' Trust in BPL

**Proposition 3:** *The greater the employees trust in commercial hybrid organizations, the more effective the organizational performance.*

The data appear to suggest that employees' trust needs to be continuously sustained through consideration and involvement of stakeholders' needs, whether this is by the actions of the chairman/CEO or by policies regularly enacted by management, to ensure continuous improvement of organizational identification, effectiveness and performance. Exploration of this objective formed part of a strategy aimed at answering the overall research question as well as the supporting research question: *How can employees' trust in commercial hybrid organizations be sustained for improved effective organizational performance?*

## 6.12 Summary and Conclusions

The overall empirical findings in this chapter have provided further insights into the experiences of the interviewees and their views on organizational hybridity in practice. Section A descriptively analysed the perception and views provided by the different interviewees as relevant to this study, and the key themes that emerged from the data are illustrated in Table 22. Section B explored the organizational hybridity in practice within BPL using document analysis, which provides support for the findings from Section A.

The overall findings in this chapter are summarised as follows. Firstly, BPL operates as a contested commercial hybrid organization by incorporating commercial and family logics as the dominant logics, while others such as philanthropic and religious logics are embodied peripherally. These logics play a role in influencing the behaviours and actions of the employees of BPL. The family-orientated business model of BPL may have enabled the religious and philanthropic logics within the organization, introducing an extra level of complexity not specifically dealt with in Besharov and Smith's (2014) four-way classification.

Secondly, BPL operates an organic but centralised leadership structure, where the decision-making power is centralised at the top of the organizational hierarchy, which happens to be the chairman/CEO. The governance structure of BPL indicates a "dual ownership and control" governance structure, which allows for the multiple roles of the chairman and CEO to be embodied by one individual. However, as a contested commercial hybrid organization, the tensions experienced within BPL appear to be minimal, which could be a result of its inclusive leadership/governance structure.

Thirdly, organizational hybridity fostered both positive and dysfunctional employee behaviours at BPL. However, religious logic appears to play a significant role in supporting employees' trust in the organization, which has helped to foster identification with the its prescribed values.

Finally, the data pointed to the need for continuous sustenance of employees' trust in the organization, based on clear and undistorted communication channels, so as to facilitate a shared identity between the employees and the organization. In conclusion, the overall findings point to recommendations on how to address the tensions posed by organizational hybridity. They also provide evidence that will contribute towards filling identified gaps in the current knowledge on the relationship between organizational hybridity and organizational trust. These findings are discussed extensively in the next chapter.

**Table 22: Summary of Emerging Themes**

| Research objectives | Research propositions | Emerging issues |
|---|---|---|
| *Objective 1* | *Proposition 1* | |
| To explore the influence of organizational hybridity on specific organizational attributes, including governance, organizational culture, leadership and intra-organizational relations of commercial hybrid organizations. | The more extensive the tensions associated with organizational hybridity, the greater the likelihood of negative behavioural responses by employees. | • Identity distress<br>• Employee disengagement<br>• Insubordinate behavior<br>• Rule-following behaviour |
| *Objective 2* | Proposition 2 | • Conflicting expectations<br>• Mixed messages<br>• High trust<br>• Distrust |
| To shape an understanding of the implications of organizational hybridity for employees' trust in commercial hybrid organizations, with particular attention to those implications having a plausible relationship to organizational effectiveness. | The greater the tensions produced by multiple logics, the less likely it becomes that employees of commercial hybrid organizations will trust their employers. | |
| *Objective 3* | Proposition 3 | • Communication gap<br>• Improved organizational effectiveness and performance<br>• Improved organizational identification |
| To develop research-based recommendations for sustaining employees' trust in the commercial hybrid organizations. | The greater the employees' trust in commercial hybrid organizations, the more effective the organizational performance. | |
| *Objective 4* | Proposition 4 | • Honest behaviour<br>• Commitment<br>• Servant leadership style<br>• Philanthropic behaviour<br>• Unethical behaviour |
| To understand the influence of non-market-orientated institutional logics on commercial hybrid organizations. | The stronger employees' affiliations to religious logics, the greater the influence of such logics on employees' behaviour and trust in commercial hybrid organizations. | |

# CHAPTER 7

# DISCUSSION OF FINDINGS

## 7.1 Introduction

Figure 17: The Research Cycle (Phase 5)

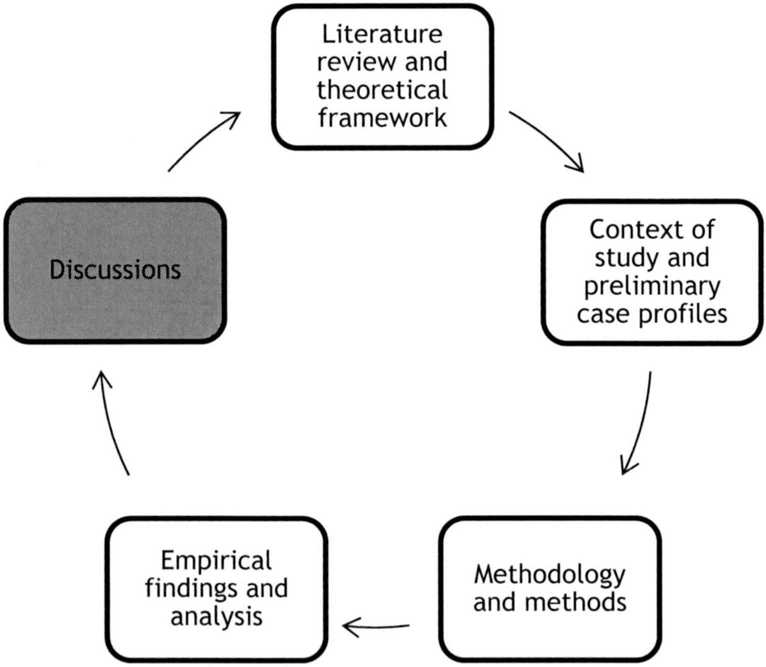


The previous two chapters presented the empirical findings of this study. The purpose of this chapter is to provide interpretive insights into these findings, which are critically analysed within the context of other studies. The chapter can thus be seen as a discussion of the key findings of the study (see Figure 17), organizing the emerging evidence from the preceding chapters in line with the research objectives, propositions and questions. The chapter is divided into five main sections. It concludes with a summary of recommendations for the future effectiveness of commercial hybrid organizations.

## 7.2 Overview of the Research

A number of studies have contributed to knowledge on organizational hybridity. More specifically, they have contributed to how contemporary organizations, in the face of institutional complexity, adopt such survival mechanisms as embodying multiple logics to effectively achieve organizational goals and objectives (Thornton et al., 2012; Battilana and Dorado, 2010; Greenwood et al., 2010; Battilana and Lee, 2014; Karré, 2011; Besharov and Smith, 2014; Pache and Santos, 2010, 2013; Battilana et al., 2012; Jay, 2013; Haigh and Hoffman, 2012; Foreman and Whetten, 2002). However, while organizational hybridity can provide valuable outcomes for the organizations, it may also create tensions for employees by facing them with alternative courses of action, as suggested by Besharov and Smith (2014), Pache and Santos (2010, 2013), Oliver (1991) and Seo and Creed (2002).

Despite the existence of this body of knowledge, individual responses to organizational hybridity and the implications that the phenomenon may have for employees' trust have largely passed beneath the academic radar. Therefore, drawing on available insights in organizational trust and institutional logics, this study represents an initial step towards a more finely tuned empirical understanding of the implications of organizational hybridity for employees' trust in commercial hybrid organizations. Furthermore, it attempts to extend the body of knowledge focused on "building the link between institutional logics and their instantiation in human actions [and behaviours]" (Pache and Santos, 2013:7).

With this overall aim, the research was directed towards four specific objectives:

1. To explore the influence of organizational hybridity on specific organizational attributes, including governance, organizational culture, leadership and intra-organizational relations, in commercial hybrid organizations.
2. To understand the influence of non-market-orientated institutional logics on commercial hybrid organizations.
3. To shape an understanding of the implications of organizational hybridity for employees' trust in commercial hybrid organizations,

with particular attention to those implications having a plausible relationship to organizational effectiveness.
4. To develop research-based recommendations for sustaining employees' trust in commercial hybrid organizations.

The study began with the following primary research question: *What are the implications of organizational hybridity for employees' trust in commercial hybrid organizations?* The supporting research questions are as follows:

1. To what extent does organizational hybridity influence specific attributes of commercial hybrid organizations?
2. What role does religion play in influencing employees' behaviour and shaping other organizational attributes of commercial hybrid organizations?
3. How does organizational hybridity affect the level of employees' trust in commercial hybrid organizations?
4. How can employees' trust in commercial hybrid organizations be sustained for improved effective organizational performance?

The literature review focused on analysing current knowledge on organizational hybridity – more specifically, the institutional logics perspective and research into organizational trust, identifying gaps therein. Results of this analysis informed the proposed theoretical framework in Chapter 2, and the research design and methods in Chapter 4. The theoretical framework comprised the following key propositions that were identified as being fundamental to understanding the relationship between organizational hybridity and organizational trust:

1. The more extensive the tensions associated with organizational hybridity, the greater the likelihood of negative behavioural responses by employees.
2. The greater the tensions produced by multiple logics, the less likely it becomes that employees of commercial hybrid organizations will trust their employers.
3. The greater the employees' trust in commercial hybrid organizations, the more effective the organizational performance.
4. The stronger employees' affiliations to religious logics, the greater the influence of such logics on employees' behaviour and trust in commercial hybrid organizations.

These key propositions provided the basis for the empirical data analysis and will also guide this discussion chapter. Thus, to discuss the research findings in a way that is meaningful and directly useful in achieving the overall research goal, the empirical findings are discussed in relation to the research objectives, questions and propositions shown above.

## 7.3 Exploring the Influence of Organizational Hybridity on Specific Organizational Attributes of Commercial Hybrid Organizations

The data suggested that organizational hybridity is likely to influence the governance, leadership, culture and intra-organizational relations of commercial hybrid organizations, by producing tensions that trigger both positive and negative behavioural responses among employees. At this juncture, it is important to note that although there are multiple institutional logics embodied by both ASL and BPL, only the prominent logics are discussed in this study. The influence of organizational hybridity on these specific organizational attributes and how these tensions were triggered are discussed in turn next. Exploration of this objective formed part of a strategy aimed at answering the overall research question as well as the supporting research question: *To what extent does organizational hybridity influence specific attributes of commercial hybrid organizations?* The empirical findings in relation to this question are summarised in Table 23.

The empirical data showed major differences in the governance, leadership structures and organizational culture of ASL and BPL; these differences could be seen to relate to the business model of the organization in each case. An evolutionary perspective such as Day's (1998) would lead us to expect that commercial hybrid organizations under fierce competitive pressure would tend to choose the structures and mechanisms that work for their competitive advantage. Such unrelenting structural change, dictated by features of the competitive environment, is consistent with real-world tensions in the context of these core organizational attributes. The interview data attested to such tensions in the form of "contradictory messages", "unclear communication of values", "mismatch of values", "value disjuncture" and "conflicting expectations". Hence, this leads to the following research proposition:

**Proposition 1:** *The more extensive the tensions associated with organizational hybridity, the greater the likelihood of negative behavioural responses by employees.*

**Table 23: Summary of Empirical Findings Associated with Exploring the Influence of Organizational Hybridity on Specific Attributes of Commercial Hybrid Organizations.**

| **Proposition 1:**<br>The more extensive the tensions associated with organizational hybridity, the greater the likelihood of negative behavioural responses by employees | | | |
|---|---|---|---|
| **Supporting question** | **Summary of empirical findings** | **Data from ASL** | **Data from BPL** |
| To what extent does organizational hybridity influence specific attributes of commercial hybrid organizations? | ➢ Organizational hybridity is likely to condition flexibility in the adoption of distinctive organizational attributes by commercial hybrid organizations in relation to governance, leadership and organizational culture.<br>➢ Organizational hybridity is likely to trigger various degrees of tension across core governance, leadership and culture of commercial hybrid organizations.<br>➢ Organizational hybridity is likely to produce behavioural responses both positive (rule-following behaviour) and negative (employee disengagement, opportunism, distress, insubordination, resigning from the organization) due to the tensions it presents. | ➢ The hybridity of professional and commercial logics at ASL may have led to the adoption of a formal, highly bureaucratic and hierarchical structure, where power is concentrated at the top of the organizational hierarchy, and distributed between the board of directors and executive management team.<br>➢ Organizational hybridity may have triggered extensive tensions at ASL.<br>➢ Organizational hybridity may have produced dysfunctional behaviours among employees at ASL as a result of extensive tensions. | ➢ The hybridity of commercial, family, religious and philanthropic logics at BPL may have brought about the adoption of an organic (with dual ownership and control), informal governance structure, where power is concentrated with the chairman/CEO.<br>➢ Organizational hybridity may have triggered minimal tensions at BPL.<br>➢ Organizational hybridity may have enabled positive and dysfunctional behaviours among employees at BPL as a result of minimal tensions. |

### 7.3.1 The influence of organizational hybridity on the governance of commercial hybrid organizations

The data pointed to the likelihood of organizational hybridity influencing the governance of commercial hybrid organizations, as shown in Table 23. Specifically, it was found that organizational hybridity influenced the adoption of distinctive patterns of governance structures and mechanisms, and various degrees of tension in both ASL and BPL. To sum up, the distinctive structural difference between the two organizations' responses to hybridity can be seen as one of the degrees of formality: this is discussed in the next section. The finding in this section corresponds with the assertions of Battilana et al. (2012), Ebrahim et al. (2014) and Battilana and Lee (2014) on the governance of hybrid organizations. These studies argued in favour of the unique role played by governance in enacting mechanisms that will ensure hybrid organizations do not deviate from their stated objectives. However, as noted in Chapter 2, in Battilana and Lee's (2014) study, governance was addressed as a sub-dimension of organizational design, which I argue is insufficient owing to the overall impact of governance regimes on organizations and the key role they play in ensuring that hybrid organizations thrive in their performances (Aguilera and Jackson, 2010; Westphal and Zajac, 2013; Davis et al., 1997; Anheier, 2011; Billis, 2010; Martin et al., 2016; Ebrahim et al., 2014).

#### 7.3.1a Distinctive patterns of governance: formal versus informal structures

Governance emerged as an important organizational attribute where tensions are experienced in commercial hybrid organizations. As argued by previous studies, governance plays a major role in ensuring that commercial hybrid organizations thrive in their performance and do not deviate from their primary objectives, since they are likely to be continuously challenged by external pressure and market forces (Aguilera and Jackson, 2010; Karré, 2011; Ebrahim et al., 2014; Mair et al., 2015; Battilana et al., 2012). Moreover, governance helps to determine how organizational resources are used and how stakeholders' expectations are balanced, as suggested by Freeman (1984). Regarding the governance of both commercial hybrid organizations, the data in this study underscore three issues. Firstly, there is a risk of ineffective organizational performance as a result of the adopted governance structure. Secondly, there is a challenge of effectively balancing multiple interests, resulting in tensions between conflicting interests, as noted by Jensen and Meckling (1992). Thirdly, there is a need to urgently seek remedies for the problems posed by hybridity in this area.

Looking at ASL and BPL, the data showed that both commercial hybrid organizations had a functional governing board in charge of policies, strategic decision-making, the balancing of objectives, and monitoring and controlling employees. In both cases, the board of directors functions to align stakeholders' interests with the organization's interest and to curtail managerial opportunism, along the lines contemplated by Williamson (1985), while the role of the executive management team in each organization is to manage the day-to-day activities of employees.

However, the distinction between the two organizations in terms of governance structure is stark. Even though both organizations have functioning governing boards, dissimilarities were apparent at the level of the governance structure and its mechanisms. This was perceived to have been influenced by the type of institutional logics embodied in each case by these commercial hybrid organizations. For example, ASL (embodying commercial and professional logics at its core) showed a formalised governance structure with clear separation of ownership and control, supported by a strict code of conduct, policies, frameworks, guidelines and a leadership style that appears to be transactional. BPL, on the other hand, (embodying family, religious, commercial and philanthropic logics at its core) evidenced an informal governance structure with a dual ownership and control mechanism, supported by an open-door policy and a leadership style that takes the form of servant leadership.

Furthermore, the data showed that both structures, each unique in its own right, reflected the core logics embodied by each of the organizations, which, as expected, contribute to shaping stakeholders' perceptions of the organization (Sharkie, 2009). A majority of the interviewees from BPL were strongly of the view that the informal structure adopted by the organization may have been a result of the influence of the core family logic, which, by its emphasis on paternalistic values, made for a strong internal sense of solidarity within the organization and allowed them to see the chairman/CEO as a "father figure". This suggests that the power balance in the governance of commercial hybrid organizations may play an important role in the organizational identification process. There is a theoretical reason to expect such a finding (James, 2006), but future research could look to explore this further. On the other hand, data from ASL suggest that the embodiment of commercial and professional logics may have favoured the formalised governance structure used, which is an affinity nicely caught in the company's mission statement in Chapter 5.

### 7.3.1b Tensions in governance

The interviewees highlighted both conflict of values and conflict of interests as the main facilitators of tension in the governance of both ASL and BPL. However, while it is possible to make a conceptual distinction between conflicts of interest and conflicts of values, the data showed that deeply held values may trigger tensions of conflicting interests. The general perception among interviewees regarding tensions of conflicting interests is that most individuals' interests are interpreted and shaped by their deeply held values, so that value disjuncture could be said to generate conflicts around attempts to balance multiple interests within an organization. Future research may need to investigate this further.

The data also showed that these tensions in governance could occur in the form of "contradictory messages", "conflicting messages" and "conflicting expectations" as a result of inconsistent values for actions prescribed by the embodied logics, which could make it challenging to achieve organizational goals collectively. The data from ASL and BPL provided support for this finding, which is consistent with the theories of Ebrahim et al. (2014), Besharov and Smith (2014), and Pache and Santos (2010, 2013) regarding how tensions manifest within hybrid organizations.

Moreover, there were suggestions that even though professional logic was embodied peripherally to support the dominant commercial logic at ASL, strong affiliations to deeply held professional values on the part of some of the executive management team members resulted in rejection of the values prescribed by the commercial logic, producing extensive tensions within the organization. This value disjuncture generated "a growing sense of tensions" among the executive management team and board members in charge of governing the organization. As a result, employees at the bottom of the hierarchy were faced with "conflicting expectations", which made it difficult to balance organizational goals collectively and achieve effective outcomes. This finding is consistent with Siebert and Costley's (2013) findings. Similarly, their study showed how inconsistent values for actions resulted in tensions between the values of employees and the organizations, and also between the employees' professionalism and the managerialism of the organizations.

Despite these challenges, the data suggest the perception that the use of strategic mechanisms tailored to the specific needs of the organization could help mitigate these growing tensions. More specifically, developing mechanisms for improving organizational identification through value alignment could be an effective way of facilitating employees' commitment to the organization, which is in line with the recommendations of Pratt and Foreman (2000), and Foreman and Whetten (2002). Although this study, restricted as it was by time limitations, may lack more fine-grained data to unpack the specific governance approaches and practices employed by the two commercial hybrid organizations studied, the data provide qualified support for the theoretical assertions of Battilana and Lee (2014), Battilana et al. (2012) and Ebrahim et al. (2014) regarding governance as an important dimension where tensions are experienced in hybrid organizations. The occurrence of "conflicting messages" and "conflicting expectations", on the other hand, emerged as sources and forms of tension in hybrid organizations, which is consistent with the line of argument in studies by Pache and Santos (2010, 2013). In total, a majority of the interviewees from both organizations reported experience supporting this finding, with very few contrary opinions expressed.

### 7.3.2 The influence of organizational hybridity on the leadership style/structure of commercial hybrid organizations

The data suggested that organizational hybridity is likely to influence the leadership structure or style of commercial hybrid organizations, as shown in Table 23. In fact, there was a general perception that organizational hybridity might have influenced the two distinctive leadership styles (transactional and servant leadership) adopted by ASL and BPL, as well as enabled some of the tensions experienced within the organizations. The distinctive leadership styles and related tensions are discussed in turn next. However, unlike the studies by Battilana et al. (2012), Ebrahim et al. (2014), and Battilana and Lee (2014), which failed to discuss leadership in detail as an important dimension of organizational hybridity, the data in this study point to leadership playing an important role in ensuring that employees understand and make sense of the logics embodied within the commercial hybrid organizations. As other studies have shown, leadership plays a crucial role in constructing meanings, building trust, allowing effective communication and shaping how employees interpret the governance of organizations (Creed and Miles, 1996; McAllister, 1995; Battilana and Lee, 2014; Haigh and Hoffman, 2012). Thus, it should not be ignored in organizational studies. The data from both ASL and BPL provided support for this finding.

### 7.3.2a Distinctive leadership styles: transactional versus servant leadership approach

One of the challenges surrounding the leadership of hybrid organizations, as stated in the literature review, is the problem of adopting the appropriate leadership style/structure fit for the organization (see Section 2.7.2 Leadership structure). The data showed that organizational hybridity played a role in influencing the adoption of different leadership styles and structures by both organizations. Regarding leadership structure, for example, the interviewees argued that the hierarchical arrangement (with a relatively less bureaucratic structure) in use at BPL depicts the leadership's readiness to include and listen to employees across various levels, regardless of status. According to the interviewees, this "inclusive structure" shows remarkable features of the servant leadership approach, i.e. "I serve" as opposed to "I lead", in the formula of Sendjaya and Sarros (2002). This is perceived by the interviewees as being shaped by the values prescribed by the logics of family, philanthropy and religious logics embodied in the organization. According to the interviewees, some of the values prescribed by these logics are "humility", "empathy", "commitment", "trust", "concern", "integrity" and "openness". These values are consistent with Spears's (2010) characteristics of servant leadership. The interview data showed perceptions that the emphasis on family enabled "involvement", "inclusiveness", "participation" and "mutual purpose" within the organization.

This finding lends support to Haigh and Hoffman's (2012) assertion that hybrid leaders could adopt a leadership style that reflects participative management, with a focus on driving the organization to a high level of achievement. Moreover, it also provides support for James's (2006) argument regarding the role of the paternalistic approach in promoting a strong sense of solidarity in family businesses, leading employees to a perception of the chairman/CEO as a "father figure", as depicted in Chapter 6. In total, a majority of the interviewees from BPL occupied a strong position that was affirmatory of James's (2006) argument, with no contrary feelings.

In contrast to the data from BPL, there were suggestions that the embodiment of both commercial and professional logics may have influenced ASL's adoption of a bureaucratic structure and a transactional leadership approach that emphasises strict monitoring and control of employees, leading in turn to employees' isolation from decision-making. This finding aligns with Weber's (1947) assertions about the adoption of a bureaucratic (hierarchical) structure by large organizations, which enables jobs to be specialised, and employees to be monitored and controlled. According to Weber (1947), bureaucratic organizations adhere to the following prescriptions: formal selection, rules, procedures, impersonality, job specialisation, hierarchical authority, monitoring and control. The interviewees argued that this structure resulted in a lack of shared sense of mission. Moreover, this finding is consistent with the argument of Erkutlu and Chafra (2015). In their study, they found that power distance between top management and employees, and rigid hierarchical arrangements, enabled weak organizational identification. Therefore, it is not surprising that the majority of the interviewees from ASL occupied a strong position concerning the feeling of "disregard for employees". However, future research may need to investigate this finding further.

### 7.3.2b Tensions in leadership style/structure

The data suggested that the hierarchical arrangements adopted by commercial hybrid organizations are likely to contribute to existing tensions in governance. In fact, multiple inputs from various levels of the leadership hierarchy, mostly the board of directors and executive management team, favoured by their strong affiliations to the logics embodied within ASL, may have triggered extensive tensions, which made it more challenging to pursue a common goal collectively. For example, the data showed that even though ASL embodied professional and commercial logics that prescribed consistent values for actions, various organizational leaders had different preferences over what they perceived as important managerial tasks. Furthermore, each of these leaders encouraged their employees to perform best in these tasks, which facilitated a recipe for endemic tensions within the organization. Moreover, the bureaucratic structure is likely to produce a slower resolution of conflicts, which are likely to run for longer and produce wide-reaching tensions.

By contrast, even though BPL embodies commercial and family logics that prescribe contradictory values for actions (Besharov and Smith, 2014; Foreman and Whetten, 2002), the findings showed that the tensions generated by these contradictory logics were easily and quickly resolved due to the less bureaucratic structure of the organization. Moreover, the preponderance of power within the hands of the chairman/CEO enabled him to make uncontested and faster decisions, resulting in minimal tensions within the organization. Alternatively, this finding may also be seen as reflecting the that employees are more likely to be receptive to logics when the organizational members espousing them have more power within the organization. Nevertheless, the data showed that the degree of tension experienced within BPL is minimal, which runs contrary to Besharov and Smith's (2014) conceptualisation.

In other words, this finding suggests that a bureaucratic leadership structure is most likely to trigger extensive tensions, given that multiple decision-makers may be strongly affiliated to various institutional logics and may be in a position to reject the values prescribed by contradictory logics. Such a situation is a recipe for organizational tension, as suggested by Pache and Santos (2013), and Mangen and Brivot (2014). This study thus provides an insight into how the leadership structure could influence the degree of tension experienced within commercial hybrid organizations. Overall, findings on the influence of organizational hybridity on the leadership structure of commercial hybrid organizations underscore the desirability of moving towards "participative leadership" and "employees' involvement" for improved organizational performance. The data from both ASL and BPL provided support for these findings.

### 7.3.3 The influence of organizational hybridity on the organizational culture of commercial hybrid organizations

The data suggested organizational hybridity is likely to influence the organizational culture of commercial hybrid organizations, as shown in Table 23. Organizational culture can be defined as "the pattern of basic assumptions that a given group has invented, discovered, or developed in learning to cope with its problems of external adaptation and internal integration, and that have worked well enough to be considered valid, therefore, to be taught to new members as the correct way to perceive, think, and feel in relation to those problems" (Schein, 1984:3). Organizational culture emerged as a critical means by which multiple logics are communicated in commercial hybrid organizations (Battilana et al., 2012). This may be as a result of its role in ensuring that employees share a mutual sense of mission with the organization, as speculated by Schein (1984) and Battilana et al. (2012). Research on organizational culture has argued that for organizations to be functional and effective, the organizational culture, structure, procedures and ideologies should be formally stated, which enables it to adapt to internal integration and a changing external environment (Schein, 1984). In this regard, the data showed that organizational hybridity may have influenced the adoption of distinctive patterns of assumptions at ASL and BPL, as well as producing distinctive patterns of tension within both organizations. These are discussed in turn next.

#### 7.3.3a Distinctive patterns of basic assumptions

The data from interviews and document analysis showed distinctive patterns of organizational culture consistent with the logics embodied by both ASL and BPL. This suggests that the embodied logics may have influenced the various patterns of basic assumptions and values espoused within both organizations, as proposed by Friedland and Alford (1991). For example, the embodiment of family logic and peripheral philanthropic logic at BPL underlie the all-inclusive/philanthropic culture espoused within it. This culture shaped the employees' interpretation of the organization as "empathetic", "concerned", "benevolent" and marked by "genuine interest to build trust". Leading informants report a "sense of belonging", "sense of shared purpose" and "employees' commitment". Moreover, employees' identification with the values prescribed within the organizations seemed to have played a role in forming employees' positive interpretation of these logics. This is consistent with studies that highlighted identification as a mechanism by which institutional logics exert an influence on individuals (Thornton and Ocasio, 2008; Ashforth et al., 2008; Weaver and Agle, 2002; Whetten, 2006). Moreover, it provides a consistent line of argument with a study by O'Reilly et al. (2014) that showed how values manifest within an organization, most especially by the CEO shaping its cultural norms. However, the values prescribed by commercial and professional logics shaped the employees' interpretation of ASL's culture as "money-focused", "exclusive" and "isolating", which militates strongly against their desire to understand, make sense of or identify with the values prescribed within the organization.

#### 7.3.3b Tensions in organizational culture

The majority of the interviewees raised the issue that the tensions influenced by organizational hybridity in governance, leadership and organizational culture are interrelated. The data suggested that the hybridity of professional and commercial logics produced a "lack of cultural fit" and "value disjuncture" at ASL as a result of employees' strong allegiance to other logics. More so, strong affiliations to professional logics by executive management team members triggered the rejection of some of the values prescribed by the dominant commercial logic. The consequent absence of a "common sense of purpose" and "value disjuncture" at the management level militates strongly against employees' desire to identify with the culture of the organization. However, contrary to the above, data showed that even though BPL embodied logics that prescribe contradictory values, identification with the embodied logics – most especially the non-market-orientated logics such as philanthropic and religious logics – enabled a "mutual purpose" within the organization. This finding comes as a surprise in the light of Besharov and Smith's (2014) postulation that professional and commercial logics prescribe compatible values for actions, and thus are likely to support rather than contradict each other. However, it is consistent with the position of Thornton et al. (2012) regarding the possibility that strong allegiance to societal-level logics can empower individuals to serve as carriers of those logics inside organizations.

In contrast to Besharov and Smith's (2014) theorising that contested hybrid organizations experience more conflict than the dominant hybrid organizations, empirical findings from this study offer an alternative line of argument. The data showed that ASL, which fits the dominant hybrid organization type, experienced extensive tensions, while BPL, which fits the contested hybrid organization type, experienced minimal tensions even though it embodied logics that prescribed contradictory values (see Section 2.5.5 Typology of hybrid organizations). This suggests that the degree of tension experienced in hybrid organizations may vary depending on key variables yet to be determined, such as the degree to which the organization is market focused. Besharov and Smith's (2014) study was based on social enterprise, which, according to them, is a perfect hybrid organization with both market and social goals central to the organization's functioning. However, their analysis of the social enterprise organization may have influenced their findings. Data from the current study pointed to the possibility that hybrid organizations that are more market focused, such as ASL and BPL, may experience tensions differently. For example, even though BPL (contested hybrid organization type) has the potential for triggering extensive conflicts or tensions due to the embodiment of incompatible logics, as suggested by Besharov and Smith (2014), the sense of mutual purpose, which was activated by employees' identification with the non-market-orientated logics, led to situations where conflicts were easily resolved. Thus, the overall level of tensions experienced at BPL was minimal, which is contrary to Besharov and Smith's (2014) theory. Thus, this finding addresses gaps in the literature regarding whether the tensions experienced within hybrid organizations would remain the same if the organizations were more market focused (see Section 2.2.1 Organizational hybridity: Theoretical background).

Furthermore, the variation in my finding from Besharov and Smith's (2014) study may have been as a result of the contextual focus of this study. More specifically, employees' strong affiliations to logics dominant in the Nigerian institutional environment may have contributed to the degree of tension experienced. Individuals are likely to take into account historical aspects of the values that are institutionalised in the society before making a strategic choice on how to act, as suggested by Pache and Santos (2013). For example, regarding the issue of bribery and corruption in Nigeria, employees of both ASL and BPL seemed to be aware of bribery and corruption as a socially acceptable way of life in the Nigerian context. Hence, this might be the reason they engage in the act although it may be against their religious or personal values to accept a bribe. Their decision on how to act – in this case, to accept a bribe – is based on the justification that it is an acceptable way of life in Nigeria. This suggests that the degree of tension in commercial hybrid organizations is likely to vary depending on the context and the dominant institutional logics embedded within the context. This finding is consistent with Farrell and Knight's (2003) theorising that an individual could use information derived from institutions to develop behavioural expectations. However, despite the above findings, one lesson that could be drawn here is that if these tensions are not adequately treated, they could generate real problems for the organization. The data from both ASL and BPL provided support for this view.

### 7.3.4 The influence of organizational hybridity on intra-organizational relations

The data also suggested that organizational hybridity is likely to influence intra-organizational relations in commercial hybrid organizations. In fact, the data suggests that the assemblage of social and individual factors contributes to the functioning of commercial hybrid organizations, and is itself subject to modification by organizational hybridity. Thus, understanding the influence of organizational hybridity on employees' behaviour and how employees make sense of, interpret and respond to the complexities can be a first step towards understanding its implications for employees' trust. According to Binder (2007), the key to understanding here is that intra-organizational relations can be expected to substantiate the material-symbolic nature of institutional logics. At the same time, studies on the responses to situations where multiple logics are in play have so far focused on the organizational level of analysis. For example, studies by Pache and Santos (2010) and Oliver (1991) pointed to compromise, defiance and avoidance as organizational responses to a multiplicity of logics. This study seeks to contribute to the individual level of analysis, arguing that employees' behavioural responses may not always be negative, as commercial hybrid organizations are likely to embody logics that employees may identify with, which could, in turn, enable positive behavioural responses.

However, to achieve the objective of this study, I take into account previous studies on organizational-level response (Pache and Santos, 2010), while stressing that individual-level response may differ from it, as suggested by Pache and Santos (2013) and similar studies.

This finding embraces Binder's (2007:568) view that "logics are not purely top-down, real people, in real contexts with consequential past experiences of their own, play with them, question them, combine them with institutional logics from other domains, take what they can use from them and make them fit their needs". Hence, this study takes the stance that organizational hybridity is likely to (negatively or positively) influence employees' behavioural responses, which are strongly determined by their sense-making and interpretations of, and identification with, the multiple logics prescribed within the organizations (see Section 2.4 The Institutional Logics Perspective: Philosophical Background). Most importantly, it contributes to empirical knowledge on how various logics shape individuals' behaviours, as suggested by Tracey (2012). Such behavioural responses that emerged from the data are the displays of employee disengagement, insubordinate behaviour, resigning from work and synergic behaviour (opportunistic or rule-following behaviour), as shown in Table 23. These are discussed in turn next.

### 7.3.4a Employee disengagement

The perception of employee disengagement articulated a view consistent with Kahn's (1990:694) definition of the term: "the uncoupling of selves from work roles". Employee disengagement was displayed through the observable expression of nonchalant attitudes to work, withdrawal and negligence about assigned duties. According to the majority of the interviewees, such withdrawal from work was displayed in the form of constant "sick leave", "extended leave days", "lateness to work", "not paying attention to work" and "avoidance of work". The data showed employee disengagement as the most common deviant behaviour displayed by disgruntled employees of commercial hybrid organizations.

Specific roots of such behaviour are not hard to find. Commercial hybrid organizations may prescribe logics that have contradictory values, such as family and business (commercial) logics, which could generate tensions, as suggested by Foreman and Whetten (2002). In attempting to interpret these tensions, employees may become distressed and therefore become disengaged from work, as suggested by BM10 (see Section 6.3.6 Behavioural responses to organizational hybridity). Despite this testimony, there were also strong suggestions that employee disengagement can be contained and managed if the organizations apply appropriate tools during the early distress stage. The adoption of clear communication strategies, as well as employees' involvement in the decision-making process, were some of the strategies suggested by the interviewees to mitigate this kind of behaviour. The data from both ASL and BPL provided support for this finding. More generally, this finding supports Pache and Santos's (2010) theorising that, in the face of conflict, actors are likely to resort to disregard for rules, avoidance and defiance. Although Pache and Santos's (2010) study was at the organizational level of analysis, the finding in the current study provides a consistent line of argument with their work.

### 7.3.4b Display of "insubordinate" behaviour

The data also showed evidence of where the rejection of prescribed logics, whether outright or subtle, by employees takes the form of non-compliance or disregard for rules and leadership authority. This definition is consistent with Pache and Santos's (2013) definition of defiant behaviour. The data showed that "insubordinate" behaviour, as suggested by AT6, emerges as a result of employees' lack of commitment to embodied logics, which leads them to resist the given logics or to explicitly contradict them. In the case of ASL, the failure by employees to identify with the prescribed logics operated along the lines of the "detachment" of the employees from the organization, as described by Pache and Santos (2013), resulting in constant challenges to the prescribed logics. However, data from BPL showed that some employees displayed "insubordinate" behaviours due to unfamiliarity with the prescribed logics. This might be because an employee related to his colleagues more or less exclusively on the basis of a family or philanthropic logic, so that the application of a commercial logic could seem strange or unexpected, as demonstrated by BM16. However, as stated earlier, these conflicts did not amount to extensive tensions at BPL as they were quickly resolved due to the power balance within the organization. The problem of unfamiliar logic was not unique to BPL: data from ASL also provided support for this finding.

This situation finds echoes in studies by Townley (1997) and McCourt and Moores (2007), which illustrated how stakeholders within organizations could reject unfamiliar logics. Townley's (1997) study focused on the outright rejection of managerial logic by academics at UK universities due to its contradiction with the academic professional logic they were familiar with. Despite the similarity between insubordinate behaviour and defiance, as suggested by Oliver (1991), Pache and Santos (2010, 2013), and Townley

(2002), insubordinate behaviour emerges as a novel discovery in the study of organizational hybridity at the individual level of analysis. Nevertheless, future research may need to verify these claims.

#### 7.3.4c Resigning from the organization

Another behavioural response that emerged from the data concerns the resignation stage. The majority of the interviewees took the view that employees who are distressed are likely to become "insubordinate", "nonchalant" and "opportunistic" as a coping mechanism, which may result in them walking away from the organization. This view reflected the folk wisdom, which holds that tensions, if left unchecked, could lead to massive turnover, as employees who can no longer cope with the conflicts tend to look for something better elsewhere. In so doing, commercial hybrid organizations may end up losing valuable employees who would otherwise contribute to the effectiveness of the organization, as suggested by AM10. The data from ASL provided support for this finding. Moreover, this finding is echoed in Battilana and Dorado's (2010) study. Similarly, their study showed how extensive conflicts and tensions in BancoSol led to significant employee turnover, including the resignation of the CEO.

However, contrary to the above assertions, data from BPL showed low employee turnover, which appeared to be a result of employees' identification with the non-market-orientated logics embodied within the organization which thus reinforced their commitment to it. Even though there were slight inconsistencies regarding employees' likeliness to resign from either ASL or BPL, the overall findings strongly supported the idea that resigning was perceived as the final behavioural response to the tensions posed by organizational hybridity.

#### 7.3.4d Display of synergic behaviour

In addition to the above behavioural responses, a rather complex alternative response also emerged from the data. A synergic response emerged as a type of behaviour displayed by employees who are familiar with or have in-depth knowledge of the values prescribed by the logics they are exposed to within the organization. In other words, this group of employees who are familiar with or acutely aware of the logics embodied within the organizations make attempts to alternate the values prescribed by these logics when they deem it necessary. However, while being fully adept with multiple logics may not seem like a bad idea, this group of employees could choose to respond in one of two ways: opportunistically or by adopting the rule-following behaviour, as illustrated in Figure 18. The data from ASL and BPL provided support for this finding.

Figure 18: Synergic Behavioural Response

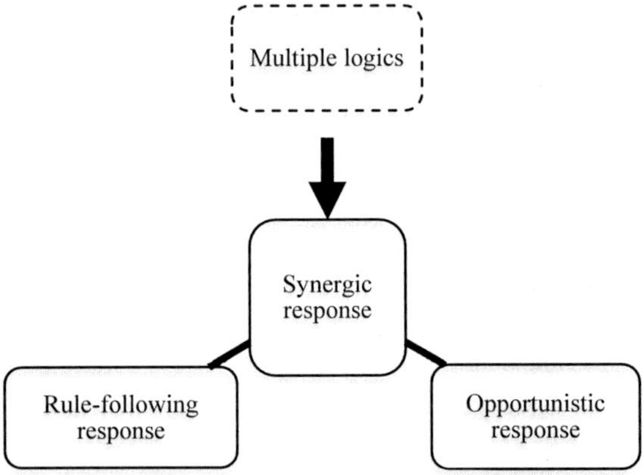


***Opportunistic and rule-following responses***

Some of the interviewees occupied a position that strongly emphasised opportunistic behaviour, in line with predictions of agency theory as developed by Eisenhardt (1989). The opportunistic response was described as being enacted by employees who are familiar with the logics prescribed in the system and who sometimes make desperate attempts to take advantage of loopholes discovered within the system. On the other hand, employees could also adopt rule-following behaviour, meaning that they optimise the loopholes discovered within the system for the benefit of the organization. In other words, instead of taking advantage of the loopholes, employees provide appropriate justifications for the loopholes for the common good of the organization. This finding corresponds with Pache and Santos's (2013) proposal that individuals might resort to complex responses, such as combination (which refers to blending values, norms and practices prescribed by the multiple logics) and compartmentalisation (which refers to displaying a behaviour compliant with a given logic and rejecting the competing logic, and vice versa), when faced with multiple logics.

However, while this finding was developed from an organizational-level perspective, it contributes to knowledge at the individual-level of analysis.

Moreover, the rule-following response may have been a result of the alignment of employees' identity with organizational identity, which is likely to reduce opportunism and enable positive behaviours, as suggested by Pratt and Foreman (2000). Furthermore, the rule-following synergic response is in line with Pastoriza and Ariño's (2008) theorising that employees learn as they interact and can change their behaviours for the good of the organization; they do not necessarily feel frustrated or betrayed by the organization. Such employees are perceived as stewards of the organization. The theoretical approach here is a generalisation of stewardship theory, which argues that managers' behaviours are aligned with the interests of the principal.

However, a majority of the top management employees from both organizations were strongly of the view that the rule-following response was likely to be displayed by employees with longer service, since they fully identify or are familiar with the logics prescribed within the organization; while those with fewer years of service who have not identified with the logics are likely to display the opportunistic response. Again, this is what we should expect on the basis of Pache and Santos's (2013) theorising that an individual who is a novice with respect to a given logic has no knowledge about it and thus is likely to be detached from its prescriptions. On the other hand, an individual who has identified with a given logic is committed to it "since that individual has not only been socialised into the logic's worldviews but has developed through training and experience" (Pache and Santos, 2013:10). However, whether or not an employees' length of service influences their identification process or responses to organizational hybridity represents yet another gap for future research. Nevertheless, one thing that is glaringly obvious in this study is that employees' identification with logics may play a major role in determining how logics are made sense of, interpreted and responded to.

In summary, the overall findings show that organizational hybridity tends to influence commercial hybrid organizations to the extent it produces various tensions in governance, leadership, culture and intra-organizational relations, as well as provoking both positive and negative behavioural responses from employees. Hence, the research proposition of "*The more extensive the tensions associated with organizational hybridity, the greater the likelihood of negative behavioural responses by employees*" is supported by the findings from both ASL and BPL.

## 7.4 Understanding the Influence of Non-Market-Orientated Logics in Commercial Hybrid Organizations

The data showed that deeply embedded non-market-orientated logics, such as religious logics, emerged as likely to influence employees' behaviour in terms of commitment, honesty and trust in commercial hybrid organizations in Nigeria. However, the data also showed that religious logics might enable self-deceiving variants by employees, especially in justifying morally reprehensible acts that promote unethical behaviours such as bribery and corruption in both commercial hybrid organizations. Exploration of this objective formed part of a strategy aimed at answering the overall research question as well as the supporting research question: *What role does religion play in influencing employees' behaviour and shaping other organizational attributes of commercial hybrid organizations?* The empirical findings in relation to this objective are summarised in Table 24.

Religion emerged as a dominant institution that plays a unique role in influencing the behaviours of actors in Nigerian society (see Section 2.4.3 Applicability of institutional logics in non-Western society: The case of Nigeria); a situation recognised by the tacit acceptance of religion within contemporary organizations in the Nigerian institutional environment, as suggested by Mazumdar and Mazumdar (2005). It is also important to note that data showed that religious logics were notably promoted by the family logic at BPL. The explanation for this may borrow from Tomes's (1985) insight that religion is so deeply embedded within some societies that it forms part of family values, personal values and culture, to an extent where it may be almost impossible to separate religious values from family or personal values. Hence, this leads to the following research proposition:

**Proposition 4:** *The stronger employees' affiliations to religious logics, the greater the influence of such logics on employees' behaviour and trust in commercial hybrid organizations.*

**Table 24: Summary of Empirical Findings Associated with Understanding the Influence of Non-Market-Orientated Logics on Commercial Hybrid Organizations**

| **Proposition 4:**<br>The stronger employees' affiliations to religious logics, the greater the influence of such logics on employees' behaviour and trust in commercial hybrid organizations | | | |
|---|---|---|---|
| **Supporting question** | **Summary of empirical findings** | **Data from ASL** | **Data from BPL** |
| What role does religion play in influencing employees' behaviour and shaping other organizational attributes of commercial hybrid organizations? | ➢ Non-market-orientated institutional logics, such as religious logics, are likely to play a role in influencing positive behaviours in terms of commitment, honesty and trust.<br>➢ Religious logics are likely to develop self-deceiving variants that promote unethical behaviours, such as bribery and corruption in commercial hybrid organizations. Other paradoxical effects are possible. | ➢ Religious logics may have influenced honest behaviours by some employees of ASL.<br>➢ Religious logics may have influenced the acceptance of unethical behaviour by some employees of ASL. | ➢ The dominant family logic may have fostered religious and philanthropic logics within the organization, which played a role in promoting employees' commitment, honesty and trust in BPL.<br>➢ Religious logics may have enabled the acceptance of unethical behaviour by employees of BPL. |

### 7.4.1 The tacit acceptance of religion in the commercial hybrid organizations

Institutions such as families, states, religion and the professions prescribe logics that shape individual and group behaviours in societies where they are dominant, as suggested by Friedland and Alford (1991) and Thornton et al. (2012). Even though religious logics were not conspicuously engraved in the corporate documents and policy statements, the data from both ASL and BPL pointed to the acceptance and influence of these logics within both organizations. Drawing on a study by PEW Research Center (2010) on the influence of religion on individuals' behaviours in Nigeria, it was not surprising that a majority of the interviewees from both ASL and BPL declared the importance of their faith, and spiritual and religious affiliations by making references to "God", "religious values", "personal values" and "Christianity" during the course of the interviews. This perception corresponds with studies by Friedland and Alford (1991), Thornton et al. (2012) and Omeje (2006) about religion and its influence on actors' behaviours. According to Friedland and Alford (1991), religion is one of the core institutions that provides prescriptions that form a basis for individuals' lives and as such its influence is deeply rooted. This research made it clear that the influence of religion in the commercial hybrid organizations can be observed throughout the organizational culture, governance, leadership and employees' behaviour. These are now discussed in turn.

#### 7.4.1a The influence of religion on organizational culture

In line with the definitions used by Cash and Gray (2000:127) religion was conceptualised as any institutionalised spirituality or strongly held values that assume the existence of supernatural entities. Therefore, the use of words such as "God", "Christianity", "spiritual values" and "personal values" were considered as references to religious convictions during data analysis for both organizations. The data showed a prominent influence of religious logic (although as a peripheral logic) on the organizational culture of BPL, which informed the reflection of "humility", "empathy", "philanthropy" and "charity" in its core values. The majority of the interviewees were strongly of the view that this conjuncture was a result of the chairman/CEO's strong affiliations with religion. Moreover, there were suggestions that the chairman/CEO's dual role as the majority owner and CEO enabled him to act as a carrier of religious logic into the organization. Since the chairman/CEO owns the business and makes all the strategic business decisions within it, his deeply integrated religious values were likely to be reflected in its core values, even under adverse circumstances.

An example from the literature is relevant here: Weaver and Agle's (2002) study showed how the CEO of Malden Mills cited his religious convictions among the reasons why he continued paying his employees even after the factory burned down. This suggests that religion may have informed the benevolent culture at Malden Mills. In a similar fashion, data from the current study showed the perception that the emphasis on integrity, honesty and benevolence towards stakeholders, which marks the philosophical stance and culture of BPL, are directly derived from the chairman/CEO, as suggested by BT6. This finding is consistent with assertions by Day (2005) and Wagner-Marsh and Conley (1999) on religion/spirituality in the workplace. Moreover, it echoes the insight of Tracey et al.'s (2014) assertion that organizational members do not set aside their religious values and beliefs when they become employees.

In a religious society, the workplace cannot be untouched by religious influences. Wagner-Marsh and Conley (1999) found that organizations committed to spirituality (religion) tend to be extremely open in the declarations of their philosophical commitment to their employees and anyone else with whom they do business. These organizations placed quality and service first in their organizational goals, while also being profitable and competitive. Such a quality-centred approach is detectable on BPL's website: "The primary strategic goal of the organization is to offer an exceptional combination of superior quality and value…achieved through well researched, innovative and efficient production methods."

The data from ASL were very different. The interview data showed the perception that since the decision-making authority was centralised with a group of individuals (the board of directors and executive management team) with diverse motives and religious affiliations, rather than with an individual, their respective religious prescriptions were unlikely to permeate through the organization's culture. In other words, the formalised bureaucratic structure of ASL made it impossible for religious logic to influence the prescribed organizational culture. Nor did ASL's corporate documents give any hint of the broadly religious logics discussed by, for example, Wagner-Marsh and Conley (1999). Overall, data suggested that the influence of religion on organizational culture is likely to be more prominent if power rests with an individual rather than a group of individuals.

### 7.4.1b The influence of religion on governance

Regarding the influence of religion on the governance of commercial hybrid organizations, a majority of the interviewees from BPL painted the chairman/CEO's governance role in the light of what Nash (1994) depicted as the perception of many religious individuals. According to Nash (1994), self-identified religious CEOs typically assume that their religious commitments guide their business decisions. Consistent with Nash's (1994) argument, the data showed a belief among the interviewees that the self-identification of the chairman/CEO of BPL as a Christian may have informed his adoption of an organic governance structure that makes him accessible to the lower-level employees, instead of the adoption of a bureaucratic structure that isolates employees. This stance of the chairman/CEO was translated as "being humble" and "being a brother's keeper" by a majority of the interviewees. A religious leader is acclimatised to certain values in the service of which he is both constrained and enabled to serve others, as suggested by Fry (2003) and Neal and Vallejo (2008). Moreover, this finding is consistent with the servant leadership philosophy, which theorises that good leaders put other people's needs above their own and in that way ensure that other people's needs are being served (Greenleaf, 1977).

Of course, all governance arrangements come with a cost: Jensen and Meckling (1992) argued that a dual ownership and control structure could be disadvantageous as the impartiality of the board is compromised when the CEO is also the chairman of the board of directors. The data from BPL provided support for this finding. By contrast, the data showed no support for the influence of religion on ASL's governance. Perhaps this may be a result of the ownership structure of the organization, which is at least ostensibly owned by multiple shareholders since it is listed on the NSE. If this is the case, it makes sense that ownership and control are separated, to ensure effective monitoring and control of employees and to maximise shareholders' investments.

### 7.4.1c The influence of religion on leadership style/structure

Furthermore, the data showed that religion is likely to influence the leadership approach of commercial hybrid organizations. In fact, data from BPL showed a strongly supported view that the chairman/CEO's self-perception as a religious individual informed the servant leadership style emphasised within the organization. Because of the chairman/CEO's strong allegiance to religion, it was held that religious logic is seamlessly carried into the organization and underlies the adoption of approaches such as "open-door policies", which allow him to listen to his employees and, in this elementary and indispensable way, to serve them; for example, "We had breakfast with the CEO this morning; he is open for discussions freely" (BT6). In other words, he serves God by serving others.

This is consistent with previous studies by Fry (2003) and Day (2005). According to Fry (2003), a leader who has absorbed and integrated Christian values can be expected to embody a degree of humility, which allows him to be free and open with those he leads. This finding is somewhat consistent with a study by Chaston and Lips-Wiersma (2014). In their study on spiritual leadership, they found that the spiritual values of the leader fostered empathetic and participative leadership, which resulted in a trusted working relationship between the leader and followers within the organization. This is in line with Sendjaya and Sarros's (2002) account of the servant leadership philosophy. These writers give great weight to the Christian scriptures, in particular on Christ's actions in washing his disciples' feet, symbolically taking on the role of the servant. Since the chairman/CEO of BPL is a self-identified Christian who regards his religious prescriptions as a basis for his actions, it is not unreasonable to suppose that he may have drawn his leadership style from Jesus's biblical example. Such a relationship between leadership style and core religious commitments suggest that the source of a servant leader's motivational base lies in deeply held beliefs, values and spiritual insights. Furthermore, there were suggestions that the chairman/CEO perceived his job as a higher calling from God, along lines described by Nash (1994), and that he saw this calling as inconsistent with poor business practice, as suggested by BT1.

These views are important because they provide a direct link between the chairman/CEO's exemplary leadership style and his religious values. More generally, the findings are consistent with Wagner-Marsh and Conley's (1999:293) insight that "a sense of higher purpose without ego" is a dominant attribute of religion-driven leaders. This suggests that the chairman/CEO holds his religious beliefs so sacred, with such respect, that they can form a sort of fixed point that anchors his behaviour within and outside the organization. At the same time, there were suggestions that the chairman/CEO's religious integration with work is good for business, as suggested by Toney and Oster (1998). Overall, data from BPL provided support for this finding. By contrast, no evidence supporting analogous results came to light in data from ASL. This again may be as a consequence of the ownership or leadership structure of ASL, which is essentially a formal structure, making it impossible for religious or personal values to influence the already scripted and controlled system. Nevertheless, future research may be required to contribute to the understanding of the influence of religion on the leadership, governance and organizational culture of commercial hybrid organizations.

### 7.4.1d The influence of religion on employees' behaviours

The data showed that religion may play an important role in influencing employees' behaviours by shaping the way they construct their reality in environments where a particular institution is dominant, as suggested by Brotheridge and Lee (2007), Day (2005), Friedland and Alford (1991), and Mazumdar and Mazumdar (2005). The data derived from both organizations showed that religion is likely to influence employees' behaviour and trust in commercial hybrid organizations, both negatively and positively. Religion was found to influence positive behaviours such as "commitment" and "honesty" through identification with the religious values espoused within the organization. This is in line with Weaver and Agle's (2002) insight that religion could influence actors' behaviour through identification. However, data also showed that religion might contribute to "unethical behaviours". These behavioural consequences, positive and negative, are now discussed in turn.

***The influence of religion on employees' commitment***

The data suggest that religion might positively influence employees' behaviour to the extent of generating employee identification. Here, the term 'identification' refers to "an individual's sense of oneness or belongingness with an organization" (Puusa and Tolvanen, 2006:30) or "the degrees to which members define [themselves] by the same attributes that [they] believe define the organization" (Dutton et al., 1994). In other words, it relates to the relationship between an employee and the organization, based on the core values of the organization and how well the employees identify with them (Shockley-Zalabak et al., 2010; Puusa and Tolvanen, 2006; Besharov, 2014; Albert and Whetten, 1985). Identification emerged from the data as a connection based upon congruity perceived by employees between the organization's core values and values they recognised as their own, and its importance in this study cannot be overemphasised.

In the case of BPL, for example, data showed that the employees assessed the values prescribed within it and compared them with the values to which they felt a strong personal attachment. Identification with the prescribed values, regardless of whether these were part of their own religious world view or not, were held not only to trigger their commitment to the organization but also to indirectly strengthen their trust in the organization in the long run.

The data from the interviews also unveiled a strongly held view that individual allegiance to religion may have facilitated identification with similar values within the organization and thus increased commitment to it. This is consistent with Pache and Santos's (2013) insight that when individuals come to accept the relationships between values, which constitute a logic in this sense, they are led to identify with these relationships in the strong sense of perceiving themselves as one with the logic, as indissolubly linked to its prescriptions. This suggests that identification with values similar to their own, such as "integrity", "humility" and "empathy", enabled the employees to remain committed to the organization, as these values provided a basis for action consistent with the logics they are strongly affiliated to as individuals. This finding lends support to Barrett's (2009) conjecture that employees are more likely to stay with an organization that is in alignment with their own deepest values. However, data showed that employees' commitment might also deteriorate if, for some reason, they cease to identify with the logic in question; this has been suggested by Day (2005) and Vandenberghe (2011). However, while BPL showed support for this finding, ASL showed no such relationship.

### *The influence of religion on employees' honesty*

The data from both case studies show that religion might also influence employees' behaviour by promoting honesty. Religious affiliations typically prescribe various behavioural expectations from their members such as honesty and responsibility, which guide their daily behaviours outside the place of worship, as Day (2005) and Westerman et al. (2013) have observed. Therefore, when an individual identifies with a religion, he/she is likely to accept the expectations prescribed by the religion, as demonstrated by some of the interviewees. In the case of BPL, some of the employees reported choosing to be honest at work as a result of their religious self-identification, as well as their identification with the organization's core values of honesty and integrity, which are in any case similar to their religious prescriptions, as suggested by Farrell and Knight (2003). This suggests that employees' identification with BPL's core values of honesty and integrity reinforced their ability to remain honest within the organization. Thus, in this case, religious values played a role in influencing employees' ability to remain honest at work through identification with similar values prescribed within the organization – as well as perhaps by directly promoting honest behaviour. This finding aligns with Wagner-Marsh and Conley's (1999) assertion that religion may influence socially constructed positive behaviours, such as honesty (see Section 2.5.3 Types of institutional logics embodied by commercial hybrid organizations).

This finding gains support from Neal and Vallejo's (2008) theory that identifying with similar values promotes behaviour that reaffirms the values and shared mission within the organization. However, data from ASL articulated this point differently. Some of the interviewees who had strong affiliations to religion reported choosing to activate their religiously prescribed behaviours within the organization, irrespective of the contradictions it created with the values prescribed within the organization. Specifically, the data highlighted the tacit acceptance of dishonesty as one of the contradictions experienced by employees with strong affiliations to religion. Undeterred by such contradictions, these employees choose to use religious prescriptions to guide their behaviours. Inevitably, such choices triggered some level of resistance to authority, as suggested in AM8's statement: "I am not lying anymore." Thus, employees who self-identified as religious at ASL were likely to have experienced difficulties in identifying with contradictory values prescribed within the organization and this may well have resulted in the display of behaviour that would be deviant in the organization's terms. The overall data makes it hard to disagree with Tracey et al.'s (2014) suggestion that religion is a fundamental source of identity with unique dynamics. The data from both organizations provided support for this finding.

***The influence of religion on unethical behaviour***

As well as these positive outcomes, the data showed potentially dysfunctional consequences of religion on employees' behaviour. Though some previous studies, such as Weaver and Agle (2002), demonstrated a positive relationship between religion and ethical behaviour, the connection between religion and unethical behaviour remains unclear in the literature. However, data from the current study showed that religion and unethical behaviour might be linked, especially with regard to bribery and corruption. There was a strong suggestion that the presence of religious logics within both ASL and BPL created an environment where religion was used as an excuse for the acceptance of unethical behaviours in the form of bribery and corruption. Since corruption is deeply embedded in the Nigerian institutional environment, there is sense in the argument that it cannot be avoided while doing business in the country, as suggested by Ezekwesili (2011), Pierce (2006), and Osaghae and Suberu (2005). The above statements illustrate the extent to which corruption is prominent in the Nigerian institutional environment. This is a milieu in which accepting to give/take bribes, as well as engaging in corrupt practices, might be the only way for organizations to survive.

Unfortunately, employees who are strongly affiliated to religious logic are the same employees who engage in these corrupt acts on behalf of the organizations. They may then have no other recourse than to undertake some religiously symbolic action: "praying to God". Recourse to "praying to God" highlights an interesting cultural strategy: the need is felt to present the situation to the transcendent for judgement while perpetrating the act. Therefore, in this situation, religion is used as a coping mechanism and a means of transferring the problem-solving responsibility to God, while the act is being perpetrated by the employees, as suggested by Day (2005). This finding suggests that certain actions such as deferring, which gives God the problem-solving responsibility, are adopted as coping mechanisms by employees who self-identify as religious. Since corruption is deeply rooted within Nigeria, these employees have to accept it too, while praying to the transcendent to intervene.

However, a few of the interviewees from both organizations represented a view that favoured mentally isolating their religious values to achieve organizational goals. For example, statements like "going philosophical", doing "the needful" to get results and "God is the rewarder" emerged from the data as mechanisms for isolating religious values. This suggests that God is acknowledged as "the rewarder", while the importance of doing "the needful" is dwelt upon. From these statements, it is evident that self-identified religious employees may come very close to using their religion to justify their unethical behaviours.

Using phrases such as "the needful" indicates a clear denial and avoidance of speaking the truth, in a bid to isolate religious values from reality. Therefore, although employees may be aware that their actions contradict the prescriptions of their religion, they still go ahead to commit these actions, believing they are doing their jobs as employees, because every employee is obligated to contribute to the achievement of organizational goals no matter the circumstances, as suggested by AT2. Such Machiavellian realism is not automatically to be rejected, in business or elsewhere; the alternative idea that truthfulness may never be compromised for the greater good is just not always practical, nor will people believe it if you tell them that is your policy.

A parallel difficulty surfaces in the context of trust. It is not wise to trust anyone 100%, as Rosaci et al. (2012) pointed out when they argued that trust can morph into blind faith, which could leave the trustor in a state of satisfied ignorance even as the trustee fails to perform as expected. Moreover, Yip and Schweitzer (2015) also argued that trust could enable exploitation and unethical behaviour, especially when trust is misplaced. This may be the case with the employees at BPL, as a majority of them claimed that they have a high level of trust for the chairman/CEO due to his religious convictions, even though they may be strategically taken advantage of, as suggested by Yip and Schweitzer (2015).

All in all, the data show that non-market-orientated logics, such as religious logics, are likely to influence employees' behaviours in commercial hybrid organizations. This influence could be positive in terms of promoting trust, commitment and honesty, as well as negative in terms of enabling the acceptance of unethical behaviour. Hence, the research proposition of "*The stronger employees' affiliations to religious logics, the greater the influence of such logics on employees' behaviour and trust in commercial hybrid organizations*" is true. The overall data from both ASL and BPL provided support for this finding.

## 7.5 Understanding the Implications of Organizational Hybridity for Employees' Trust in Commercial Hybrid Organizations

The overall data showed both negative and positive consequences of organizational hybridity for employees' trust in commercial hybrid organizations. The data from both ASL and BPL provided support for these findings. Regarding the positive implications, the data from the interviews yet again unveiled a view consistent with Pache and Santos's (2013) insight that when individuals come to accept the relationships between values, which constitute a logic in this sense, they are led to identify with these relationships in the strong sense of perceiving themselves as one with the logic (see Section 7.4.1d). In other words, when employees identify with familiar logics, especially non-market-orientated logics such as religious and family logics embodied by commercial hybrid organizations, their trust in the organization is likely to increase. This results in a progressive behavioural response as illustrated in Figure 19.

On the other hand, the data showed that if employees are unable to identify with, or see themselves as one with, the multiple logics embodied by commercial hybrid organizations due to the contradictory values they prescribe, the employees' trust in the organization is likely to decrease. This results in a retrogressive behavioural response as illustrated in Figure 20. This negative implication is further supported by the insight that the primary cause of extensive tensions in hybrid organizations is the embodiment of conflicting/contradictory logics (Besharov and Smith, 2014). Hence, this leads to the following research proposition:

**Proposition 2:** *The greater the tensions produced by multiple logics, the less likely it becomes that employees of commercial hybrid organizations will trust their employers.*

Furthermore, there were suggestions from the data that organizational hybridity may also foster both trust and distrust in the same relationship, as theorised by Saunders et al. (2014). However, due to time limitations, this finding was not explored further. Extensive research is required to understand how this may occur within commercial hybrid organizations. The empirical findings in relation to this objective are summarised in Table 25. Exploration of this objective formed part of a strategy aimed at answering the overall research question as well as the supporting research question: *How does organizational hybridity affect the level of employees' trust in commercial hybrid organizations?* These findings are extensively discussed next.

**Table 25: Summary of Empirical Findings Associated with Understanding the Implications of Organizational Hybridity for Employees' Trust in Commercial Hybrid Organizations**

| **Proposition 2:**<br>The greater the extent of tensions produced by multiple logics, the less likely it becomes that employees of commercial hybrid organizations will trust their employers | | | |
|---|---|---|---|
| **Supporting question** | **Summary of empirical findings** | **Data from ASL** | **Data from BPL** |
| How does organizational hybridity affect the level of employees' trust in commercial hybrid organizations? | ➢ Organizational hybridity is likely to have both positive and negative implications for employees' trust in commercial hybrid organizations. Organizational hybridity is likely to foster either a high level of employees' trust in commercial hybrid organizations through identification with embodied logics, or distrust as a result of extensive tensions.<br>➢ Organizational hybridity is likely to trigger both retrogressive and progressive behavioural responses by employees.<br>➢ Religion is likely to play a unique role in influencing the construction of employees' trust in commercial hybrid organization. | ➢ Organizational hybridity may have caused levels of employees' trust to decrease.<br>➢ Lack of identification with embodied logics may have promoted distrust.<br>➢ Organizational hybridity may have triggered retrogressive behavioural responses at ASL due to extensive tensions. | ➢ Organizational hybridity may have fostered trust in BPL through identification.<br>➢ Identification with embodied non-market-orientated logics, especially religious logics, may have promoted employees' trust in BPL.<br>➢ Organizational hybridity may have triggered progressive behavioural responses at BPL. |

### 7.5.1 Positive implications of organizational hybridity for employees' trust

On this point, the overall perception of trust by the interviewees fell under four themes: "competence", "integrity", "benevolence" and "job security". This is consistent with the definition of trust in the literature. In fact, competence, integrity and benevolence are consistent with the theorising by Mayer et al. (1995) on organizational trust, while job security is in conformity with Rosaci et al.'s (2012) dimensions of trust. Even though there have been suggestions by Karré (2011) and Pache and Santos (2010) that organizational hybridity may generate tensions such as "conflicting messages" and "conflicting expectations" that could diminish employees' trust due to inconsistent values prescribed by the embodied multiple logics, the data showed that identifying with the non-market-orientated logics (family, philanthropic and religious logics) embodied by BPL may have served to produce a sense of "mutual sense of mission", "commitment" and "trust", resulting in low employee turnover as suggested by BT1. The above finding is illustrated in Figure 19.

This suggests that BPL is trusted because employees can make sense of, interpret and identify with the values (integrity, humility, empathy, charity, honesty, trust) prescribed within the organization by the chairman/CEO, which they consider to be similar to deeply held values of their own. However, it highlights an element of vulnerability, since some fragility must be ascribed to a situation in which any unjustifiable act could turn the existing employees' trust to distrust, as suggested by Jones and George (1998). On the face of it, however, these findings are consistent with Foreman and Whetten's (2002) theory that employees' identification with shared values increases commitment to the organization.

Also, the situation at BPL is consistent with Fry's (2003) assertion that an organization's leader with a religious identity may establish a culture with mutual understanding and trust, which enables employees to give up selfish goals and remain committed. Furthermore, it also supports Bachmann and Inkpen's (2011:285) conceptualisation of how an institution (institutional logics), which in this case is religion, acts "like a personal third-party guarantor [and is] capable of reducing the risk that a trustee will behave untrustworthily, allowing the trustor to make the leap of faith and invest trust in a relationship". Bachmann and Inkpen's (2011) argument may be helpful in explaining why the employees of BPL allowed themselves to be vulnerable to the organization, believing that the chairman/CEO who shares similar "inherent" (religious) values with them will not go against the institutional logic that he is strongly affiliated to. However, even though Bachmann and Inkpen's (2011) study was focused on community norms, and professional and legal arrangements, they neglected how the institutional basis of trust is formed by actors. Thus, this study extends knowledge on institutionally based trust by highlighting the importance of religion in the construction of trust. While data from BPL provided support for this finding, data from ASL showed no support for it.

Figure 19: Progressive Behavioural Process

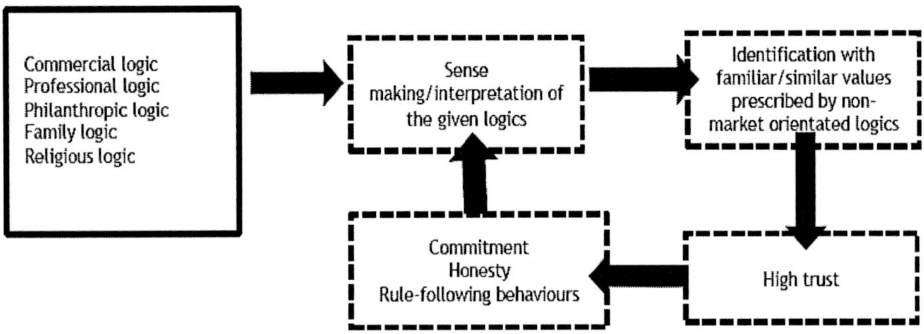


## 7.5.2 Negative implications of organizational hybridity for employees' trust

Contrary to the data derived from BPL, data from ASL showed that extensive tensions generated by organizational hybridity may foster employees' distrust in commercial hybrid organizations, as speculated by Karré (2011) and Pache and Santos (2010). In fact, the data showed that the embodiment (meaning the inclusion or adoption of multiple logics in the organizational functioning) of professional and commercial logics triggered extensive tensions at ASL resulting in employees' distrust. This finding deviates from Besharov and Smith's (2014) conjecture that both logics could support rather than contradict each other due to the consistency in the values they prescribe, as discussed in Chapter 2.

Data showed that employees' strong affiliations to professional logic or commercial logic produced "value disjuncture" as employees who were strongly affiliated to the former logic rejected some of the unfamiliar values prescribed by the latter logic, leading to extensive conflicts and tensions within the organization. Consequently, the organization's core values were interpreted as "distrustful", having "no integrity" and were seen as leading to "high employee turnover" as employees who could no longer cope with the conflicts and tensions resigned, as suggested by AM11. This finding is supported by Gillespie and Dietz's (2012) thesis that trust could be unintentionally damaged during many interactions within organizations. Data from ASL points strongly to the view that employees' trust could have been unintentionally damaged as a result of various interactions between management and employees in an attempt to balance the multiple logics embodied by the organization. An example of this is when the firm allowed employees to lie to customers in an effort to maintain the organization's professional identity, which may have influenced AM8's perception of the organization as untrustworthy and dishonest.

Moreover, there was a strong perception that distrust lay at the root of subsequent retrogressive behavioural responses by employees within the organization. This suggests a retrogressive behavioural cycle, as illustrated in Figure 20. In other words, employees may experience identity distress as a result of tensions, which diminishes their trust in the organization. Employees caught in this cycle become insubordinate, disengaged from work and opportunistic, and in the long run they resign, which could affect the overall effectiveness and performance of the organization. Distrust could breed destructive behaviours, negating any desire to contribute to the productivity of the organization, as suggested by Shockley-Zalabak et al. (2010). Such possibilities highlight the need to gain/sustain employees' trust in commercial hybrid organizations, as proposed by AM12. Hence, the research proposition of "*The greater the tensions produced by multiple logics, the less likely it becomes that employees of commercial hybrid organizations will trust their employers*" is true.

In summary, this study confirms Karre's (2011) and Pache and Santos's (2010, 2013) speculations regarding the implications of organizational hybridity for employees' trust. However, while organizational hybridity may trigger employees' distrust in commercial hybrid organizations, it was found that organizational hybridity might foster employees' trust by their identification with non-market-orientated logics, which may benefit commercial hybrid organizations. The data from both ASL and BPL provided support for this finding.

Figure 20: Retrogressive Behavioural Cycle

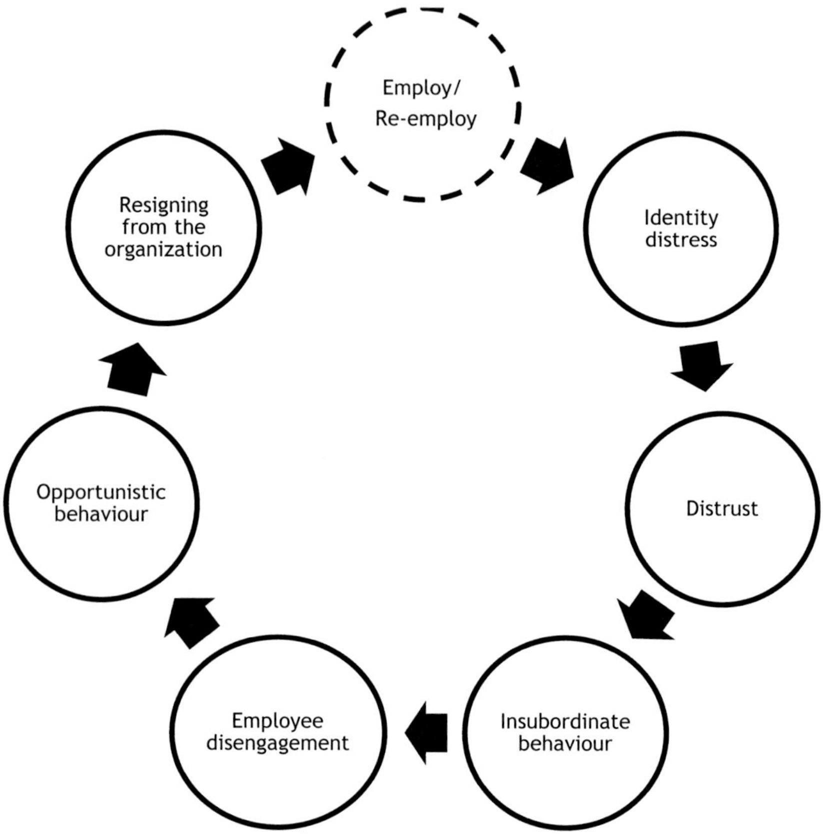


### 7.5.3 The role of religion in the construction of employees' trust

The role of religion in this study cannot be overemphasised. The data showed that religion played a role in influencing not only positive employee behaviour but also negative behaviour. For example, a few of the interviewees at ASL took the view that their strong affiliations to religion influenced their decision to "stop lying to customers". However, at the same time, there is evidence of the tacit acceptance of unethical business practices by religiously motivated employees (AM8 and AM11); a conflictual situation that may have triggered their enactment of deviant behaviours within the organization. Thus, their religious beliefs may have informed their intolerance of unethical (dishonest) values, and in so doing, may have triggered their "lack of identification" with those values and subsequent "distrust". However, there are also indications that some employees may separate the prescriptions of their religion from their work. Also, the data showed no direct relationship between religion and employees' trust in ASL, which could have fostered negative behaviours and been detrimental to the construction of trust.

On the other hand, data from BPL showed a direct relationship between religion and trust. This is based on the identification demonstrated by employees with religious logics prescribed by the chairman/CEO. However, there were suggestions that the high trust placed on the chairman/CEO by the employees may have been fostered by shared inherent spiritual values rather than mere institutionalised prescriptions offered by religion. However, this creates an avenue for future research. As stated earlier, identifying with shared values such as humility, integrity, honesty, benevolence and empathy, which the interviewees argued were supported by the chairman/CEO's religious convictions, formed the basis of employees' commitment and trust in the organization, as suggested by BT6. Moreover, engaging in communal religious rituals, such as "praying during meetings", facilitated the reaffirmation of shared values and beliefs, and this tended to reinforce employees' commitment to and trust in the organization.

This finding lends considerable support to Sosis's (2005) observation that religious rituals can signal trustworthiness, stability and harmony, even to non-group members. However, at this point, it is still unclear whether employees would give the same level of trust to a leader who is not one of their own co-religionists. Future research would need to explore this gap. Nonetheless, based on these findings, religion is likely to play a role in the construction of employees' trust in commercial hybrid organizations.

### 7.5.4 The role of identification in the construction of employees' trust

Like Besharov's (2014) study, identification played a major part in determining how employees of both ASL and BPL interpreted and responded to the multiple logics prescribed within the organizations. As the cases show, employees' identification with values emphasised by the non-market-orientated logics espoused within BPL informed their commitment to and trust in the organization; this is very much along the lines of the perception of oneness between employees and logics, as suggested by Pache and Santos (2013). In other words, employees of BPL are committed to the organization, since their deeply held values are reflected as core values of the organization. This echoes the observation of Shockley-Zalabak et al. (2010) of "identification" as a key driver of organizational trust across various types of organizations; this is also supported by Puusa and Tolyanen's (2006) work on organizational identity and trust, which puts similar weight on shared values.

On the other hand, the lack of identification with prescribed logics may be at the bottom of "employees' distress" and subsequent retrogressive behaviour (see Figure 20), as suggested by a majority of the interviewees from ASL. In fact, the data showed that the lack of identification with the prescribed commercial logic by some of the employees at ASL triggered conflicts, which informants saw as destructive of trust within the organization. For example, the perception emerged that while the board of directors' targets were focused on generating income and shareholder wealth, the executive management team's target was focused on delivering added value to customers through professionalism, which resulted in "conflicting expectations" and the perception of ASL as an organization with "no integrity". This finding provides a consistent line of argument with Besharov's (2014) view that dis-identification could arise during interactions with individuals with divergent values.

Thus, the roles of religion and more generally of identification have been shown in this study to be centrally important. However, further research may be needed to understand in detail the role of both identification and religion in the construction of employees' trust and distrust in commercial hybrid organizations. The data from both ASL and BPL provided support for this finding.

## 7.6 Towards Developing Research-Based Recommendations for Sustaining Employees' Trust in Commercial Hybrid Organizations

The overall findings showed that employees of commercial hybrid organizations regard trust as an essential element in their relationship with their employers, which conditions their overall organizational performance. This can be seen as consonant with the insight that trust is "fundamental for bottom line results" (Shockley-Zalabak et al., 2010:21), or as BM9 put the matter: "Trust really improves the activities of every company in the sense that if you trust a company, you will do everything possible as an employee to see there is less waste, you will do everything possible to see there is high productivity, you will do everything possible to even protect the company with your last drop of blood until you leave that place." In such dramatic terms, this informant supports the idea that when there is trust, employees are more committed and keener to take risks for the organizations they work for. This is an idea fielded in the literature by Thorgren and Wincent (2011), Lewicki et al. (1998), and Puusa and Tolvanen (2006), suggesting that trust is a condition of organizational effectiveness. The empirical findings in relation to this objective are summarised in Table 26.

**Table 26: Summary of Empirical Findings Associated with Developing Research-Based Recommendations for Sustaining Employees' Trust in Commercial Hybrid Organizations**

| **Proposition 3:** The greater the employees' trust in commercial hybrid organizations, the more effective the organizational performance | | | |
|---|---|---|---|
| **Supporting question** | **Summary of empirical findings** | **Data from ASL** | **Data from BPL** |
| How can employees' trust in commercial hybrid organizations be sustained for improved effective organizational performance? | ➢ Employees' trust in commercial hybrid organizations is essential for improved effective organizational performance.<br>➢ Employees' trust in commercial hybrid organizations is likely to be sustained through employees' involvement and undistorted/open communication channels. | ➢ There may be the need to regain employees' trust in ASL through employees' involvement, establishment of clear communication channels and a cultural reorientation, to stimulate identification and to achieve effective organizational performance. | ➢ There may be the need for continuous sustenance of employees' trust in BPL through clearer communication channels and continuous involvement, for improved effective organizational performance. |

Exploration of this objective formed part of a strategy aimed at answering the overall research question as well as the supporting research question: *How can employees' trust in commercial hybrid organizations be sustained for improved effective organizational performance?* However, before making recommendations based on the findings (see Section 8.3), the most important preliminary is to highlight the key challenges limiting employees' trust in commercial hybrid organizations before effective solutions can be generated. Hence, this leads to the following research proposition:

**Proposition 3:** *The greater the employees' trust in commercial hybrid organizations, the more effective the organizational performance.*

## 7.6.1 Challenges limiting employees' trust in commercial hybrid organizations

Based on data from ASL and BPL, the lack of clear communication and lack of employees' involvement are the key challenges that are likely to inhibit employees' trust in commercial hybrid organizations. These are discussed in turn next.

### 7.6.1a Lack of clear communication

The data underscores the need to proffer solutions to the communication gap generated by organizational hybridity. One of the common problems of commercial hybrid organizations that emerged from the data is the "lack of clarity" in the communication of the multiple objectives pursued by the organizations, as suggested by Battilana et al. (2012) and Battilana and Lee (2014). Some of the interviewees from ASL maintained that information was not effectively communicated to them, leaving them "conflicted" about which goals to pursue (professional versus commercial goals) and how to pursue them; a situation that clearly implies the need to put in place appropriate and clear communication channels. This suggests that when employees have a clear understanding of management expectations through "undistorted open and honest information channels", they feel a "sense of belonging", and in that way they become "satisfied", "trusting" and "committed" to achieving organizational objectives. This is a state of affairs that shows in the overall performance of the organization, as suggested by AE20.

Therefore, since commercial hybrid organizations are likely to embody multiple logics that may generate tensions due to inconsistencies in the values they prescribe, efforts to ensure that communication gaps are closed, with tasks, goals and objectives clearly defined, could help to dissolve brooding tensions and facilitate the development of employees' trust in the organization. This finding is supported by Shockley-Zalabak et al.'s (2010:14) suggestion that "It is through communication processes that individuals can describe an ideal organizational life." In other words, organizational experience with defective communication processes is always going to be unsatisfactory and less than ideal. The data from both ASL and BPL provided support for this finding.

### 7.6.1b Lack of employees' involvement

In addition to the lack of clear communication, the data pointed to the lack of employees' involvement as another key challenge that may be faced by commercial hybrid organizations. Data affirm Ezekwesili's (2011) view regarding the need for employees' involvement, especially in an unstructured environment where expectations have little institutional protection and in particular where, as in the Nigerian situation, the rights of employees are not duly respected. This suggests that involving employees in decision-making sends a signal that their opinions are valued, and thus triggers a "sense of belonging" and a "sense of shared purpose", which in turn builds trust and contributes to the overall organizational effectiveness, as suggested by BM17. However, if the employees feel that the organization is not keeping to its obligations, a perception of distrust and lack of integrity could set in, which is likely to reflect negatively on the overall effectiveness and performance of the organization. The data from both ASL and BPL provided support for this finding.

## 7.7 The Future of Commercial Hybrid Organizations

The challenges and tensions identified in organizational hybridity have been amply discussed in previous research (Battilana and Lee, 2014; Battilana et al., 2012; Karré, 2011; Besharov and Smith, 2014; Pache and Santos, 2013). The overall empirical findings contribute to knowledge by affirming some of the tensions posed by organizational hybridity, and its implications for employees' behaviour and trust. Furthermore, employees' responses to these tensions could manifest in the form of opportunistic behaviour (Farrell and Knight, 2003), insubordinate behaviour or employee disengagement, which are likely to develop as employees' goals no longer appear to be aligned with the organizations' goals – a situation that could compromise the effectiveness of these organizations (Kahn, 1990; Pache and Santos, 2013; Karré, 2011; Reay and Hinings, 2009; Karré, 2011; Seo and Creed, 2002; Greenwood and Hinings, 1996; Marquis and Lounsbury, 2007; Battilana et al., 2012).

It is evident from this study that technology, innovation and management alone do not guarantee the effectiveness of the hybrid organization; trust is equally important because it facilitates effective performance by employees (Dirks and Ferrin, 2002; Sharkie, 2009). Thus, this study suggests the need to improve employees' trust so as to reap the benefits associated with it by such writers as Dirks and Ferrin (2002), Shockley-Zalabak et al. (2010), Jones and George (1998), Mayer et al. (1995), and Rousseau et al. (1998). At the same time, it is maintained that employees' trust in commercial hybrid organizations can be sustained in line with the findings and recommendations of this study.

The key challenges experienced by employees in interpreting and making sense of multiple logics may be used as a point of departure in defining the problems to be addressed. The main emphasis of these tensions is around "conflicting messages", "conflicting expectations", "value disjuncture", "lack of identification" and "unclear communication channels"; all these are problems that can easily be seen to influence levels of employees' trust in commercial hybrid organizations. Hence, the research proposition of "*The greater the employees' trust in commercial hybrid organizations, the more effective the organizational performance*" is confirmed, at least to the extent that many essential elements militating against trust are also factors counting against effective performance by the organization.

In a positive sense, where employees identify with non-market-orientated logics prescribed within the organization, this is likely to encourage them to trust the organization and remain committed to it, which positively influences overall organizational effectiveness. In other words, the degree to which commercial hybrid organizations can claim to be effective could be related to the level of trust employees have in the organizations; thus, the need arises to sustain employees' trust in commercial hybrid organizations through appropriate mechanisms for effective organizational performance. Hence, the key propositions are supported by empirical data derived from both ASL and BPL. The recommendations from these findings are discussed in Chapter 8.

# CHAPTER 8

# RECOMMENDATIONS AND CONCLUSIONS

## 8.1 Introduction

This final chapter summarises the knowledge and understanding gained from the research process, and also the findings and discussions contained in the preceding chapters. The implications of the findings and evidence-based strategies for improving the effectiveness and performance of commercial hybrid organizations are presented. Finally, the limitations of the study are highlighted and areas for future research re-emphasised.

## 8.2 Summary of the Empirical Findings

This study set out to understand *the implications of organizational hybridity for employees' trust in commercial hybrid organizations*. With this overall aim, the research was directed towards four specific objectives:

1. To explore the influence of organizational hybridity on specific organizational attributes, including governance, organizational culture, leadership and intra-organizational relations of commercial hybrid organizations.
2. To understand the influence of non-market-orientated institutional logics on commercial hybrid organizations.
3. To understand the implications of organizational hybridity for employees' trust in commercial hybrid organizations, with particular attention to those implications having a plausible relationship to organizational effectiveness.
4. To develop research-based recommendations for sustaining employees' trust in the commercial hybrid organizations.

The study began with the primary research question: *What are the implications of organizational hybridity for employees' trust in commercial hybrid organizations?* The supporting research questions were as follows:

1. To what extent does organizational hybridity influence specific attributes of commercial hybrid organizations?
2. What role does religion play in influencing employees' behaviour and shaping other organizational attributes of commercial hybrid organizations?
3. How does organizational hybridity affect the level of employees' trust in commercial hybrid organizations?
4. How can employees' trust in commercial hybrid organizations be sustained for improved effective organizational performance?

The research propositions and gaps were identified through the literature review in Chapter 2. The knowledge gained from the findings of this chapter informed the philosophical framework underpinning the study and the development of the proposed theoretical framework. The theoretical framework comprised the following four key propositions, identified as fundamental for understanding organizational hybridity from an institutional logics perspective and its implications for employees' trust in commercial hybrid organizations:

1. The more extensive the tensions associated with organizational hybridity, the greater the likelihood of negative behavioural responses by employees.
2. The greater the tensions produced by multiple logics, the less likely it becomes that employees of commercial hybrid organizations will trust their employers.
3. The greater the employees' trust in commercial hybrid organizations, the more effective the organizational performance.
4. The stronger employees' affiliations to religious logics, the greater the influence of such logics on employees' behaviour and trust in commercial hybrid organizations.

These key propositions provided the framework for the empirical research, data analysis and discussion of findings. The research context, Nigeria and more specifically Abuja, was explored in Chapter 3. The gaps in knowledge identified in Chapter 2 and Chapter 3 were empirically investigated in this study. The research design and approach to fieldwork and data analysis were explained in detail in Chapter 4. The analysis of the data collected from empirical studies was presented in Chapters 5, 6 and 7. These three chapters provide insights into the tensions experienced within commercial hybrid organizations, as well as how employees made sense of, interpreted and responded to multiple institutional logics. Also, challenges that could compromise the effectiveness of commercial hybrid organizations were discussed in these chapters. Guided by the theoretical framework and research findings, this current chapter proposes three key recommendations for improving the effectiveness and performance of commercial hybrid organizations. Finally, the practical implications of this study, its limitations, the contributions claimed for it, suggested lines of future research and a generalisation of findings are also presented. The overall research findings, as well as the research questions and propositions, are summarised in Table 27.

**Table 27: Summary of Overall Empirical Findings**

| **Key research question:**<br>What are the implications of organizational hybridity for employees' trust in commercial hybrid organizations? | | |
|---|---|---|
| **Supporting research questions** | **Research propositions** | **Research findings** |
| To what extent does organizational hybridity influence specific attributes of commercial hybrid organizations? | The more extensive the tensions associated with organizational hybridity, the greater the likelihood of negative behavioural responses by employees. | ➢ Organizational hybridity is likely to condition flexibility in the adoption of distinctive organizational attributes by commercial hybrid organizations in relation to governance, leadership and organizational culture.<br>➢ Organizational hybridity is likely to trigger various degrees of tension across the core governance, leadership and culture of commercial hybrid organizations.<br>➢ Organizational hybridity is likely to produce behavioural responses both positive (rule-following behaviour) and negative (employee disengagement, opportunism, distress, insubordination, resignation) due to the tensions it presents. |
| What role does religion play in influencing employees' behaviour and shaping other organizational attributes of commercial hybrid organizations? | The stronger employees' affiliations to religious logics, the greater the influence of such logics on employees' behaviour and trust in commercial hybrid organizations. | ➢ Non-market-orientated institutional logics, such as religious logics, are likely to play a role in influencing positive behaviours in terms of commitment, honesty and trust.<br>➢ Religious logics are also likely to develop self-deceiving variants, which promote unethical behaviours such as bribery and corruption in commercial hybrid organizations. Other paradoxical effects are possible. |

| How does organizational hybridity affect the level of employees' trust in commercial hybrid organizations? | The greater the tensions produced by multiple logics, the less likely it becomes that employees of commercial hybrid organizations will trust their employers. | ➢ Organizational hybridity is likely to foster either a high level of employees' trust through identification with embodied logics or distrust as a result of tensions in commercial hybrid organizations.<br>➢ Organizational hybridity is likely to trigger both progressive and retrogressive behavioural responses by employees.<br>➢ Religion is likely to play a unique role in influencing the construction of employees' trust in commercial hybrid organizations. |
|---|---|---|
| How can employees' trust in commercial hybrid organizations be sustained for improved effective organizational performance? | The greater the employees' trust in commercial hybrid organizations, the more effective the organizational performance. | ➢ Employees' trust in commercial hybrid organizations is essential for improved effective organizational performance.<br>➢ Employees' trust in commercial hybrid organizations is likely to be sustained through employees' involvement and undistorted/open communication channels. |

## 8.3 Recommendations for Improving the Effectiveness and Performance of Commercial Hybrid Organizations

The idea that organizational hybridity could be essential in achieving optimum organizational effectiveness through its innovative combinations of multiple logics has gained academic momentum (Kraatz and Block, 2008; Jay, 2013). However, its implications for employees' behaviours and trust, especially in the context of the Nigerian institutional environment, remain underexplored. Thus, this study makes both theoretical and practical contributions to address the gaps identified in the literature (see Section 8.7 Reflections on the Knowledge Gained from the Research). Most importantly, this study addresses a gap in the literature regarding the influence of religious logics in the construction of trust. It shows how religious logics can be used as a basis for employees' behaviours and actions; a conclusion that is easy to draw thanks to the profound embeddedness of such logics in Nigerian life.

Against a background of the literature and in view of the findings from this study, it is possible to conclude that commercial hybrid organizations require constant vigilance because of the high risk of internal tensions and conflicts arising out of, and feeding into, the ways employees make sense of, interpret and respond to multiple logics embodied within these organizations. To manage these tensions and to achieve organizational effectiveness, commercial hybrid organizations may need to put in place processes, structures and mechanisms to ensure that decisions are clearly communicated across the employment hierarchy. This will help to stimulate a mutual sense of purpose, foster identification, and encourage trust, commitment and other positive behaviours associated with organizational hybridity evident in the literature.

However, I also propose that the impacts of the constantly changing institutional environment on commercial hybrid organizations should be assessed, to generate new ideas for managing the tensions posed by organizational hybridity. More specifically, drawing values from non-market-orientated logics, such as religious logics, can help to foster employees' identification, commitment and trust in commercial hybrid organizations. Scholarly investigation of such matters as the influence of non-market-orientated logics, e.g. religious logics, in commercial hybrids can be expected to sharpen debates and possibly provide an incentive for sharpening the effectiveness of commercial hybrid organizations (Tracey et al., 2014).

The overarching recommendation that emerged from the data can be summed up as follows. Trust is an indispensable element of effective organizations; thus, sustaining employees' trust through their involvement, and using clear communication to address them and, where appropriate, to respond to their concerns, are fundamental for improved effective performance of commercial hybrid organizations. This points towards three themes: sustaining employees' trust, employees' involvement and clear communication channels. These themes are essential for managing the tensions posed by hybridity, as well as for the overall performance of commercial hybrid organizations. These desiderata are now discussed in turn.

### 8.3.1 Sustaining employees' trust

Sustaining employees' trust emerged from the data as a legitimate means of coping with the uncertainties posed by institutional complexities in Nigeria (Bachmann, quoted in Kramer, 2006). However, societal factors that have historically hampered the development of the Nigerian economy appear to operate as major constraints on sustaining employees' trust in the Nigerian context, as depicted in Chapter 3. Owing to political, religious, social, cultural and ethical challenges, as well as mediocre organizational processes and a lack of standardised structures and mechanisms as highlighted in this study, the general perception of Nigerian commercial hybrid organizations by their employees is that they are "untrustworthy". For example, the analysis of data from ASL indicates that the existing mechanisms relating to governance, leadership and organizational culture may be insufficient for managing the tensions posed by organizational hybridity. Such insufficiency may lie at the heart of the perception of the organization's processes as "contradictory" or "conflicting", and thus generating concerns regarding the organization's "integrity" and "trustworthiness", which may have contributed to a retrogressive behavioural cycle and high turnover among employees, as suggested by AE18. In contrast, data from BPL showed a rather trustworthy organization as a result of the chairman/CEO's role in the organization. This is because, according to BM7, trust starts with leadership and, in this case, power rests in the hands of a "near-perfect gentleman" whom the employees consider to be trustworthy. However, although data from BPL showed an organization perceived to be rather trustworthy, organizational processes were not viewed as perfect and there were suggestions for their further improvement by the majority of the interviewees. The interviewees recognised the need for increasing employees' trust, taking the view that any unjustifiable act could quickly turn their existing trust to distrust; a view that is in line with Jones and George (1998).

A majority of the interviewees took the view that sustaining employees' trust in the organization could encourage "loyalty", "job satisfaction" and "commitment", which will improve effectiveness and overall organizational performance. This finding is consistent with previous studies on organizational trust. These studies have argued that trust between an organization and an employee is highly beneficial for the employee's workplace attitude, behaviour and overall performance (Dirks and Ferrin, 2002; Mayer et al., 1995; Shockley-Zalabak et al., 2010; Neal and Vallejo, 2008; Jones and George, 1998). Specifically, trust may increase job satisfaction, as suggested by Dirks and Ferrin (2001). This is because, when employees trust organizations, they are more willing to accept the organization's culture (Shockley-Zalabak et al., 2010), take risks, take the mental leap of faith (Möllering, 2001), suspend doubts about the organization and carry out tasks that lead towards the achievement of a common goal (Burke et al., 2007).

However, in the face of behaviour that violates expectations of the company's integrity, as occurred in the case of ASL, verbal promises may be insufficient to regain employees' trust. Substantive actions such as the implementation of appropriate organizational processes and mechanisms may prove to be more useful (Gillespie and Dietz, 2009). Furthermore, the adoption of stringent rules or practice protocols may also turn out to be insufficient, especially in the Nigerian institutional environment where religion prescribes values for individuals' actions and behaviours (Eberl et al., 2015; Friedland and Alford, 1991; Thornton et al., 2012). Therefore, value inconsistencies may need to be addressed directly, as suggested by Sitkin and Roth (1993), before the implementation of practical organizational processes. In addition to the above suggestions, constant cultural reorientation or reform of the organization's pattern of assumptions emerged as a necessary step towards sustaining employees' trust in commercial hybrid organizations:

According to the interviewees, cultural reorientation could help identify value inconsistencies that may be triggering tensions. It is important for commercial hybrid organizations to keep their values under review in the light of changing pressures from the institutional environment as such a review could help prevent misinterpretation of embodied logics. In this way, employees can make sense of what is expected from them, as well as identify with the organization's underlying values, which will encourage trust and commitment to the organization, as suggested by Foreman and Whetten (2002) and Shockley-Zalabak et al. (2010). Training and workshops may occasionally be conducted to ensure all employees are aware of the prescribed multiple logics. For example, data from the interviews showed that it was entirely possible for employees to be unaware of values officially prescribed in the organization, suggesting that for cultural reorientation to take place effectively some training would be needed. Research-based benchmarking tools may be used for evaluating the organizational culture to ensure employees' values are in line with the organization's values.

### 8.3.2 Employees' involvement in decision-making

The involvement of all employees in the decision-making process was perceived as a highly effective strategy for improving the effectiveness of commercial hybrid organizations. As stated earlier, one of the challenges of commercial hybrid organizations may be the inability of employees to identify with the prescribed logics embodied by the organization (Dutton et al., 1994). This problem appeared to relate to the lack of employees' involvement in the decision-making process (Bussing, 2002; Spreitzer and Mishra, 1999); a link that was traceable in the testimonies of a majority of the interviewees from ASL. For example, there were strong indications that employees of ASL made limited or no contribution at all to the overall strategic decisions taken within the organization. This is a situation that is not unreasonable to suppose might have triggered feelings of "disregard", "isolation" and "lack of concern" for employees. Moreover, employees' isolation may have been encouraged by the bureaucratic structure adopted by the organization, which militates strongly against their ability to understand, make sense of or identify with the prescribed logics, leading to "value disjuncture" and "extensive tensions", as suggested by AT3 and AE20.

However, a majority of the interviewees took the view that involving employees in the decision-making process could help generate: a sense of belonging and mutual sense of purpose, which in turn could build employees' trust and commitment to the organization, as suggested by AT6; and shared identification with the values prescribed within the organization, which may help prevent misinterpretations and rejection of prescribed values. Thus, such participatory processes could stimulate positive attitudes and be useful, independently of any financial incentive, for improving employees' commitment and the overall organizational effectiveness of commercial hybrid organizations. This is consistent with Spreitzer and

Mishra's (1999) study. Indeed, Spreitzer and Mishra (1999) argued that involving lower-level employees could increase organizational performance.

Although data from BPL showed a certain degree of employee involvement through participatory leadership, the overall finding suggests that a more systematic or continuous involvement may be required to sustain employees' commitment. In other words, the involvement of employees would automatically strengthen and bring to life their loyalty and commitment to the organizational goals. Various studies have argued about the importance of employees' involvement in strategic decision-making. For example, Freeman's (1984) stakeholder theory suggests a line of argument consistent with that proposed here. Stakeholder theory emphasises the importance of investing in stakeholder relationships, which involves sharing of values with the parties concerned (including employees) and involving them in the strategic decision-making process. Freeman (1984) argued that stakeholders should not only be treated as a means to an end but also be considered as an important part of the organizational life, and thus should not be ignored. Therefore, for commercial hybrid organizations to be effective, there may be an urgent need to involve employees, which may contribute to improving the effectiveness of the organizations in the long run. However, management needs to consider whether such approaches best meet the contextual needs of the employees before implementation (Ji and Dimitratos, 2013).

### 8.3.3 Clear communication channels

The importance of clear communication emerges clearly in this study. The data indicated that the way multiple organizational objectives – which are clearly influenced by multiple logics – are communicated to employees may determine how they make sense of and interpret the institutional logics in question (compare, for example, the testimony of BT2). According to Weick et al. (2005), communication is a central component of sense-making, which draws on resources of language. Thus, to mitigate conflicting messages and expectations, which were shown in Chapter 7 to be strongly corrosive of employees' trust in the organization, clear communication channels should be implemented to ensure that there is undistorted communication across all levels of the employment hierarchy. This makes it possible for lower-level employees to understand clearly the challenges faced by the organization and the rationale for organizational responses, leading – it may be hoped – to the strengthening of employee commitment to the organization. This finding is consistent with other studies (Guzley, 1992; Smidts et al., 2001). Guzley (1992) argued that communicating to employees could positively affect their involvement and loyalty to the organization. This is because a positive communication climate strengthens identification, which provides support for the data in the current study.

However, a lack of identification with prescribed values emerged as the core tension that occurs in commercial hybrid organizations and, as such, more effort should be made by these organizations to communicate their values to employees, including a clear explanation of what the organization is and what it stands for. For example, data from ASL showed that unclear communication of values resulted in a "communication gap" and "conflicting expectations" from employees. Lack of clarity, in this case, seemed to arise from the affiliations of the board and executive members to different logics; a value disjuncture that meant that employees received conflicting messages about what ASL's core values are and what they stand for as an organization. There is reason to believe, therefore, that clear communication across all levels of the employment hierarchy, using properly structured and undistorted channels that are respected by those in authority, as suggested by BT3, BT1 and BT4, may succeed in telling a consistent story that employees can believe – even if such a story has to include multiple value orientations. This may enable the employees across the various levels of the employment hierarchy to understand new challenges faced by commercial hybrid organizations.

Thus, a majority of the interviewees from ASL expressed general dissatisfaction with the communication mechanisms currently in place. The following suggestions emerged from the data: firstly, setting up a standardised communication timeline with feedback mechanisms to ensure that information is clearly sent, received and interpreted by employees without disruption; and secondly, setting up standardised organizational processes with clear objectives and goals to neutralise contradictions. There were signs of lapses in the effectiveness of the organizational processes of both ASL and BPL as a result of a "communication gap", which led the interviewees to suggest the establishment of a proper structural mechanism to reduce contradictions. Furthermore, they suggested that communicating a strong ethical culture, with zero tolerance for corruption, may help to change employees' perceptions of commercial hybrid organizations as being untrustworthy, especially in an institutional environment like Nigeria's where the issue of corruption is endemic.

### 8.3.4 Barriers limiting the future of commercial hybrid organizations

It is imperative to note that using the recommendations outlined above as a point of departure for improving the effectiveness and performance of commercial hybrid organizations is unlikely to succeed without addressing barriers unique to the institutional environment where the organizations are located; for example, the reality of an extreme culture of bribery and corruption in Nigerian society, which was highlighted as the major problem faced by commercial hybrid organizations in this institutional environment. Therefore, it is recommended that commercial hybrid organizations in similar contextual backgrounds should consider bribery and corruption as a fundamental issue that needs to be dealt with from the top to the bottom of the employment hierarchy. This could be achieved by adopting a corruption-proof organizational culture that will resist any form of unethical pressure from the external institutional environment (Bachmann et al., 2015). Indeed, Corruption flourishes on the opportunities we create, therefore commercial hybrid organizations need to avoid creating these opportunities by establishing solid cultures that will not give room for corruption.

## 8.4 Future Research

This study has identified many gaps in previous research in understanding the concept of organizational hybridity and its relationship with organizational trust. In addition, the study has drawn attention to various tensions posed by organizational hybridity across core organizational attributes such as governance, leadership, organizational culture and intra-organizational relations. This has fed into a current debate on the practical and behavioural implications of organizational hybridity for employees' trust in hybrid organizations. The key gaps that have emerged from this study are suggested as a guide for future research. In addition to some of the gaps already mentioned in previous chapters, these shortcomings are summarised under six headings below:

- *Organizational hybridity and individual-level analysis*
    - Very few studies have shown how individuals respond to organizational hybridity and the tensions it presents (Pache and Santos, 2013; Reay and Hinings, 2009; Karré, 2011; Farrell and Knight, 2003). The majority of studies on organizational hybridity are on an organizational-level of analysis and focus on

social enterprises (Besharov and Smith, 2014; Battilana and Lee, 2014; Battilana et al., 2012; Ebrahim et al., 2014; Jäger and Schröer, 2014). Future research may need to explore individual responses to organizational hybridity more widely across the hybrid spectrum, as suggested by Besharov and Smith (2014).

- *Organizational hybridity and trust*
    - Future research could examine the implications of organizational hybridity for individual dispositions to bestow or withhold trust in contexts where commercial hybrid status is an issue. Specifically, research could investigate to what extent employees of conventional commercial organizations can trust a commercial hybrid organization in the framework of an impending merger or acquisition.
    - In a context where religious affiliations feed the multiplicity of logics embedded in a hybrid organization, there may be the need to explore whether a leader whose affiliation differs from that of employees can command their trust to the same extent as one who belongs to the same religious tradition.

- *Organizational hybridity and managerial decision-making*
    - Future research could examine the extent to which multiple institutional logics count in the context of decision-making. Specifically, it could examine how far the beliefs, vocabularies and practices that come into play in the context of boardroom decisions in hybrid organizations reflect deep commitments to multiple logics. Understanding the concept of organizational hybridity requires investigation of such key opportunities to deploy multiple institutional logics.
    - Future research may also need to investigate the extent to which non-market-orientated logics may influence the decisions of directors of commercial hybrid organizations; this is an area that such research should attempt to investigate empirically.
    - Future research may need to investigate further how logics with similar values may enable each other within hybrid organizations.

- *Organizational hybridity, tensions and core organizational attributes*
    - Future research may need to investigate empirically how tensions are experienced in various specific elements of organizational structure, such as leadership and power structure, across various types of hybrid organizations.

- *Organizational hybridity and religion*
    - Future research may need to contribute to the understanding of the influence of religion on the leadership, governance and organizational culture of commercial hybrid organizations.
    - Future research may need to distinguish clearly between religion and spirituality, especially their roles in influencing employees' behaviour and trust relations in contemporary organizations.

- *Organizational hybridity and organizational identification*
    - How far, if at all, the work experiences of employees influence their identification process with the hybrid organization, or their responses to organizational hybridity, creates yet another gap for future research.

## 8.5 Approaches to Generalisation of Research Findings

As stated in Chapter 2, the institutional logics perspective was used as the theoretical underpinning for this study, since employees of commercial hybrid organizations are likely to be influenced by logics prescribed by dominant institutions such as religion, family, community, the capitalist market and profession (Friedland and Alford, 1991; Thornton et al., 2012). This is because individuals use the vocabularies, practices and prescriptions that make up institutional logics as a basis to make sense of the world. However, just like the Western societies depicted by Friedland and Alford (1991), non-Western societies are also formed and shaped by various institutional logics derived from dominant institutions, which infuse actors' social realities with values and meaning. Nigeria, for example, is a country dominated by institutions and institutional logics that are consistent with Friedland and Alford's (1991) conceptualisation. Thus, the theoretical possibility exists of the generalisation of these research findings and recommendations based on the institutional logics perspective. However, it is also very important to note that the generalisability of findings derived from this study must be treated with caution owing to the specific contextual needs of commercial hybrid organizations and the various institutional logics that are dominant in the Nigerian environment. Nevertheless, it is not unreasonable to suppose that empirical findings related to trust, effectiveness and performance of commercial hybrid organizations could be applied to developing countries with similar geographical, social, political, cultural, economic and environmental contexts.

## 8.6 The Significance of the Study and its Contribution to Knowledge

The overall empirical findings from this study have made noteworthy contributions to both theory and practice. The findings from this study contribute to knowledge of organizational hybridity, institutional logics and organizational trust. The research contributions are summarised in Table 28. The significance of the study and its contributions to knowledge are summed up as follows. Firstly, this study advances knowledge on organizational hybridity by focusing on another spectrum of hybrid organizations, *commercial hybrid organizations*, which could help gain research-based knowledge towards understanding the concept and its implications for employees' behaviour, as well as developing strategies for the effectiveness and sustainability of these organizations.

Secondly, this study addresses gaps in knowledge in the literature relevant to organizational hybridity by extending on Battilana and Lee's (2014) framework, highlighting governance, leadership, organizational culture and intra-organizational relationships as core organizational attributes in the context of which issues may arise in commercial hybrid organizations. Furthermore, the study addresses the gap in knowledge relevant to Besharov and Smith's (2014) framework regarding how tensions are experienced within hybrid organizations by providing an alternative line of argument focused on understanding how tensions manifest within these organizations (see Section 2.5.4 The coexistence of multiple institutional logics). Moreover, it argues that the context, power balance and leadership structures of commercial hybrid organizations contribute to the level of tensions experienced within the organizations and how employees make sense of and identify with these logics. Data showed that the bureaucratic leadership structure of ASL, for example, encouraged the isolation of employees, which contributed to their lack of identification with the values prescribed within the organization and thus fostered extensive tensions.
Thirdly, this study also focuses on the continent of Africa, specifically Nigeria, which is often ignored in management and organizational research. Thus, it addresses a gap in knowledge relevant to understanding the multiplicity of logics; in this case, organizational hybridity in the African context.

Fourthly, the research attempts to revive religion as a non-market-orientated institution that influences aspects of economic activity, including – *among other things* – employees' behaviour and trust, in societies where it is dominant and as such it should not be ignored in organizational research.

The literature on organizational trust fails to take into account key contextual variables, the most significant of which is religion. Thus, this study provides improved understanding of the influence of religion on employees' trust in commercial hybrid organizations.

Finally, this study contributes specifically to knowledge on organizational hybridity by exploring the individual level of analysis (the individual responses to organizational hybridity) and the research methodology can be used for similar studies in similar contextual backgrounds, while future studies can reference the data and information gathered through this research.

**Table 28: Summary of Research Contributions**

| **Key research contributions** |
|---|
| 1. The research addresses gaps in knowledge in literature relevant to organizational hybridity by extending on Battilana and Lee's (2014) framework on hybrid organizing, highlighting governance, leadership, organizational culture and intra-organizational relationships as key attributes through which tensions can be experienced in commercial hybrid organizations. |
| 2. The research addresses gaps in knowledge in literature relevant to organizational hybridity by providing an alternative line of argument to Besharov and Smith's (2014) framework. This research argues that contextual factors as well as the organizational culture, governance and leadership structures of commercial hybrid organizations may contribute to the level of tensions experienced within these organizations. |
| 3. The research attempts to revivify religion as a non-market-orientated institution that influences employees' behaviours and trust in societies where it is dominant, and as such it should not be ignored in organizational research. |
| 4. The literature on organizational trust fails to take into account key contextual variables, the most significant of which is religion. This research provides improved understanding of the influence of religion on employees' trust in commercial hybrid organizations. |
| 5. The research methodology can be used for similar studies in similar contextual background, while future studies can reference the data and information gathered through this research. |

## 8.7 Reflections on the Knowledge Gained from the Research

To understand the implications of organizational hybridity for employees' behaviour and trust in commercial hybrid organizations, the study started off by exploring its influence on five specific organizational attributes (leadership, governance, organizational culture, intra-organizational relations and trust relations). Looking at these attributes enabled the understanding of how the tensions postulated by previous research occur within commercial hybrid organizations, which led to the conclusion that embodying multiple institutional logics may no longer be conceived as sufficient for achieving innovativeness and organizational effectiveness, as suggested by Jay (2013), Karré (2011), and Kraatz and Block (2008). Instead, investing in strategies focused on improving employees' trust may enable commercial hybrid organizations to improve overall organizational effectiveness and performance. In fact, the data showed that for commercial hybrid organizations to remain effective, there is an urgent need to evaluate and sustain employees' trust in the organizations by involving them in the decision-making process, and clearly communicating the organization's values, goals and objectives to avoid misinterpretations.

However, as shown in this study, the tensions experienced across governance, leadership, organizational culture, intra-organizational relations and trust relations of commercial hybrid organizations may be minimal or extensive, which is a result consistent with the conceptualisations of Battilana and Lee (2014), and Besharov and Smith (2014). However, this study has shown that these tensions may also be perceived as contradictory expectations by employees, which may negatively influence their behaviour and trust in the organizations in the long run. Nevertheless, the findings also showed that employees' identification with embodied logics, especially the non-market-orientated logics such as religious logics, may enable them to interpret, make sense of and positively respond to hybrid organizations, even if they are more market focused. This indicates that there may be the need for commercial hybrid organizations to embody non-market-orientated logics peripherally to stimulate employees' identification and foster their trust in the organization. However, further research may be needed to substantiate this conjecture.

Religion emerged from the data as an important institution that contributed to employees' positive responses. For example, the data showed that employees' identification with the religious logics embodied by the chairman/CEO at BPL activated their honesty, commitment and trust in the organization. Regarding the relationship between religion and trust, there were suggestions that the high trust placed on the chairman/CEO by the employees may have been fostered by similarities in shared inherent spiritual values rather than institutionalised prescriptions (religious logics) offered by religion. This calls for further research.

Furthermore, the data showed that religious logics are capable of influencing the leadership style, governance structure and organizational culture of commercial hybrid organizations. However, this may depend on individuals' affiliations to religion and the extent to which they act as carriers of religious logics into the organization. Looking at BPL, for example, the data showed that the chairman/CEO's strong affiliations to family and religious logics, of which he served as a carrier into the organization, might have influenced his servant leadership style, as well as favouring the embodiment of other religiously affiliated logics such as philanthropic logic. Thus, religion should not be ignored in the study of individual-level responses to the multiplicity of logics embedded within organizations, especially in an environment where it is perceived as a dominant institution. The study thus addresses the gap highlighted in the review of the literature regarding the limitation in available studies focused on understanding the influence of religion in contemporary organizations and its influence on employees' behaviour within these organizations.

Furthermore, this study has shown a contrasting line of argument to Besharov and Smith (2014), who theorised dominant hybrid organizations as experiencing minimal conflict (since the embodied logics provide consistent values for action), while contested hybrid organizations experience extensive tensions (since the embodied logics provide contradictory values for actions) (see Figure **4**: The Ideal Types of Hybrid Organizations (Besharov and Smith, 2014). In contrast, this study revealed extensive tensions within ASL (a dominant commercial hybrid organization), while minimal tensions were evidenced in BPL (a contested commercial hybrid organization). This suggests that the degree of conflict over logics experienced within commercial hybrid organizations may be influenced by both contextual factors and deeply embedded institutional logics in the institutional environment where the organization is located. For example, the tacit acceptance of corruption and unethical practices as a socially acceptable way of life in Nigerian society by some of the employees of ASL may have contradicted the professional prescriptions, triggering the outright rejection of professional values by this group of employees. The tensions at ASL may have been potentiated by the way the two allegedly consistent logics were embodied in different elements of the organization and personnel: the board of directors was strongly affiliated to the commercial logic, while the executive management team was strongly affiliated to the professional logic. This resulted in value disjuncture, distrust and extensive tensions experienced within ASL, as both teams set contradictory targets for the employees.

On the other hand, data from BPL showed minimal conflict even though the embodied logics provide inconsistent values for action, which provides a counter-example to Besharov and Smith's (2014) conceptualisation. The data showed that BPL embodied commercial, family and philanthropic logics, which are argued by the literature to prescribe contradictory values – a recipe for extensive tensions (Besharov and Smith, 2014). However, there were strong suggestions that the leadership/balance of power in the governance of both commercial hybrid organizations may have influenced the degree of tensions experienced across core organizational attributes. The justification for this is that tensions were easily resolved at BPL since power was vested in an individual – the chairman/CEO – instead of a group of individuals with different interests and motivations.

The variation between findings from this study and earlier conceptualisations of organizational hybridity highlights the inadequacies surrounding the constant use of social enterprise as a case study for understanding the dimensions of hybridity. Thus, this study addresses this gap by advancing knowledge on organizational hybridity through the study of another spectrum of hybrid organization: the commercial hybrid organization. Moreover, the context of study – Nigeria – addresses the gap constituted by the limited attention to Africa in management and organizational research, as noted by Zoogah et al. (2015). However, future research may need to investigate these findings to fully understand the concept of organizational hybridity, and its implications for employees' behaviour and trust in the commercial hybrid organization.

For now, this study provides a stepping stone towards the advancement of knowledge regarding employees' responses to organizational hybridity. It provides answers to the primary research question: *What are the implications of organizational hybridity for employees' trust in commercial hybrid organizations?* In conclusion, the data showed that there are real consequences of organizational hybridity for employees' behaviour and trust in commercial hybrid organizations. Also and most importantly, the data showed that there is a need for commercial hybrid organizations to sustain employees' trust in order to reap the benefits associated with it for improved organizational effectiveness and performance.

# APPENDICES

## Appendix A: Interview Schedule for ASL

| Fieldwork interview schedule for Alter securities limited (26th of May to 6th of June, 2014) | May 26th | May 27th | May 28th | May 29th | May 30th | May 31st | June 1st | June 2nd | June 3rd | June 4th | June 5th | June 6th |
|---|---|---|---|---|---|---|---|---|---|---|---|---|
| A1, A2, A3, A4 | ■ | | | | | | | | | | | |
| A5, A6, | | ■ | | | | | | | | | | |
| A7, A8, A9, A10 | | | | | ■ | | | | | | | |
| A11, A12, A13 | | | | | | | | ■ | | | | |
| A14, A15 | | | | | | | | | ■ | | | |
| A16, A17, A18, A19, A20 | | | | | | | | | | | | ■ |

# Appendix B: Interview Schedule for BPL

| Fieldwork interview schedule for Barak petroleum limited (13th to 17th of June, 2014) | June 13th | June 14th | June 15th | June 16th | June 17th | June 18th |
|---|---|---|---|---|---|---|
| B1, B2, B3, B4, B5, B6, | ■ | | | | | |
| B7, B8 | | | | ■ | | |
| B9, B10, B11, B12, B13, B14 | | | | | ■ | |
| B15, B16, B17, B18, B19, B20 | | | | | | ■ |

# Appendix C: Data Display Format

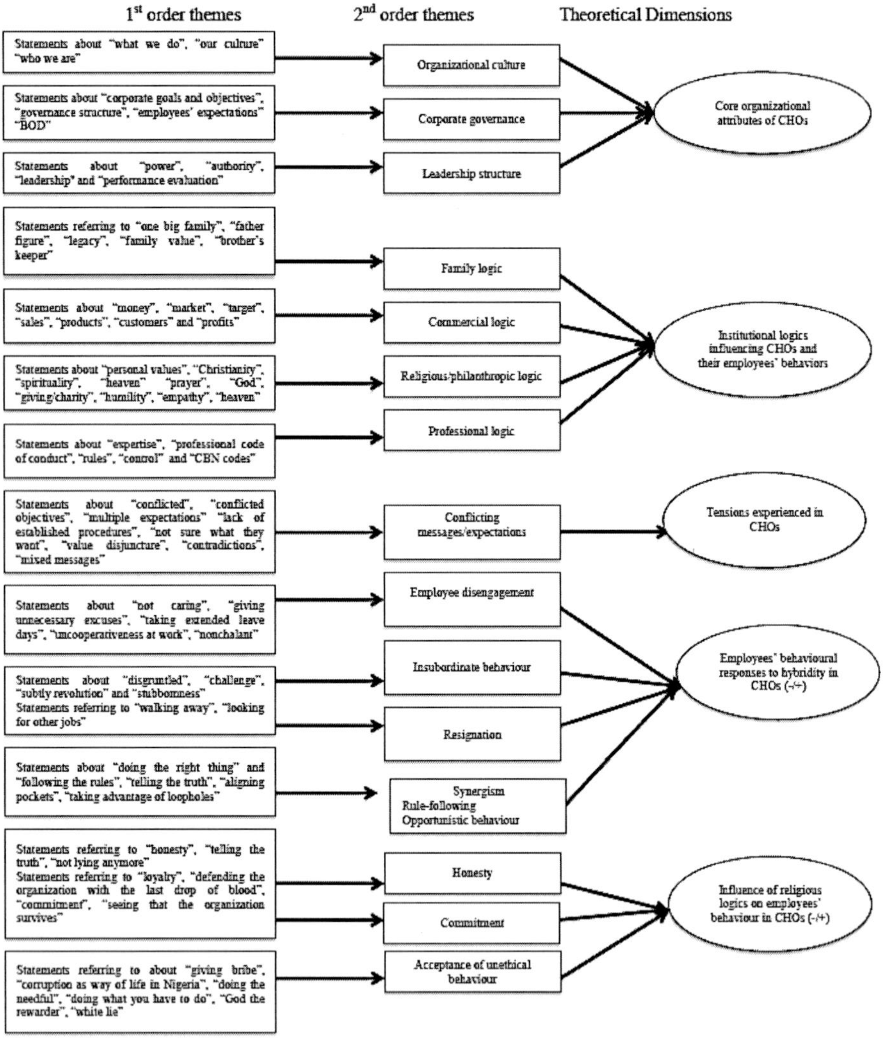


**Adapted from Gioia et al (2012) Seeking Qualitative Rigor in Inductive Research**

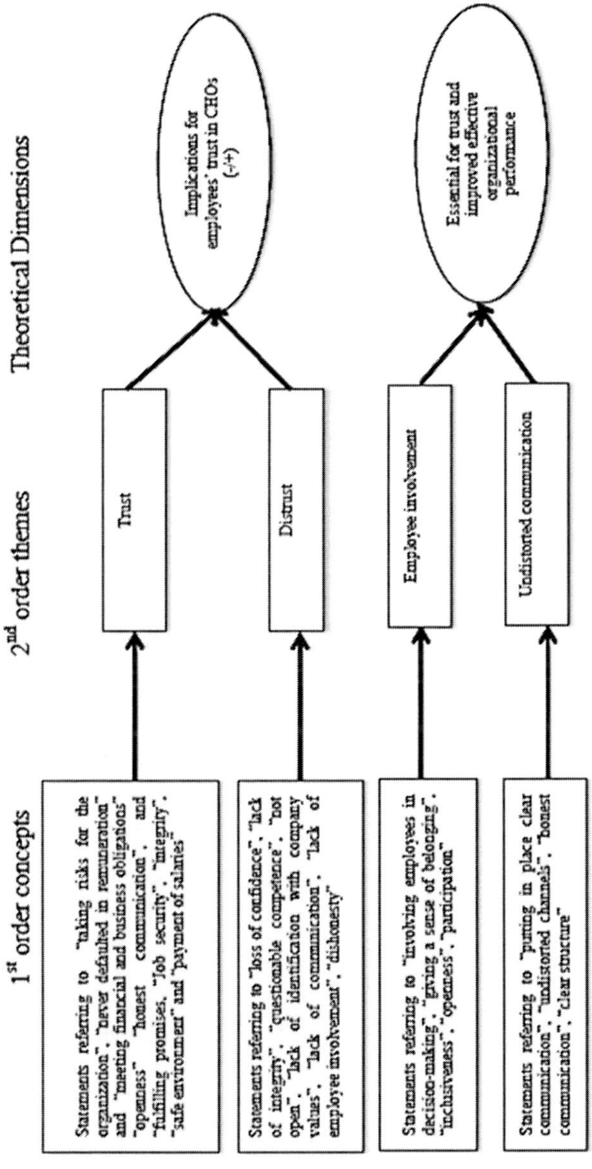
1st order concepts
2nd order themes
Theoretical Dimensions
Statements referring to "taking risks for the organization", "never defaulted in remuneration" and "meeting financial and business obligations" "openness" "honest communication", and "fulfilling promises, "Job security", "integrity", "safe environment" and "payment of salaries"
Statements referring to "loss of confidence", "lack of integrity", "questionable competence", "not open", "lack of identification with company values", "lack of commnication", "lack of employee involvement", "dishonesty"
Statements referring to "involving employees in decision-making", "giving a sense of belonging", "inclusiveness", "openness", "participation"
Statements referring to "putting in place clear communication", "undistorted channels", "honest communication", "clear structure"
Trust
Distrust
Employee involvement
Undistorted communication
Implications for employees' trust in CHOs (-/+)
Essential for trust and improved effective organizational performance

# REFERENCES


Adekoya, A. and Ekpenyong, E. (2009). Corporate Governance and Environmental Performance: Three Point Strategy for Improving Environmental Performance Among Corporations in Africa. In: IAIA 09 Conference Proceedings, Impact Assessment and Human Wellbeing.

Aguilera, R., Filatotchev, I., Gospel, H. and Jackson, G. (2008). An Organizational Approach to Comparative Corporate Governance: Costs, contingencies, and complementarities. *Organization Science*, 19(3), pp. 475–492.

Aguilera, R. and Jackson, G. (2010). Comparative and International Corporate Governance. *The Academy of Management Annals*, 4(1), pp. 485–556.

Aguilera, R., Williams, C., Conley, J. and Rupp, D. (2006). Corporate Governance and Social Responsibility: A comparative analysis of the UK and the US corporate governance. *An International Review*, 14(3), pp. 147–158.

Alade, S. and Tule, M. (2017). The Nigerian Financial System at a Glance. Central Bank of Nigeria, Monetary Policy Department. Retrieved from https://www.cbn.gov.ng/Out/2017/CCD/THE%20NIGERIAN%20FINANCIAL%20SYSTEM.pdf [last accessed 10th April 2021].

Albert, S., and Whetten, D. A. (1985). Organizational Identity. *Research in Organizational Behaviour*, 7, 263-295.

Alford, R. and Friedland, R. (1985). Powers of Theory: Capitalism, the State, and Democracy. Cambridge: Cambridge University Press.

Alter, K. (2007). Social Enterprise Typology. *Virtue Ventures LLC*, 12, pp. 1–124.

Alvesson, M. (2011). Interpreting Interviews. United Kingdom: Sage Publications Ltd.

Amao, O. (2008). Corporate Social Responsibility, Multinational Corporations and the Law in Nigeria: Controlling multinationals in host states. *Journal of African Law*, 52(1), pp. 89–113.

Amnesty International (2009). Nigeria: Petroleum pollution and poverty in the Niger Delta. London: Amnesty International Publications.

Anheier, H. (2011). Governance and Leadership in Hybrid Organizations. *Comparative & Interdisciplinary Perspectives*, pp. 1–7.

Ashforth, B., Harrison, S., and Corley, K. (2008). Identification in Organizations: An examination of four fundamental questions. *Journal of Management*, 34(3), pp. 325–374.

Babalola, J. and Adegbite, M. (2001). The Performance of the Nigerian Capital Market since Deregulation in 1986. *Central Bank of Nigeria Economic and Financial Review*, 39(1), pp. 1–19.

Bachmann, R. (2001). Trust, Power and Control in Trans-Organizational Relations. *Organization Studies*, 22(2), pp. 337–365.

Bachmann, R., Gillespie, N. and Priem, R. (2015). Repairing Trust in Organizations and Institutions: Toward a conceptual framework. *Organization Studies*, 36(9), pp. 1123–1142.

Bachmann, R. and Inkpen, A. (2007). Trust and Institutions. Research Paper 84, *Sociological Series*. Institute for Advanced Studies, Vienna.

Bachmann, R. and Inkpen, A. (2011). Understanding Institutional-based Trust Building Processes in Inter-organizational Relationships. *Organization Studies*, 32(2), pp. 281–301.

Baluch, A., Salge, T. and Piening, E. (2013). Untangling the Relationship Between HRM and Hospital Performance: The mediating role of attitudinal and behavioural HR outcomes. *The International Journal of Human Resource Management*, 24(16), pp. 3038–3061.

Barrett, R. (2009). What's Right and Wrong with Spirituality in the Workplace? *Journal of Management, Spirituality & Religion*, 6(3), pp. 261–268.

Battilana, J. (2006). Agency and Institutions: The Enabling Role of Individuals' Social Position. *Organization*, 13(5), pp. 653–676.

Battilana, J. and Dorado, S. (2010). Building Sustainable Hybrid Organizations: The Case of Commercial Microfinance Organizations. *Academy of Management Journal*, 53(6), pp. 1419–1440.

Battilana, J. and Lee, M. (2014). Advancing Research on Hybrid Organizing – Insights from the Study of Social Enterprises. *Academy of Management Annals*, 8(1), pp. 397–441.

Battilana, J., Lee, M., Walker, J. and Dorsey, C. (2012). In Search of the Hybrid Ideal. *Stanford Social Innovation Review*, 10(3), pp. 50–55.

Bell, J. (2005) Doing Your Research Project: A Guide for First-Time Researchers in

Education and Social Science, 4th edition. London: Open University Press.

Berger, P. and Luckmann, T. (1967). The Social Construction of Reality: A treatise in the sociology of knowledge. Great Britain: The Penguin Press.

Besharov, M. (2014). The Relational Ecology of Identification: How organizational identification emerges when individuals hold divergent values. *Academy of Management Journal*, 57(5), pp. 1485–1512.

Besharov, M. and Smith, W. (2012). Multiple Logics within Organizations: An Integrative Framework and Model of Organizational Hybridity. Ithaca, NY: Cornell University working paper.

Besharov, M. and Smith, W. (2014). Multiple Institutional Logics in Organizations: Explaining their varied nature and implications. *Academy of Management Review*, 39(3), pp. 364–381.

Bhattacharya, R., Devinney, T. and Pillutla, M. (1998). A Formal Model of Trust Based on Outcomes. *Academy of Management Review*, 23(3), pp. 459–472.

Billis, D. (2010). Towards a theory of Hybrid Organizations. *In Hybrid Organizations and the Third Sector: Challenges for Practice, Theory and Policy*. Houndmills Basingstoke Hampshire, New York: Palgrave Macmillan, pp. 46-69.

Binder, A. (2007). For Love and Money: Organizations' creative responses to multiple environmental logics. *Theory & Society*, 36(6), pp. 547–571.

Bjerregaard, T. and Jonasson, C. (2013). Organizational Responses to Contending Institutional Logics: The moderating effect of group dynamics: contending institutional logics. *British Journal of Management*, 25(4), pp. 651–666.

Blaikie, N. (2007). Approaches to Social Enquiry: Advancing knowledge. Cambridge: Polity Press.

Blaikie, N. (2009). Designing Social Research: The logic of anticipation, 2nd edition. Cambridge: Polity Press.

Blumer, H. (1969). Symbolic Interactionism: Perspectives and Methods. New Jersey: Prentice-Hall Inc.

Blumer, H. (1986). Symbolic Interactionism: Perspective and method. California: University of California Press.

Borys, B. and Jemison, D. (1989). Hybrid Arrangements as Strategic Alliances: Theoretical issues in organizational combinations. *Academy of Management Review*, 14(2), pp. 234–249.

Bowen, G. A. (2009). Document analysis as a qualitative research method. *Qualitative Research Journal*, 9(2), pp. 27 – 40.

Boyd, B., Henning, N., Reyna, E., Wang, D. and Welch, M. (2009). Hybrid Organizations: New business models for environmental leadership. Sheffield: Greenleaf Publishing Limited.

Brandsen, T. and Karré, P. (2011). Hybrid Organizations: No cause for concern? *International Journal of Public Administration*, 34(13), pp. 827–836.

Brickson, S. (2000). The Impact of Identity Orientation on Individual and Organizational Outcomes in Demographically Diverse Settings. *Academy of Management Review*, 25(1), pp. 82–101.

Brotheridge, C. and Lee, R. (2007). Hands to Work, Heart to God: Religiosity and organizational behaviour. *Journal of Management, Spirituality & Religion*, 4(3), pp. 287–309.

Bryman, A. (2004). Social Research Methods, 2nd edition. Oxford: Oxford University Press.

Bryman, A. (2012). Social Research Methods, 4th edition. Oxford: Oxford University Press.

Bryman, A. and Bell, E. (2011). Business Research Methods, 3rd edition. New York: Oxford University Press Inc.

Burke, S., Sims, D., Lazzara, E. and Salas, E. (2007). Trust in Leadership: A multi-level review and integration. *The Leadership Quarterly*, 18(6), pp. 606–632.

Bussing, A. (2002). Trust and its Relations to Commitment and Involvement in work and Organizations. *SA Journal of Industrial Psychology*, 28(4), pp. 36–42.

Cash, K. and Gray, G. (2000). A Framework for Accommodating Religion and Spirituality in the Workplace. *The Academy of Management Executive*, 14(3), pp. 124–133.

Central Intelligence Agency (2013). Africa: Nigeria. The World FactBook. Retrieved from https://www.cia.gov/library/publications/the-world-factbook/geos/ni.html [last accessed 31st March 2016]

Chaston, J. and Lips-Wiersma, M. (2014). When Spirituality Meets Hierarchy: Leader spirituality as a double-edged sword. *Journal of Management, Spirituality & Religion*, 12(2), pp. 111–128.

Child, J. and Rodrigues, S. (2004). Repairing the Breach of Trust in Corporate Governance. *Corporate Governance*, 12(2), pp. 143–152.

Chung, C. and Luo, X. (2008). Institutional Logics or Agency Costs: The influence of corporate governance models on business group restructuring in emerging economies. *Organization Science*, 19(5), pp. 766–784.

Clarke, T. (2007). Corporate Governance: A comparative approach. London, UK: Routledge.

Cloutier, C. and Langley, A. (2013). The Logic of Institutional Logics Insights from French Pragmatist Sociology. *Journal of Management Inquiry*, 22(4), pp. 360–380.

Cook, K. S., Levi, M., and Hardin, R. (Eds.). (2009). Whom can we trust?: How groups, networks, and institutions make trust possible. Russell Sage Foundation.

Creed, W. and Miles, R., Eds. (1996) Trust in Organizations: A Conceptual Framework. Sage Publications, London.

Crombie, N. (2013). Institutional Logics of Corporate Governance and the Discourse on Executive Remuneration (Unpublished PhD thesis, University of Canterbury, New Zealand). Retrieved from http://ir.canterbury.ac.nz/handle/10092/8202 [last accessed 11th April 2016).

Currie, G. and Spyridonidis, D. (2015). Interpretation of Multiple Institutional Logics on the Ground: Actors position, their agency and situational constraints in professionalized contexts. *Organization Studies*, 37, pp. 77–97.

Davis, J., Schoorman, D. and Donaldson, L. (1997). Toward a Stewardship Theory of Management. *Academy of Management Review*, 22(1), pp. 20–47.

Day, G. (1998). What Does it Mean to be Market-driven? *Business Strategy Review*, 9(1), pp. 1–14.

Day, G. (1999). The Market Driven Organization: Understanding, attracting, and keeping valuable customers. New York: The Free Press.

Day, N. (2005). Religion in the Workplace: Correlates and consequences of individual behaviour. *Journal of Management, Spirituality & Religion*, 2(1), pp. 104–135.

Dietz, G. and Gillespie, N. (2012). Recovery of Trust: Case studies of organizational failures and trust repair (Vol. 5). *Institute of Business Ethics*.

DiMaggio, P. (1988). Interest and agency in institutional theory. In L. Zucker (Ed.), Institutional patterns and culture (pp. 3-32). Cambridge, MA: Ballinger.

Dirks, K. and Ferrin, D. (2001). The Role of Trust in Organizational Settings. *Organization Science*, 12(4), pp. 450–467.

Dirks, K. and Ferrin, D. (2002). Trust in Leadership: Meta-analytic findings and implications for organizational research. *Journal of Applied Psychology*, 87(4), pp. 611–628.

Doherty, B., Haugh, H. and Lyon, F. (2014). Social Enterprises as Hybrid Organizations: A review and research agenda. *International Journal of Management Reviews*, 16(4), pp. 417–436.

Donaldson, T. and Preston, L. (1995). The Stakeholder Theory of the Corporation: Concepts, evidence, and implications. *The Academy of Management Review*, 20(1), pp. 65–91.

Dunn, M. and Jones, C. (2010). Institutional Logics and Institutional Pluralism: The contestation of care and science logics in medical education, 1967–2005. *Administrative Science Quarterly*, 55(1), pp. 114–149.

Dutton, J., Dukerich, J. and Harquail, C. (1994). Organizational Images and Member Identification. *Administrative Science Quarterly*, 39(2), pp. 239–263.

Dyer Jr, W. G., & Whetten, D. A. (2006). Family firms and social responsibility: Preliminary evidence from the S&P 500. *Entrepreneurship Theory and Practice*, 30(6), 785-802.

Eberl, P., Geiger, D. and Aßländer, M. (2015). Repairing Trust in an Organization after Integrity Violations: The ambivalence of organizational rule adjustments. *Organization Studies*, 36(9), pp. 1205–1235.

Ebrahim, A., Battilana, J. and Mair, J. (2014). The Governance of Social Enterprises: Mission drift and accountability challenges in hybrid organizations. *Research in Organizational Behaviour*, 34, pp. 81–100.

Effoduh, J. O. (2014). The economic development of Nigeria from 1914 to 2014. Nigerian Institute of Advanced Legal Studies. Retrieved from http://www.casade.org/economic-development-nigeria-1914-2014/ [last accessed 29th March 2021].

Eisenhardt, K. (1989). Agency Theory: An assessment and review. *Academy of Management Review*, 14(1), pp. 57–74.

Erkutlu, H. and Chafra, J. (2015). Impact of Behavioral Integrity on Organizational Identification: The moderating roles of power distance and organizational politics. *Management Research Review*, 39(6), pp. 672–691.

Falola, T. and Heaton, M. (2008). A History of Nigeria. Cambridge: Cambridge University Press.

Farrell, H. and Knight, J. (2003). Trust, Institutions, and Institutional Change: Industrial districts and the social capital hypothesis. *Politics & Society*, 31(4), pp. 537–566.

Flick, U., Kardorff, E. and Steinke, I. (2004). A Companion to Qualitative Research. Sage Publications.

Ford, J. and Ford, L. (1994). Logics of Identity, Contradiction, and Attraction in Change. *Academy of Management Review*, 19(4), pp. 756–785.

Foreman, P. and Whetten, D. (2002). Members' Identification with Multiple-Identity Organizations. *Organization Studies*, 13(6), pp. 618-635.

Fox, A. (1974). Beyond Contract: Work, trust and power relations. Faber and Faber.

Freeman, R. (1984) Strategic Management: A stakeholder approach. University of Minnesota: Cambridge University Press.

Freeman, R. (1994). The Politics of Stakeholder Theory: Some future directions. *Business Ethics Quarterly*, 4(4), pp. 409–421.

Freidson, E. (2001). Professionalism, the Third Logic: On the Practice of Knowledge. University of Chicago Press.

Friedland, R. and Alford, R. (1991). Bringing Society Back in: Symbols, Practices, and Institutional Contradictions. In: Powell, W. W. and DiMaggio, P. J. (eds.), The New Institutionalism in Organizational Analysis. University of Chicago Press, pp. 232–266.

Fry, L. (2003). Toward a Theory of Spiritual Leadership. *The Leadership Quarterly*, 14(6), pp. 693–727.

Fuglsang, L. and Jagd, S. (2015). Making Sense of Institutional Trust in Organizations: Bridging institutional context and trust. *Organization*, 22(1), pp. 23–39.

Fukuyama, F. (1995). Trust: The Social Virtues and the Creation of Prosperity. New York: The Free Press.

Fulmer, C. and Gelfand, M. (2012). At What Level (and in Whom) We Trust: Trust across multiple organizational levels. *Journal of Management*, 38(4), pp. 1167–1230.

Galaskiewicz, J. (1997). An Urban Grants Economy Revisited: Corporate charitable contributions in the twin cities, 1979–81, 1987–89. *Administrative Science Quarterly*, 42, pp. 445–471.

Gao, G. (2015). How do Americans Stand Out from the Rest of the World. *PEW Research Center*. Retrieved from http://www.pewresearch.org/fact-tank/2015/03/12/how-do-americans-stand-out-from-the-rest-of-the-world/ [last accessed 25th May 2016].

Gawer, A. and Phillips, N. (2013). Institutional Work as Logics Shift: The case of intel's transformation to platform leader. *Organization Studies*, 34(8), pp. 1035–1071.

Gibbs, G. (2007). Analysing Qualitative Data. Great Britain: Sage Publications Ltd.

Gillespie, N. and Dietz, G. (2009). Trust Repair After an Organization-level Failure. *Academy of Management Review*, 34(1), pp. 127–145.

Gillespie, N. and Mann, L. (2004). Transformational Leadership and Shared Values: The building blocks of trust. *Journal of Managerial Psychology*, 19(6), pp. 588–607.

Gioia, D., Corley, K. and Hamilton, A. (2013). Seeking Qualitative Rigor in Inductive Research: Notes on the Gioia Methodology. *Organizational Research Methods*, 16(1), pp. 15–31.

Gioia, D. and Pitre, E. (1990). Multiparadigm Perspectives on Theory Building. *Academy of Management Review*, 15(4), pp. 584–602.

Gioia, D., Schultz, M. and Corley, K. (2000). Organizational Identity, Image, and Adaptive Instability. *Academy of Management Review*, 25(1), pp. 63–81.

Glynn, M. A. (2000). When cymbals become symbols: Conflict over organizational identity within a symphony orchestra. *Organization Science,* 11, 285-298.

Gray, B. (1985). Organizations as Constructions and Destructions of Meaning. *Journal of Management*, 11(2), pp. 83–98.

Greenleaf, R. (1977). Servant Leadership. New York: Paulist Press.

Greenwood, R., Raynard, M., Kodeih, F., Micelotta, E., and Lounsbury, M. (2011). Institutional Complexity and Organizational Responses. *Academy of Management Annals*, 5(1), pp. 317 – 371.

Greenwood, R., Díaz, A., Li, S. and Lorente, J. (2010). The Multiplicity of Institutional Logics and the Heterogeneity of Organizational Responses. *Organization Science*, 21(2), pp. 521–539.

Greenwood, R. and Hinings, C. (1996). Understanding Radical Organizational Change: Bringing together the old and the new institutionalism. *Academy of Management Review*, 21(4), pp. 1022–1054.

Grix, J. (2010). The Foundations of Research, 2nd edition. Palgrave Macmillan.

Guzley, R. (1992). Organizational Climate and Communication Climate Predictors of Commitment to the Organization. *Management Communication Quarterly*, 5(4), pp. 379–402.

Haigh, N. and Hoffman, A. (2012). Hybrid Organizations. *Organizational Dynamics*, 41, pp. 126–134.

Hardin, R. (2002). Trust and Trustworthiness. New York: Russell Sage Foundation.

Hirsch, P. and Lounsbury, M. (2015). Toward a More Critical and “Powerful” Institutionalism. *Journal of Management Inquiry*, 24(1), pp. 96–99.

Hoge, D., Petrillo, G. and Smith, E. (1982). Transmission of Religious and Social Values from Parents to Teenage Children. *Journal of Marriage & the Family*, 44, pp. 569–580.

Holton, R. (1994). Deciding to Trust, Coming to Believe. *Australasian Journal of Philosophy*, 72(1), pp. 63–76.

Holtz, B. (2013). Trust Primacy: A Model of the reciprocal relations between trust and perceived justice. *Journal of Management*, 39(7), pp. 1891–1923.

Hosmer, L. (1995). Trust: The connecting link between organizational theory and philosophical ethics. *Academy of Management Review*, 20(2), pp. 379–403.

Ibrahim, J. (1991). Religion and Political Turbulence in Nigeria. *The Journal of Modern African Studies*, 29(1), pp. 115–136.

Iledare, W. (2008). An Appraisal of Oil and Gas Industry Reform and Institutional Restructuring in Nigeria. *International Association for Energy Economics*, Fourth Quarter, pp. 23–26.

Imaga, E. (2003). Comparative Management System: Nigeria and some Selected Countries, Rhyce Kerex Publisher: Enugu.

Ituma, A. and Simpson, R. (2009). The Boundaryless Career and Career Boundaries: Applying an institutionalist perspective to ICT workers in the context of Nigeria. *Human Relations*, 62(5), pp. 727–761.

Jäger, U. and Schröer, A. (2014). Integrated Organizational Identity: A Definition of Hybrid Organizations and a Research Agenda. *VOLUNTAS: International Journal of Voluntary and Nonprofit Organizations*, 25(5), pp. 1281–1306.

James, H. (2006). Family Capitalism, Wendels, Haniels, Falks, and the Continental European Model. Belnap Press of Harvard University: Cambridge

Press, Cambridge, MA.Jay, J. (2013). Navigating Paradox as a Mechanism of Change and Innovation in Hybrid Organizations. *Academy of Management Journal*, 56(1), pp. 137–159.

Jensen, M. (2001). Value Maximisation, Stakeholder Theory and the Corporate Objective Function. *Journal of Applied Corporate Finance*, 14(3), pp. 8–21.

Jensen, M. and Meckling, W. (1992). Specific and General Knowledge and Organizational Structure. In: Lars, W. and Hans, W. (eds.), Contract Economics. Blackwell, pp. 251–274.

Ji, J. and Dimitratos, P. (2013). An Empirical Investigation into International Entry Mode Decision-making Effectiveness. *International Business Review*, 22, pp. 994–1007.

Jones, G. and George, J. (1998). The experience and evolution of trust: Implications for cooperation and teamwork. *Academy of Management Review*, 23(3), pp. 531–546.

Jones, T. (1998). Interpretive Social Science and the "Native's Point of View": A closer look. *Philosophy of the Social Sciences*, 28(1), pp. 32–68.

Kahn, W. (1990). Psychological Conditions of Personal Engagement and Disengagement at Work. *The Academy of Management Journal*, 33(4), pp. 692–724.

Kam, T-K. (2009). Implicit Theories and the Trust Repair Process. In: *22nd Annual IACM Conference Paper*.

Karré, P. (2011). Heads and tails: both sides of the coin: an analysis of hybrid organizations in the Dutch waste management sector. The Hague: Eleven international Publishing.

Karré, P. (2012). Conceptualizing hybrid organisations. In A public administration approach. Paper written for symposium "Neither Public nor Private: Mixed Forms of Service Delivery around the Globe". University of Barcelona. Retrieved from http://www.ub.edu/graap/Final%20Papers%20PDF/Philip%20Karre.pdf [last accessed 30th March 2021].

Kodeih, F. and Greenwood, R. (2014). Responding to Institutional Complexity: The role of identity. *Organization Studies*, 35(1), pp. 7–39.

Kolapo, F. and Adaramola, A. (2012). The Impact of the Nigerian Capital Market on Economic Growth (1990–2010). *International Journal of Developing Societies*, 1(1), pp. 11–19.

Kolawole, B. O. and Omobitan, O. A. (2014). Determinants of Private Sector Performance in Nigeria. *Developing Country Studies*, 4, pp. 41–49.

Kraatz, M. S. (2009). Leadership as institutional work: A bridge to the other side. In T. B. Lawrence, R. Suddaby, & B. Leca (Ed.), Institutional work: Actors and agency in institutional studies of organizations: 59-91. New York: Cambridge University Press.

Kraatz, M. S. and Block, E. S. (2008). Organizational implications of institutional pluralism.

In R. Greenwood, C. Oliver, K. Sahlin, & R. Suddaby (Eds.), The Sage handbook of organizational institutionalism (pp. 243–275). Thousand Oaks, CA: Sage.Kramer, R. (1999). Trust and Distrust in Organizations: Emerging perspectives, enduring questions. *Annual Review of Psychology*, 50(1), pp. 569–598.

Kramer, R. (ed.) (2006). Organizational Trust: A reader. Oxford: Oxford University Press.

Lee, B. and Cassell, C. (2013). Research Methods and Research Practice: History, Themes and Topics: Research methods and research practice. *International Journal of Management Reviews*, 15(2), pp. 123–131.

Lee, M. and Lounsbury, M. (2015). Filtering Institutional Logics: Community logic variation and differential responses to the institutional complexity of toxic waste. *Organization Science*, 26(3), pp. 847–866.

Leke, A., Fiorini, R., Dobbs, R., Thompson, F., Suleiman, A., and Wright, D. (2014). Nigeria's Renewal: Delivering Inclusive Growth in Africa's Largest Economy. The McKinsey Global Institute. Retrieved from https://www.mckinsey.com/~/media/McKinsey/Featured%20Insights/Middle%20East%20and%20Africa/Nigerias%20renewal%20Deliverin g%20inclusive%20growth/MGI_Nigerias_renewal_Full_report.pdf [last accessed 29th March 2021].

Lewicki, R., McAllister, D. and Bies, R. (1998). Trust and Distrust: New relationships and realities. *Academy of Management Review*, 23(3), pp. 438–458.

Lewis, J. and Weigert, A. (1985). Trust as a Social Reality. *Social Forces*, 63(4), pp. 967–985.

Li, P., Bai, Y. and Xi, Y. (2012a). The Contextual Antecedents of Organizational Trust: A multidimensional cross-level analysis. *Management & Organization Review*, 8(2), pp. 371–396.

Li, P., Van, M. and Smith, C. (2012b). A Holistic Framework for Trust in Online Transactions. *International Journal of Management Reviews*, 14(1), pp. 85–103.

Lounsbury, M. (2007). A Tale of Two Cities: Competing logics and practice variation in the professionalizing of mutual funds. *Academy of Management Journal*, 50(2), pp. 289–307.

MacLean, T. and Webber, S. (2015). Navigating Multiple Identities Across Multiple Boundaries A Cross-Level Model of Organizational Identification. *Journal of Management Inquiry*, 24(2), pp. 156–173.

Mair, J., Mayer, J. and Lutz, E. (2015). Navigating Institutional Plurality: Organizational governance in hybrid organizations. *Organization Studies*, 36(6), pp. 713–739.

Mangen, C. and Brivot, M. (2014). The Challenge of Sustaining Organizational Hybridity: The role of power and agency. *Human Relations*, pp. 1–26.

Marquis, C. and Lounsbury, M. (2007). Vive la Résistance: Competing logics and the consolidation of US community banking. *Academy of Management Journal*, 50(4), pp. 799–820.

Mars, M. and Lounsbury, M. (2008). Raging Against or With the Private Marketplace? Logic hybridity and eco-entrepreneurship. *Journal of Management Inquiry*, 18(1), pp. 4–13.

Martin, G., Beech, N., MacIntosh, R. and Bushfield, S. (2015). Potential Challenges Facing Distributed Leadership in Health Care: Evidence from the UK National Health Service. *Sociology of Health & illness*, 37(1), pp. 14–29.

Martin, G., Farndale, E., Paauwe, J. and Stiles, P. (2016). Corporate Governance and Strategic Human Resource Management: Four archetypes and proposals for a new approach to corporate sustainability. *European Management Journal*, 34, pp. 22–35.

Mayer, R., Davis, J. and Schoorman, F. (1995). An Integrative Model of Organizational Trust. *Academy of Management Review*, 20(3), pp. 709–734.

Mayer, R. and Gavin, M. (2005). Trust in Management and Performance: Who minds the shop while the employees watch the boss? *Academy of Management Journal*, 48(5), pp. 874–888.

Mazumdar, S. and Mazumdar, S. (2005). How Organizations Interface with Religion: A typology. *Journal of Management, Spirituality & Religion*, 2(2), pp. 199–220.

McAllister, D. (1995). Affect-and Cognition-based Trust as Foundations for Interpersonal Cooperation in Organizations. *Academy of Management Journal*, 38(1), pp. 24–59.

McCourt, W. and Moores, J. (2007). Managerial Control Versus Professional Control: The case of performance appraisal; in UK universities. Institute for Development Policy and Management, University of Manchester working paper. Retrieved from https://www.escholar.manchester.ac.uk/uk-ac-man-scw:86488 [last accessed 13th April 2016].

Ménard, C. (2011). Hybrid Organizations. In: Klein, P. and Sykuta, M. The Elgar Companion to Transaction Cost Economics. Edward Elgar, pp. 176–184.

Miles, M. and Huberman, M. (1994). Qualitative Data Analysis: An expanded sourcebook. Thousand Oaks: Sage Publications.

Misangyi, V., Weaver, G. and Elms, H. (2008). Ending Corruption: The interplay among institutional logics, resources, and institutional entrepreneurs. *Academy of Management Review*, 33(3), pp. 750–770.

Mishra, A. (1996). Organizational Responses to Crisis. *Trust in Organizations Frontiers of Theory & Research*, pp. 261–287.

Möllering, G. (2001). The Nature of Trust: From Georg Simmel to a theory of expectation, interpretation and suspension. *Sociology*, 35(2), pp. 403–420.

Moore, J. and Kraatz, M. (2011). Governance Form and Organizational Adaptation: Lessons from the savings and loan industry in the 1980s. *Organization Science*, 22(4), pp. 850–868.

Nash, L. (1994). Believers in Business. Thomas Nelson Publishers: Nashville.

Neal, J. and Vallejo, M. (2008). Family Firms as Incubators for Spirituality in the Workplace: Factors that nurture spiritual businesses. *Journal of Management, Spirituality & Religion*, 5(2), pp. 115–159.

NNPC. (2021). Joint Venture Contractors (JVCs). Retrieved from https://napims.nnpcgroup.com/our-services/Pages/Joint-Venture-Contractors.aspx [last accessed 10th April 2021].

Nooteboom, B. (2002). Trust: Forms, foundations, functions, failures and figures. Cheltenham:Edward Elgar.

Nooteboom, B. (2006). Guido Mollering Trust: Reason, Routine, Reflexivity. *Organization Studies*, 27(12), pp. 1907–1910.

Odularu, O. (2008). Crude Oil and the Nigerian Economic Performance. *Oil &Gas Business*, pp. 1–29.

Okonjo-Iweala, N. and Osafo-Kwaako, P. (2007). Nigeria's Economic Reforms: Progress and challenges. Brookings Global Economy and Development Working Paper 6. Retrieved from http://www.inter-reseaux.org/IMG/pdf_Nigeria_Economic_Reforms_Okonjo_2007.pdf [last accessed 12th April 2016].

Oliver, C. (1991). Strategic Responses to Institutional Processes. *The Academy of Management Review*, 16(1), pp. 145–179.

Omeje, K. (2006). High Stakes and Stakeholders: Oil Conflict and Security in Nigeria. Hampshire: Ashgate Publishing Limited.

OPEC. (2020). Nigeria facts and figures. Annual Statistical Bulletin. Retrieved from https://www.opec.org/opec_web/en/about_us/167.htm [last accessed 11th April 2021].

O'Reilly, C., Caldwell, D., Chatman, J. and Doerr, B. (2014). The Promise and Problems of Organizational Culture CEO Personality, Culture, and Firm Performance. *Group & Organization Management*, 39(6), pp. 595–625.

Osaghae, E. and Suberu, R. (2005). A History of Identities, Violence and Stability in Nigeria. Centre for Research on Inequality, Human Security and Ethnicity. University of Oxford.

Osemeke, M. (2011). Problems and Prospects of Private Sector Organizations in Nigeria. *International Journal of Business & Management*, 6(4), pp. 178.

Pache, A-C. (2010). When Competing Logics Enter Organizations: The Politics of Organizational Responses to Conflicting Institutional Demands. ESSEC Business School Working Paper. Retrieved from http://citeseerx.ist.psu.edu/viewdoc/download?doi=10.1.1.471.8146&rep=rep1&type=pdf [last accessed 12th April 2016].

Pache, A-C. and Santos, F. (2010). When Worlds Collide: The internal dynamics of organizational responses to conflicting institutional demands. *Academy of Management Review*, 35(3), pp. 455–476.

Pache, A-C. and Santos, F. (2013). Embedded in Hybrid Contexts: How individuals in organizations respond to competing institutional logics. *Research in the Sociology of Organizations*, 39, pp. 3–35.

Pastoriza, D. and Ariño, M. (2008). When Agents Become Stewards: Introducing learning in the stewardship theory. In: 1st IESE Conference, "Humanizing the Firm & Management Profession", Barcelona, IESE Business School.

Patton, M. (1999). Enhancing the Quality and Credibility of Qualitative Analysis. *Health Services Research*, 34(5/2), pp. 1189.

Patton, M. (2002). Qualitative Research and Evaluation Methods, 3rd edition. Thousand Oaks, CA: Sage.

Payne, G., Brigham, K., Broberg, J., Moss, T. and Short, J. (2011). Organizational Virtue Orientation and Family Firms. *Business Ethics Quarterly*, 21(2), pp. 257–285.

Pew Research Center (2010). Tolerance and tension: Islam and Christianity in Sub-Saharan Africa. Retrieved from http://www.pewforum.org/files/2010/04/sub-saharan-africa-appendix-b.pdf [last accessed 13th April 2016].

Pierce, S. (2006). Looking Like a State: Colonialism and the discourse of corruption in Northern Nigeria. *Comparative Studies in Society & History*, 48(4), pp. 887–914.

Pierre, E. and Jackson, A. (2014). Qualitative Data Analysis after Coding. *Qualitative Inquiry*, 20(6), pp. 715–719.

Pratt, M. and Foreman, P. (2000). Classifying Managerial Responses to Multiple Organizational Identities. *The Academy of Management Review*, 25(1), pp. 18–42.

Puusa, A., & Tolvanen, U. (2006). Organizational Identity and Trust. EJBO: *Electronic Journal of Business Ethics and Organization Studies*, 11(20), pp. 29-33.

Reay, T. and Hinings, C. (2009). Managing the Rivalry of Competing Institutional Logics. *Organization Studies*, 30(6), pp. 629–652.

Romanelli, E. (1991). The Evolution of New Organizational Forms. *Annual Review of Sociology*, pp. 79–103.

Rosaci, D., Sarné, G. and Garruzzo, S. (2012). Integrating Trust Measures in Multiagent Systems. *International Journal of Intelligent Systems*, 27(1), pp. 1–15.

Rousseau, D., Sitkin, S., Burt, R. and Camerer, C. (1998). Not so Different After All: A cross-discipline view of trust. *Academy of Management Review*, 23(3), pp. 393–404.

Sanusi, S. L. (2010). Growth Prospects for the Nigerian Economy. Convocation lecture delivered at the Igbinedion University eighth convocation ceremony, Okada, Edo State, 26th November.

Saunders, M., Dietz, G. and Thornhill, A. (2014). Trust and Distrust: Polar opposites, or independent but co-existing? *Human Relations*, 67(6), pp. 639–665.

Saunders, M., Lewis, P., & Thornhill, A. (2007). Research methods. Business Students 4th edition Pearson Education Limited, England.

Schatz, S. (1984). Pirate Capitalism and the Inert Economy of Nigeria. *The Journal of Modern African Studies*, 22(1), pp. 45–57.

Schein, E. (1984). Coming to a New Awareness of Organizational Culture. *Sloan Management Review*, 25(2), pp. 3–16.

Schoorman, F., Mayer, R. and Davis, J. (2007). An Integrative Model of Organizational Trust: Past, present, and future. *Academy of Management Review*, 32(2), pp. 344–354.

Schumpeter. (2009). The Rise of Hybrid Company. Retrieved from https://www.economist.com/business/2009/12/03/the-rise-of-the-hybrid-company [last accessed 5th August 2016].

Scott, W. (1995). Institutions and Organizations. Thousand Oaks: Sage.

Searle, R. and Ball, K. (2004). The Development of Trust and Distrust in a Merger. *Journal of Managerial Psychology*, 19(7), pp. 708–721.

Sendjaya, S. and Sarros, J. (2002). Servant leadership: Its origin, development, and application in organizations. *Journal of Leadership & Organizational Studies*, 9(2), pp. 57–64.

Seo, M. G. and Creed, D. (2002). 'Institutional Contradictions, Praxis and Institutional Change: A Dialectical Perspective,' *Academy of Management Review*, 27 (2): 222–247.

Serva, M., Fuller, M. and Mayer, R. (2005). The Reciprocal Nature of Trust: A Longitudinal Study of Interacting Teams. *Journal of Organizational Behaviour*, 26(6), pp. 625–648.

Shane, S. (1996). Hybrid Organizational Arrangements and their Implications for Firms Growth and Survival: A study of new franchisors. *Academy of Management Journal*, 39(1), pp. 216–234.

Sharkie, R. (2009). Trust in Leadership is Vital for Employee Performance. *Management Research News*, 32(5), pp. 491–498.

Shockley-Zalabak, P., Morreale, S. and Hackman, M. (2010). Building the High-Trust Organization: Strategies for supporting five key dimensions of trust (Vol. 7). John Wiley and Sons.

Siebert, S. and Costley, C. (2013). Conflicting Values in Reflection on Professional Practice. *Higher Education, Skills & Work-based Learning*, 3(3), pp. 156–167.

Siggelkow, N. (2007). Persuasion with Case Studies. *Academy of Management Journal*, 50(1), pp. 20–24.

Sitkin, S., & Roth, N. (1993). Explaining the Limited Effectiveness of Legalistic "Remedies" for Trust/ Distrust. Organization Science, 4(3), 367-392. Retrieved from http://www.jstor.org/stable/2634950 [last accessed 13th April 2021].

Skelcher, C. (2012). What Do We Mean When We Talk About "Hybrids" and "hybridity" in Public Management and Governance? Retrieved from http://epapers.bham.ac.uk/1601/1/Hybrids_working_paper_-_march_2011.pdf [last accessed 13th April 2016].

Smidts, A., Pruyn, A. and Van Riel, C. (2001). The Impact of Employee Communication and Perceived External Prestige on Organizational Identification. *Academy of Management Journal*, 44(5), pp. 1051–1062.

Smith, L., Amiot, C., Smith, J., Callan, V. and Terry, D. (2013a). The Social Validation and Coping Model of Organizational Identity Development: A longitudinal test. *Journal of Management*, 39(7), pp. 1952–1978.

Smith, W., Gonin, M. and Besharov, M. (2013b). Managing Social-Business Tensions: A review and research agenda for social enterprise. *Business Ethics Quarterly*, 23(3), pp. 407–442.

Snow, C. (2015). Organizing in the Age of Competition, Cooperation, and Collaboration. *Journal of Leadership & Organizational Studies*, pp. 1–10.

Sosis, R. (2005). Does Religion Promote Trust? The role of signalling, reputation and punishment. *Interdisciplinary Journal of Research on Religion*, 1(7), pp. 1–30.

Spears, L. (2010). Character and Servant Leadership: Ten characteristics of effective, caring leaders. *The Journal of Virtues & Leadership*, 1(1), pp. 25–30.

Spreitzer, G. and Mishra, A. (1999). Giving Up Control Without Losing Control: Trust and its substitutes' effects on managers' involving employees in decision making. *Group & Organization Management*, 24(2), pp. 155–187.

Suddaby, R., Elsbach, K., Greenwood, R., Meyer, J. and Zilber, T. (2010). Organizations and their Institutional Environments—Bringing meaning, values, and culture back in: Introduction to the special research forum. *Academy of Management Journal*, 53(6), pp. 1234–1240.

Symon, G. and Cassell, C. Eds. (2012). Qualitative Organizational Research: Core methods and current challenges. London: Sage Publications Ltd.

Thorgren, S. and Wincent, J. (2011). Interorganizational Trust: Origins, dysfunctions and regulation of rigidities. *British Journal of Management*, 22(1), pp. 21–41.

Thornton, P. (2004). Markets from Culture: Institutional logics and organizational decisions in higher education publishing. Standford: Standford University Press.

Thornton, P. and Ocasio, W. (1999). Institutional Logics and the Historical Contingency of Power in Organizations: Executive succession in the higher education publishing industry 1958–1990. *American Journal of Sociology*, 105(3), pp. 801–843.

Thornton, P. and Ocasio, W. (2008). Institutional Logics. *The Sage handbook of organizational institutionalism*, 840, pp. 99–128.

Thornton, P., Ocasio, W. and Lounsbury, M. (2012). The Institutional Logics Perspectives: A new approach to culture, structure and process. Oxford: Oxford University Press.

Tomes, N. (1985). Human Capital and Culture: Analyses of Variations in Labor Market Performance. *The American Economic Review*, 75(2), pp. 245-250.

Toney, F. and Oster, M. (1998). The Leader and Religious Faith: The relationship between the exercise of religious faith by CEOs, and goal achievement, self-fulfilment, and social benefits. *The Journal of Leadership Studies*, 5(1), pp. 136–147.

Townley, B. (1997). The Institutional Logic of Performance Appraisal. *Organization Studies*, 18(2), pp. 261–285.

Townley, B. (1999). Practical Reason and Performance Appraisal. *Journal of Management Studies*, 36(3), pp. 287–306.

Townley, B. (2002). The Role of Competing Rationalities in Institutional Change. *Academy of Management Journal*, 45(1), pp. 163–179.

Tracey, P. (2012). Religion and Organization: A critical review of current trends and future directions. *The Academy of Management Annals*, 6(1), pp. 87–134.

Tracey, P., Philips, N., & Jarvis, O. (2011). Bridging Institutional Entrepreneurship and the Creation of New Organizational Forms: A multilevel model. *Organization Science*, 22(1), 60-80.

Tracey, P., Phillips, N. and Lounsbury, M. (2014). Taking Religion Seriously in the Study of Organizations. In: Tracey, P., Phillips, N. and Lounsbury, M. (eds.), Religion and Organization Theory. Emerald Group Publishing Limited, pp. 3–21.

Tyler, T. (1999). Why People Cooperate with Organizations: An identity-based perspective. *Research in Organizational Behaviour*, 21, pp. 201–246.

Vandenberghe, C. (2011). Workplace Spirituality and Organizational Commitment: An integrative model. *Journal of Management, Spirituality & Religion*, 8(3), pp. 211–232.

Van Gestel, N. and Hillebrand, B. (2011). Explaining Stability and Change: The rise and fall of logics in pluralistic fields. *Organization Studies*, 32(2), pp. 231–252.

Retrieved from http://druid8.sit.aau.dk/acc_papers/eesnlnejbp1pp7q5026jfxgfveqy.pdf [last accessed 13th April 2016].

Wagner-Marsh, F. and Conley, J. (1999). The Fourth Wave: The spiritually-based firm. *Journal of Organizational Change Management*, 12(4), pp. 292–302.

Weber, M. (1947). The Theory of Social and Economic Organization, translated by T. Parsons and A.M. Henderson, with an introduction by T. Parsons, New York: Free Press.

Weaver, G. and Agle, B. (2002). Religiosity and Ethical Behaviour in Organizations: A symbolic interactionist perspective. *The Academy of Management Review*, 27, pp. 77–97.

Weick, K., Sutcliffe, K. and Obstfeld, D. (2005). Organizing and the Process of Sensemaking. *Organization Science*, 16(4), pp. 409–421.

Werder, A. (2010). Corporate Governance and Stakeholder Opportunism. *Organization Science*, 22(5), pp. 1345–1358.

Westerman, J., Whitaker, B. and Hardesty, A. (2013). Belief in God: The differential prediction of workplace values. *Journal of Management, Spirituality & Religion*, 10(4), pp. 324–341.

Westphal, J. and Zajac, E. (2013). A Behavioural Theory of Corporate Governance. *The Academy of Management Annals*, 7, pp. 605–659.

Whetten, D. (2006). Albert and Whetten Revisited: Strengthening the concept of organizational identity. *Journal of Management Inquiry*, 15(3), pp. 219–234.

Williamson, O. (1985). The Economic Institutions of Capitalism. New York: Free Press.

Willmott, H. (1995). Managing the Academics: Commodification and control in the development of university education in the UK. *Human Relations*, *48*(9), pp. 993–1027.

World Bank. (2020). Nigeria: Overview. Retrieved from https://www.worldbank.org/en/country/nigeria/overview [last accessed 12th April 2021].

Yin, R. (1994). Case Study Research. *Designing and Methods*. Thousand Oaks: Sage Publications.

Yin, R. (2003). Case Study Research Design and Methods, 3rd edition. *Applied Social Research Methods Series*. Thousand Oaks: Sage Publications.

Yip, J. and Schweitzer, M. (2015). Trust Promotes Unethical Behaviour: Excessive trust, opportunistic exploitation and strategic exploitation. *Current Opinion in Psychology*, 6, pp. 216–220.

Zajac, E. and Westphal, J. (2004). The social construction of market value: Institutionalization and learning perspectives on stock market reactions. *American Sociological Review*, 69(3), pp. 433–457.

Zoogah, D., Peng, M. and Woldu, H. (2015). Institutions, Resources, and Organizational Effectiveness in Africa. *Academy of Management Perspectives*, 29(1), pp. 7–31.